BORN TO FLY

BORN TO FLY

RYAN CAMPBELL

BROADWATER
PRESS

Ryan's books may be purchased for educational, business or sales promotional use. For information please write: info@ryancampbell.co, or visit us at www.broadwater-press.com

Production and creative provided by Epiphany Creative Services, LLC
Printed in the United States of America
Library of Congress Cataloging-in-Publication Data
Library of Congress Control Number: 2019919986

FIRST EDITION
Ryan Campbell – 1st ed.
TITLE: Born To Fly: The inspiring story of an Australian teenager's record-breaking flight around the world
             p. cm.

ISBN–13   978-1-7343821-0-5
1. BIOGRAPHY & AUTOBIOGRAPHY   2. Adventurers & Explorers

BROADWATER
P R E S S

Distributed by Broadwater Press

14   10 9 8 7 6 5 4 3 2 1

To my Family,
the biggest adventure of all.

CONTENTS

AUTHOR'S NOTE

When I first wrote *Born to Fly*, I struggled a lot in deciding how to end the narrative. How do you take more than two years of highs, lows, excitement, heartache, and lessons learned and bring them to a close worthy of a reader's time? The result, after endless nights staring at a blank page, was an emotional epilogue about life—the pathways we take and the inability to have complete certainty that any of our decisions are the right decisions.

My epilogue simply said that I hoped all my future endeavors, as with the world flight, would bring with them an opportunity for growth, not just for me but for those who travel this journey with me. The story of my world flight and subsequently *Born to Fly* went on to influence, inspire, and encourage those who crossed paths with it. Witnessing that impact on others became the highlight of the entire around-the-world project.

Fast forward to December 28, 2015. I was spending the last days of my twenty-first year flying airplanes up and down the East Coast of Australia. My pursuit of unique flying had led me away from the airlines and into the cockpit of a Tiger Moth, a yellow biplane built in the 1930s. It was my unique privilege to take passengers skyward to experience not only this piece of living history but also the beautiful sights of the Australian coastline.

A normal day. No oceans to cross. No records to break. Just a routine flight.

I pointed the vintage Tiger Moth down the grass airstrip and pushed the power lever forward, just as I had thousands of times before I took off. We began to climb away as the airstrip slipped beneath me.

Then, silence.

Shortly after takeoff, we experienced some form of engine failure. The engine fell silent at a very low level, and my instincts and training took charge. I pushed the nose forward to find a clear place to land. The low level at which the engine had failed left few options, however, and in a matter of seconds, it was all over. Despite my best efforts to navigate trees and terrain, the result was a horrific plane crash.

I was unconscious for a short while. When I awoke, my legs and feet were pinned in the wreckage, while the top half of my body hung inverted over the airplane's crumpled wing. I managed to contact emergency services, which found the wreckage from the air before directing ground crews to the swampy area where the aircraft lay. Voices surrounded the wreckage as the situation was assessed. I was the only survivor.

I was cut from the wreckage and flown to a hospital in Brisbane where I later underwent emergency surgery on my face, back, and right ankle. I had been shattered from head to toe, including five breaks in my back, broken facial bones, and a shattered and almost severed right ankle.

An unknown amount of time later, I woke up in a surgical recovery ward surrounded by the familiar faces of my family.

The pain in my body was indescribable, yet somewhat numbed by the concoction of painkillers running through my IV lines. I lay so still, scared to move, yet eager to know the extent of my injuries. Although the pain was evident across my entire body, I knew there was something especially wrong from my waist down; I could see my legs, yet

I could not move or feel them. The sensation was that of a concrete block laying across the bottom half of my body where no level of exertion would result in movement.

I was a paraplegic.

Life changed that day in more ways than I could ever imagine. I was a paraplegic plane crash survivor with my own hospital bed in a long-term spinal injury recovery ward. My mind was simply full, or "at capacity," as I regularly explain it. I was now faced with a new challenge, yet it wasn't an expedition or adventure; it was learning to walk again.

The next six months in the hospital were hard. Who would expect spinal rehabilitation to be anything but? It was a journey that tested me physically and especially mentally. It was a time of discovery, growth, and adaption fueled by unexpected adversity. It was far and away the greatest challenge I had ever faced.

My recovery, in short, was unbelievably positive. The damage to my spinal cord was severe, yet every spinal cord injury, and therefore recovery, is unique. My damaged nerves managed to repair themselves to a certain extent fueled by determination and full-time physiotherapy. Slowly but surely, my body began to wake up. At first it was a twitch of a toe, then a flicker of my leg muscles, and so on. I moved from a wheelchair to a walker, from crutches to this now runway-ready strut I show off on a daily basis. A year and a half after my accident, I was walking, albeit like I'd had a few too many Tennessee whiskeys, but I was walking!

Around that time, the progress of my recovery slowed almost to a halt, and that in itself was one of the hardest realities to accept. Constant progress and physical improvements had kept me driven and eager to see what was next, yet once that was taken away, I found myself left with the reality of my now "lifelong" body. Damaged internal systems, no calf muscles, no glute muscles, no hip flexors, no push in my feet, limited foot movement, and no feeling in half of my lower body.

This plateau in recovery forced me to reinvent the next chapter of my life. I could talk for hours about my life after the around-the-world flight, from meeting the Royals to spinal rehabilitation, my journey back to the cockpit, learning to fly a helicopter, living in the US as a keynote speaker, and everything in between, but that is a conversation for another day.

In the time since the original edition of *Born to Fly* was released, life has been a wild roller coaster, yet I have never felt so connected to my initial epilogue as I do today. I continue to make what I believe are the right decisions on a day-to-day basis in hopes that I will live a life of growth, positivity, and joy for both myself and those around me.

I now invite you to dive back into the mind of the nineteen-year-old kid I was when I wrote this book, for every page from here on out remains as it was originally written. Strap in for a wild ride with a normal Aussie kid in a tiny plane on an enormous adventure.

—Ryan Campbell, December 2019

FOREWORD

At the age of nineteen, Ryan Campbell circled the globe solo in a single-engine aircraft. At his age, I was in college and only had a private pilot's licence, hoping to someday fly jets.

There had never been a day I could remember that flying wasn't part of my life. Both my parents were pilots, and when I wasn't up in the air with them, I was hanging around the airport or flying model airplanes. Getting my private pilot's licence at sixteen, studying aeronautical engineering in college, and then becoming a naval aviator, I developed a "need for speed." What could be faster and more exciting than sitting in the front seat of Navy fighter planes traveling at the speed of sound?

Well, there was one thing—the Space Shuttle. Sitting atop millions of pounds of explosives and hearing the roar of liftoff and feeling the acceleration up to twenty-five times the speed of sound was not for the faint of heart. Flying five Shuttle flights and commanding four of them were experiences I can never forget. Those years were followed by other kinds of aviation: for the airlines, in my single-seat small plane and a four-seater with my family, to competing in the Reno Air Races - and winning!

But aviators all know that danger always lurks; aviation can be very unforgiving. Ryan, like all pilots, never thought an accident could happen to him. Yet one day when he took to the air in his Tiger Moth biplane for some fun flying, the engine quit shortly after takeoff, and he crashed violently to the ground. His injuries were so severe he thought he would never walk—or fly—again. But a love of aviation and a steely determination to once again be up in the air pushed him beyond what he thought possible. He relearned how to walk and then took to the sky once more.

Ryan's flight around the globe was inspirational in itself. His story of determination to once again walk and fly is a lesson to all of us— that in times of great adversity, we can overcome loss, fear, and physical limitation to achieve our goals.

> —Robert Lee "Hoot" Gibson,
> former American naval officer and aviator,
> test pilot, aeronautical engineer,
> and retired NASA astronaut

1

FINDING THE MAGIC

It was a calm and clear morning. It was also my fifteenth birthday. We rolled down the runway in the fabric-covered lightweight Gazelle and pointed the aircraft skywards. I was defying gravity and the laws of physics in a way that millions have only dreamed of, and I was eager to impress my instructor. My nervous hand gripped the control stick as I worked through my checklist of tasks, making sure that every phase was successful and nothing had been forgotten. My instructor Mark, with whom I had only flown twice before, sat quietly and watched, making himself as invisible as possible. He kept a keen eye on my every move.

We zoomed through the skies above the Sapphire Coast, a stunning stretch of Australia's eastern seaboard that sits about halfway between Sydney and Melbourne. We reviewed the skills absorbed throughout my flight training, testing my ability to fly the aircraft in all configurations and simulating various failures in our little two-seater machine. Finally we taxied back to the aeroclub.

'Keep her running," Mark said. The words I had been nervously waiting for. My heart began to beat faster and my grip on the control stick tightened even more. Mark slowly and calmly unplugged his headset and tidied up as if he had just been to the shops. With one last look he told me to fly three takeoffs and landings. He added that I should also remember to "lock the door and have fun." And then he climbed out of the plane.

I locked the door. Not too sure about the other thing he said. I checked and double-checked. I glanced over to a group of family members, including my very nervous Mum, and waved goodbye. I taxied through the grass to the runway and with a shaky voice I keyed the microphone and lined up on the centerline.

With a push of the throttle I hurtled down the runway. As I took off I noticed that with only one pilot the aircraft felt completely different, much lighter. And faster too: just before I reached the end of the runway it was already time to turn. Ticking off the checks as I went, I levelled off above the pristine coastline. As I took a breath, I looked to the right. For the first time the seat next to me was empty, its belts neatly folded. Now I truly felt that I was alone, that I truly was making my first solo flight.

The trees were so small and the cars zipped around on the most realistic and widespread slot car track one could imagine. The clouds were above me and the ocean lay below with boats resembling bath toys. These were all things I had seen before, all the things that had made me fall in love with aviation, but this time it was different. I no longer felt like a student constantly wondering whether the instructor had "helped you out a little bit." This time it was just the aircraft and me.

Physics had never been my strong point in high school, but I did know that what goes up must come down. I had successfully gone up, but now I had to do the other part. I reduced the power and pushed the nose towards the earth. Carefully monitoring height and speed, I glided towards the runway when a group of people caught my eye. They were all looking skyward, shielding their eyes with a salute to the sun, a sight typical of airfields the world over. With the instructor's voice ringing in my ears, I held the wheels inches from the ground and further reduced the power, and very soon heard the landing gear rumble as I met the earth once again. The relief that flowed through me was immense, and I couldn't prevent a smile that felt it was stretching from ear to ear. I had flown an aircraft solo. I was a pilot.

I have never really understood why the fact that it's possible to hurtle through the sky, to soar above the ground in a machine, is no longer magical for so many people. Now flying is a matter of going to an airport with baggage that's overweight, queuing to get into a huge metal cylinder, and settling into your seat only to realise that the baby in seat 22A is crying. A lot of people don't see that watching a 747 lift off the runway is a sort of miracle: how can something that size get into the air? On the other hand, there are pilots who, when they're not flying, are playing with model planes or maneuvering them around on the computer. There are people who are totally involved with flying and planes, and they're keeping the magic alive, taking the science away from aviation to some extent. That's what I have always tried to do.

Flying was in my genes to some degree. I was born in Cooma in southern New South Wales on 13 January 1994, the last of three boys. In the early stages of my life we lived about eighty kilometers south of where I was born, on a farm not too far from Bombala, a small rural town with a population of just over one thousand. Down the road was a farmhouse, thousands of acres and an airstrip known as Yarrawonga. The land belonged to my grandparents, and this was where my dad, Lindsay, grew up.

His father, my granddad, was a farmer, but his early dreams had involved a life that was much less bound to the earth. In the 1920s, when he was young, pioneering aviators were taking to the skies, breaking records and achieving unheard-of feats. These pilots became heroes, making headlines across the world; air races thrilled audiences and aircraft began crossing stretches of ocean and land never seen from above. And Australia's greatest hero and my grandfather's idol was the Australian pilot Sir Charles Kingsford Smith.

He was born in Brisbane in 1897, moved to Canada with his family soon after and settled back in Sydney in 1909. He turned eighteen a year after World War I broke out and joined the Australian Army, then known as the Australian Infantry Forces, and fought at Gallipoli. In 1917, he transferred to Britain's Royal Flying Corps where he undertook flight and combat training. After being wounded in aerial combat he flew as a flight instructor until he was demobilised in 1919.

Kingsford Smith knew that he wanted to keep flying more than anything else. After the war, he ran joyride flights in England and the United States, as well as barnstorming—being a stunt pilot and performing popular tricks with airplanes at fairs and shows. Barnstorming was a very popular way for former Air Force flyers to make some money; in the United States there was even a barnstorming season, which ran from early spring until after the harvest and county fairs in the autumn.

Kingsford Smith settled back in Australia in 1921. His ambition was to be the first pilot to fly across the Pacific Ocean, but he knew he would need money for that. And so he continued barnstorming in order to raise funds. He would take an aircraft around rural Australia, landing in paddocks and small airstrips in order to give ordinary Australians the experience of flying. In 1928, he achieved his ambition, making the first trans-Pacific flight from the United States to Australia in his legendary plane the *Southern Cross*. He was also the first pilot to cross the Australian mainland nonstop, he made the first flight across the Tasman Sea to New Zealand, and crossed the Pacific from Australia to the United States for the first time. Not only that, but he flew from Australia to London, setting a new record of ten and a half days for the journey.

When my grandfather was a young boy, Kingsford Smith landed the *Southern Cross* in Bombala, Granddad's home town, on a barnstorming tour. Granddad was desperate to fly, and so was the rest of the family—except his father, who was an "If I was meant to fly I would have feathers and a beak" type of man. However, he figured if his entire family was going to go down "in one of those airplane things" then he might as well go with them. And so they all climbed aboard the *Southern Cross* and set off into the sky. My family's relationship with aviation had begun.

Granddad passed on his love of flying to the rest of the family; he himself acquired his private pilot's licence and flew a total of 222 hours and 22 minutes. His son, my uncle, became a commercial pilot and now owns and runs Merimbula Air Services, and my dad is a private pilot. One of my brothers is a commercial pilot and the other one is learning to fly. I had my own first flying lesson when I was fourteen; my first solo flight at fifteen. At seventeen I studied for my private pilot's licence and passed that, and in April 2012 I passed my commercial licence.

In 1998, my parents, brothers and I packed up and moved about eighty-five kilometers east to Merimbula, a small tourist town on the Sapphire Coast surrounded by beautiful beaches and crystal-clear ocean. Dad took a job as the local milkman, and my mum, whose name is Joanne, attempted to steer three young sons in the right direction. I loved living in Merimbula, with the beach practically on our doorstep. Not only did we have a great outdoor lifestyle but we were still only an hour away from family in Bombala.

I started kindergarten in 1999 at the Bega Valley Christian College. My brother Adam was in Year 2, and my eldest brother Chris was beginning high school. The thirty-five kilometer bus ride to school was long and winding, stopping and starting every five minutes until we arrived moments before the bell. We would all gather at the morning assembly, discussing the topics of the day before we all headed to our different classrooms. Because it was a small school, we seemed to know pretty much everyone and they knew you, too. Even if people didn't know exactly who I was, they knew I was "the little Campbell."

Primary school was okay, I guess. I've always been the sort of person who likes knowing how things work, how to put them together. When I can see a practical use for something I can usually do it. But I could never learn things from textbooks. Sitting at a desk was never my favorite pastime for a start, I didn't like the hours spent learning "running writing." (I never actually received my pen licence, I should look into that.) And I never much enjoyed sports days with everyone sitting back and observing my less than perfect high jump technique. But I did make regular appearances in the swimming carnival "splash and dash," the cluttered race across the pool where the aim was not to drown yourself or others.

In retrospect, I have to say that the highlights of my primary school years were the holidays. Through various business promotions, Mum and Dad were able to take us overseas; a number of tickets towards an overseas holiday were awarded depending on the amount of dairy produce sold through Dad's work as the local milkman. When the coolrooms become overstocked with huge amounts of orange juice, we knew it was time to start packing our bags. It was a way of affording the unaffordable. Our first trip—the first time away from Australia for all of us—was to Vanuatu when I was six. I had taken a week off from Year 1. I was confident I could catch up.

I think it is fair to say that this trip changed my life forever.

I sat down in the enormous jet and strapped into my seat with no idea what was coming. The seat towered in front of me, yet if I stretched just a little I could peek out the window. The wing was so long, so much longer than I ever imagined, and when I looked closely I could see that it was covered in all sorts of doors and levers. Maybe that was how it flew?

The engines boomed to life as the flight attendants showed us how to use a life jacket. I thought that was a little strange; after all, we weren't going swimming. We bumped along the taxiway, eyes glued outside as jets disappeared from sight and wheels screeched onto the tarmac. With a shudder from the overhead lockers and a roar from the engines, we began our dash down the runway. I will never forget the feeling of being pushed back in the seat and the rumbling that suddenly turns into silence. It was thrilling then, and that sensation still remains one of the highlights of flying for me.

I looked across Sydney, absolutely blown away by its size. I had no idea cities even got that big, and definitely did not know that everyone's roof was red. We flew through a cloud, we were above the clouds. Planes flew that high?

When the flight attendant asked whether we would like to visit the flight deck and say hello to the pilots, my head nearly exploded with excitement. Like ducklings following their mother across the road, my brothers and I followed her to the front of the plane. One by one we stepped into the cockpit.

The pilots swiveled in their seats, looked back and said a quick hello. I stood wide-eyed and open-mouthed. There were so many buttons on the console and they even had to put some on the roof! How did they know which ones to press? And the steering wheel. Why was no one holding the steering wheel? I had a million questions in my mind, but I was too tongue-tied to ask any of them.

I loved our holiday in Vanuatu, but I just could not wait to get back on that airplane.

Not to go home, just to go flying. That was the day when I decided I would be a jumbo jet pilot when I grew up.

Meanwhile, primary school turned into high school. I now wore a white shirt instead of a yellow one, not only a constant reminder of my age, but also what I had eaten for lunch that day. We began to choose subjects based on our interests. One exercise book became twenty-seven and our backpacks became heavy. Someone decided to put the alphabet into mathematics, which if you asked me, was quite unnecessary. But one thing didn't change—I was going to be a jumbo jet pilot.

It was an ambition that remained unwavering, except for a short period when I wanted to venture into custom car building. I loved studying geography and tourism because I was curious about the world, and these were travel-based subjects, but I was best at D&T: design and technology, because it was practical. I had no idea how you went about being a jumbo jet pilot, but common sense said you had to have money, get a driver's licence, leave school, get a job and learn to fly. Even though my uncle, who lived just around the corner, had a lot of experience in light aircraft, I never thought to ask him how to learn how to be a pilot. And although I had heard family stories about Granddad and Kingsford Smith, Granddad had died when I was too young to ask him about all that.

When I was twelve or thirteen, between doing last-minute essays and school projects I sometimes thought were a bit pointless, I started my research.

I was never a great reader—I can only remember a couple of books I read cover to cover by choice, and one of those was nonfiction about spaceships—but I really got into aviation magazines. I wanted to know how other people had started their careers in aviation, and I read everything I could and used the internet. Unlike lots of other aviation-mad kids I never built models; I do it now, but then I was more interested in getting into the real thing. Any lunchtime at school, any spare time I had, I was thinking about and talking about planes. All my friends were sick of hearing about them. I couldn't wait to finish high school and get some sort of job that would support my flight training. Naturally I assumed I would need a driver's licence before being able to fly a plane.

One day when I was fourteen, I was wandering around the house trying to find something to do. I sat down at the kitchen table and flipped through the local newspaper, mostly to see whether there were any cool pictures or people I knew. My eyes locked onto a picture of a young guy sitting in a light aircraft, and the headline was: "Young pilot takes to the skies at 15!"

No way, I thought, it couldn't be true. But it was. This was a story about a local kid, not much older than me, who flew an aircraft solo at the age of fifteen. This was beyond anything I had ever imagined, and to say I was jealous would be an understatement. Questions crowded into my mind. The first one was simply, how did he get to the airport?

I read that article over and over again, replacing his name with mine and dreaming of achieving what he had just done. If he could do it, there was no reason why I couldn't.

Now I knew what was possible, I wanted answers. I started to research the finer details, the questions of where, when and how. It wasn't easy, but I kept at it. I have the kind of personality—ask Mum and Dad—where once I get hooked into something I'll just go with it. We were never spoiled kids, we were told to work for what we wanted, but if I had my mind set on something I just wouldn't let go.

2

A PASSION AND A GOAL

At about this time my dad had taken a huge step towards becoming a pilot himself. He had started flight training through Merimbula Air Services where Andy, his brother, had a flying instructor on hand, and after a lifetime of wishing he could fly he was now a few lessons closer to his dream. When he came home after every session, I would grab him and ask him dozens of questions about what he was doing. Soon I was tagging along. Merimbula airport was only minutes from our house. It is the base for my Uncle Andy's scenic flight business, Merimbula Air Services, but it was not somewhere I had spent a lot of time. It was housed in a large green building opposite the small regional airport terminal and faced the security fence that divided the general public from the hive of aviation activity. Scattered around the building were light aircraft of all colours, shapes and sizes.

The chief flying instructor was Alan Lindsay, a long-time family friend. Known as "Big Al," he stood well over six feet tall and I couldn't imagine how he squeezed into any small plane. I would sit and listen as Alan explained the day's lesson to Dad, where they would go and what he would teach Dad to do. I would place myself on the viewing deck, radio in hand, and just watch.

After one lesson Dad and Alan taxied off the runway and parked only meters from the fence. Dad looked up through the bubble canopy and beckoned me to come over. Alan wanted to take me up for a quick flight, even though he was in a hurry. He was busy apologising for his time constraints; I was just thrilled to be flying at all.

I climbed up and into the little Evektor Sportstar, sat in the pilot's seat on the left, and buckled in. It felt like being in a racing car. Alan's hands darted back and forth flicking switches, while at the same time he talked to me, giving me basic information about how to fly a plane, what bit makes it go up and which bit makes it go down. Before I knew it, the aircraft was alive and we were taxiing out to the runway with Alan still apologising for being so rushed. Over the microphone he gave some kind of pilot code for "We are going to take off now." The radio calls alone were exciting.

We zoomed down the runway and into the air. My eyes kept flicking between the aerial view of my hometown and the switches and levers inside the aircraft. I watched as Al turned the plane to the right and before long pushed the nose down to level. And then he let me take control. I rocked the wings to the left and right before pointing the nose to the sky and back to line up with the horizon. Apologetically, Alan took back over, flicked more switches and sent code throughout the airwaves for all the other pilots out there. We turned and lined up with the runway and I watched as it grew larger. Then, with the throttle at idle, Al brought us back to earth. I had permanent smile, stretching from ear to ear.

As I said goodbye and left the airport, I knew more than ever that this was where I belonged. And so I immediately started thinking about how to afford flying lessons.

Months before, I had started working at the local supermarket in the nearby town of Pambula. It was small, with a handful of employees governed by our boss, Darryl. I would clamber off the bus at 4:10 after school and scoot up the street, change uniforms, and head into my first duty of the afternoon. This was stacking the milk fridge. (Always remember to rotate the milk!) Working in the supermarket was a great job and Darryl looked after us well. I was there until 6pm three afternoons a week and was always paid for two hours of work, even though I arrived slightly late. At $7.65 an hour the money added up, and my first goal—to buy a new guitar, paying it off on lay-by—was achieved in no time. Now my money was accumulating in the bank, just waiting for me to find something new to spend it on. With my heart set on that second flying lesson, I cast around for other ways to make money. Washing a truck on the weekend helped out and within a fortnight I had enough for an hour in the air. I booked in with Alan and counted down the days.

Al was more relaxed this time, and took the lesson more slowly. I was perched in the left seat of a Grumman Tiger, a low-wing four-seater, and we took off, heading north along the coastline. We zoomed up and swished down and around the clouds, and I tried to improve my co-ordination as I worked out the throttle. Everything seemed so complicated, yet I could see that there was a logic to it, and I was sure I could learn.

After we landed, we had a chat about what we had done that day. I jotted the details down in my new pilot's logbook, just given to me by Uncle Andy, a logbook that would eventually carry details about every flight I made. I created a job list of the equipment to buy and forms to fill out. It was the beginning of my new life. I aimed at having a flying lesson once a fortnight so I wouldn't forget the skills I had already learned. I went to work and school with my mind set on the weekend, hoping for a still, blue-sky day.

One Sunday afternoon shortly after I started learning to fly, I went with Dad to the local aeroclub. This wasn't at Merimbula but about ten nautical miles northwest at an airport called Frogs Hollow. We pulled up alongside the clubhouse, which was halfway down the grass airstrip, to see a small group of people surrounded by hangars. Some doors were closed, some were cracked open and others had an aircraft sitting out the front just ready to go flying. From time to time a plane would take off or land—no security fences or sealed runway. To the north, the airstrip dipped down and back up again while to the south it lay flat. The clubhouse was well placed for spectators to sit back and admire the aircraft touching down. The history of the airfield hung on its walls for all to see.

Soon after introducing ourselves, we were asked whether we would like to go for a fly. That was an easy question. I clambered into a Victa Aircruiser, the only four-seat Victa in the world. Our pilot, Des, flew us around the valley in the little low-wing aircraft, asking questions and cracking jokes as he went. It was a prime example of the Frogs Hollow Aeroclub spirit.

We left full of cake and biscuits with another flight under our belt and a bunch of new friends. It was a fantastic experience and the next Sunday could not come soon enough.

Every time I took flight I learned something new, not only about flying itself but about my abilities as a person. At fourteen, I was still two years away from learning to drive a car, and even then I would only have a learner's licence. I've always been very conscious of doing things early—maybe that comes from being the youngest of three brothers and always being in a race to catch up—and I was determined to be like that local kid in the paper and fly solo at fifteen, not just at that age but on my fifteenth birthday. I just had to keep on with my flying lessons and juggling the paperwork and other bits and pieces so I would be ready in time. It was both a goal and a passion. Only days before my fifteenth birthday we drove up to Moruya, another small coastal town an hour or two north of Merimbula. Because I was so young I could only fly solo in a smaller and lighter aircraft than the one I had completed my flight training in. There was such an aircraft in Moruya and a few familiarisation flying hours later I was comfortable and as ready as I could be.

As my birthday edged closer, I kept working away and when an issue popped up, I would do my best to find a way around it. I remember being told that the paperwork I required to fly solo could not be processed until I was fifteen, so we fixed that by finding a helpful person who faxed it through on my birthday morning.

On the day I turned fifteen I woke up and ran outside. The sky was blue and the trees stood still. As a surprise, my uncle had an aircraft ready and we flew from Merimbula to Moruya instead of driving; a long drive had become a quick flight. Once there, I prepared the aircraft and got ready to fly with my new instructor, Mark.

That morning I took off and landed three times before taxiing back to the aeroclub and celebrating. It was the first time in my life I had achieved something so significant. The hard work had paid off, and with a little help from the early morning weather everything had gone to plan. I was now the youngest solo pilot in Australia.

The smile never really faded following my solo flight. The next week an article popped up in our local newspaper with the same headline that had made me determined to do what I had just achieved: "Young pilot takes to the skies at 15." This time there was no need to replace the young flyer's name with mine. I returned to school and work, aiming to make a flight every fortnight. Being back in the slightly larger aircraft I had learned on, all my flying was done with Alan until I turned sixteen. We concentrated on navigation, so we usually flew a fair way from Moruya and Merimbula. With maps spread across the cockpit I carefully compared the outside world to where I should have been. I am proud to say I only found myself geographically disorientated once.

On my sixteenth birthday, I set off solo in the Grumman Tiger. It was the second solo flight of my life. With more experience than last time I was slightly less nervous, although the excitement and rush from being up there alone were just as strong as before.

Before long I had completed the training that allowed me to take passengers within a measurable distance from Merimbula, almost as if I was on a leash. The months afterwards became some of the most enjoyable of my life to that point; I would gather the eager and daring passengers and proceed to share the magic of flight. (That is, if they drove me to the airport.) In between flying friends and family around the local area I continued to learn the art of navigation from Alan. Each flight brought something new, something exciting and unforgettable. This was especially true of my first solo navigation flight. I had the takeoff and landing parts worked out; the challenge now lay in flying away from Merimbula and then finding it again later. As I sat in a small Cessna 152 and prepared for that, I was extremely nervous. The whole flight was nerve-racking, but I managed to get down, not just in one piece, but in the right place.

As well as dealing with flight training, school and work, I had become a regular at the Frogs Hollow Aeroclub. One Sunday afternoon, Bob, a flying member of the club, suggested that I should apply for a scholarship funded by the Aircraft Owners and Pilots Association or AOPA, which offered $6000 towards flight training. It seemed like a good idea, but other things crowded in and I forgot to complete the application. With another reminder months later, I sat down and wrote the required essay, which I sent off to the AOPA together with a copy of my logbook and the newspaper article describing my first solo flight.

Each day I hopped on the AOPA website trying to see how I had done. I didn't think I would win but the sooner I knew who had, the sooner I could relax. And then, while I was visiting my brother Chris in Townsville, I had a call from AOPA. I had won the scholarship! It was amazing, I couldn't believe it. I stood in the middle of a Westpac bank telling the person on the other end of the phone just how much I loved them.

With my eyes now set on my private pilot's licence, the magic PPL, I used the AOPA funds to pay for my navigation flights. I had recently left the Pambula supermarket and upgraded my line of work, washing dishes at the local RSL club. It was a dirty job, but it paid very well. Having learned that airplanes use not just airspeed to fly but also money, earning as much as I could seemed like a good decision. Shortly after my seventeenth birthday, I passed my PPL flight test and became a private pilot. Now I could fly where, when, and with whomever I wanted. It was an exciting way to begin my final year of high school.

As I approached my Higher School Certificate as a fairly non-motivated student, life became a bit more serious. I concentrated on passing in the kinds of subjects that would allow me to have a career in the airlines. I gave up a subject or two that I thoroughly enjoyed to focus on mathematics and physics, two subjects that I was never really good at and found irritating, to say the least. With maths and physics I studied English and geography; I also worked towards a certificate in tourism and events. My aim was to pass my commercial pilot's licence exams and flight test before the middle of the year, after I finished school, allowing me to begin work as a paid pilot. I kept on working and graduated from high school in early November 2011 with my required passes in maths and physics in hand. That was a relief, and I could now look towards the future.

After I had done my final exams, I decided against schoolies—celebrating the end of school life with my mates—and headed down south to Victoria's Latrobe Valley. I spent the next three days learning to fly upside down, a cheaper and more exciting schoolies experience than the usual, I thought.

In mid January 2012, I turned eighteen and was officially old. I celebrated in the backyard with my family and friends, but not too much, because I had a long drive ahead of me. The next morning I set off for Redcliffe, a northern suburb of Brisbane, for two months of training and exams with Bob Tait, who was renowned for his classes in commercial pilot licence theory. The best thing about Bob's course was meeting other pilots, mostly around my age or a little older, who were also getting ready to take on a career in aviation. We met and chatted after classes and during lunch and morning tea, finding out where we had learned to fly and where we wanted to be in a few years time. We studied in class through the week where I was staying in Redcliffe, just north of Brisbane on the weekends, and then took on the exam the following Monday. It was a relaxing and fun atmosphere; study was intertwined with catch-ups here and there, along with the freedom of my little beachside unit and the lack of requirement to make my bed. With much relief, I knocked over the exams one by one and knew I stood very close to my goal.

In late February, I repacked my car and headed home with seven commercial pilot's licence exam passes under my belt. Eager to start work as a pilot, I jumped straight into the final phase of training, which involved a check flight or two and a flight test. I brushed up on my study once more, signed the last form, and booked the testing officer.

I hired an aircraft from my uncle, filled it with fuel and cleaned the windshield. Setting off early from Merimbula, I tracked north up the magnificent coastline to Moruya where I would pick up my testing officer. After checking the belts were neatly folded and the mats were shaken, I scooted into the aeroclub.

A handshake and hello later, Ben, my testing officer and I got down to business. I was given a limited time frame to plan a flight to a number of destinations I had just been told about. Once completed, I would take off and fly the route, treating my testing officer as a passenger. The flight was to take us to Canberra and then south through a number of locations before finally tracking north along the coast to Moruya. All the while Ben would watch closely to ensure I was meeting all the requirements and standards needed to be a commercial pilot.

We ventured into the air with what I thought was a meticulously prepared flight plan. I had a folder with a small essay of notes and flight details sitting on my knee; there was no way I was leaving anything to chance. But there was one factor I hadn't planned for. Before long the weather deteriorated well below what we had expected and we had to divert to a different airfield, landing north of the planned route. With the testing officer nearby, I set about planning a new route clear of the bad weather. Straddling the landing gear and leaning awkwardly onto the seat of the aircraft, I put together a new flight plan and new notes. Finally we took off once again, this time towards a blue sky.

Late that afternoon we touched back down at Moruya airport. A smile and another handshake later I heard the words anyone in a test situation wants to hear—pass. I was now a commercial pilot.

In our household, there was a standard way of letting you know you had been in the shower too long. Sometimes it was a light "don't run the hot water out" tap on the wall. If you had been in for much longer, you were likely to hear the kind of regular thumping noise that could have been mistaken for a small car driving through the house. I got the second sort all the time. I blame this entirely on daydreaming. The shower is a fantastic place to let your mind wander, and you can always trace a few detailed technical drawings on the shower screen. I had many different ideas and thoughts over the years, some of these thoughts came and went, but some stuck around. And the one that was most persistent was this. I wanted to fly an airplane around the world.

I had wanted to do this during most of my flight training. I was totally engrossed in aviation, not just the practicalities but the different types of planes, the eras and events that have shaped the history of man-made flight. I knew the names: Lindbergh. Hughes. Hargrave. Kingsford Smith. Batten. Hawker. Sopwith. Wilkins. Hinkler. Wright. Dumont. Earhart. Barnes. Bach. Curtiss. Lilienthal. Ader. Blériot. Houdini. All living at a time when the general public was consumed by something new and magical. Pilots breaking records and setting new standards. I knew that behind the security fences, past the paperwork and beyond the bureaucracy, the magic of flying, the sheer adventure of it, was still there.

For me, freedom was the single biggest gift of flight. The ability to go somewhere, or even nowhere, but to enjoy the ride. And for me, the greatest sense of freedom meant flying around the world by myself. All the way—taking off from an airport in a light aircraft, staying low and pointing east. Tracking over the same oceans that Kingsford Smith and all the others, the great and iconic names of aviation, had flown over. Passing over countries, so many that you would need a list to keep track. Seeing four seasons pass by, the desert, snow, ice and vast green fields as far as you can see. I wanted to do that.

As I worked my way past goal after goal, I kept on thinking about this. Not as a realistic adventure, more so a dream fueled by curiosity. I never talked to anyone else about it—I didn't want anyone thinking I wished to fly around the world myself. That would be crazy.

What made me think about this again in a different way was a conversation I had during Bob Tait's theory course. I had been the only student who was studying the full seven subjects, so I met lots of different pilots at different times. On this particular day, I wandered over to a wooden table, sat down and began chatting to a guy called Cameron. He had a country bloke's chilled-out attitude and a strong love for aviation. We exchanged the usual questions: "What do you fly?" "Where do you want to end up?" "I'm pretty sure I am going to fail the exam on Monday, are you?"

The conversation somehow turned to flying around the world. Cameron told me he knew a guy who had done it; he himself had thought about it and was very interested in the idea. I mentioned a similar interest and we shared a few "wouldn't it be cool" moments. Without another thought, we went back to class. As I sat that evening and stalled on the idea of microwaving dinner, I thought about our conversation. I was intrigued that someone had the same interest as I did, yet had been just as cautious about mentioning it. How many more people were there with the same dream?

I put my highly refined detective skills to the test. I Googled: "How do you fly around the world?" I sifted through the adverts for round-the-world commercial air tickets and found two websites. Earthrounders.com and Soloflights.org. I then found an article, "How do you fly around the world?" My excitement and enthusiasm rose as I kept reading. When I found some good information I saved it in a folder. And then suddenly I thought: what am I doing? This is ridiculous. I closed the computer and turned on the TV.

Soon after I passed my commercial licence, I received the final paperwork in the mail. After doing a few short courses on various areas of aviation, I started work as a pilot with my uncle at Merimbula Air Services. Most of the time I flew up and down the Sapphire Coast giving tourists a glimpse of one of the most spectacular coastlines in the world. The odd charter, setting off to see what was behind the hills of the Bega Valley, was a welcome adventure.

Life began to settle down and although I was forever learning, the years of constant flight training were over for the time being. I began to meet new people within the industry and think about my next move, where I would go and what I would like to experience. I looked into the sensible options, the path worn by thousands of other pilots advancing to bigger and better aircraft as experience grew. I investigated courses overseas, thinking that maybe studying in the United States would be an option, and I also looked into a few avenues at home including the Royal Australian Air Force. I also kept putting information about flying around the world in the folder I had started on the night when I had first thought it might be possible. I watched documentaries on aviation, often more than once, and used my new-found inspiration to research a little more, to dream a little more. Eventually I had found out everything about it on the internet and read all I could find. I wanted to know still more.

I sat back and thought for a while, trying to work out a way to move forward while keeping my secret from people around me. All I needed was someone to steer me in the right direction. This person had to be an Australian who knew about flying around the world, and who had done so recently: any information from a pilot who had circumnavigated the globe many years ago might be of little use. I needed a recent earthrounder. And then I had an idea. I had read about two Australian men who had taken on the aviation world and won. Nothing wrong with starting at the top, I thought. I'll just write to them.

3

CLOSER TO THE DREAM

The first person I approached was possibly the most obvious one: Dick Smith. He is a household name as an entrepreneur, businessman and adventurer. Not only has he founded Dick Smith Electronics, Dick Smith Foods and *Australian Geographic* magazine, he has dedicated many years to the betterment of Australian aviation. He started learning to fly in 1972, and only four years later competed in his first air race across Australia. In 1982, on the fiftieth anniversary of the first solo circumnavigation of the world by pioneering American aviator Wiley Post, he became the first person in history to fly a helicopter solo around the world.

Dick Smith has flown around the globe five times, once from the North Pole to the South Pole in a twin-engine aircraft, twice in a single engine Cessna Caravan, and once with his wife Pip in a turbine Augusta helicopter, snapping over 10,000 photographs along the way. As I scanned through the information online, I was amazed at what he had achieved. He had an obvious passion for Australia and for aviation and I knew he lived not too far away. And, with five email addresses in hand—surely one of them would work—I sat at my computer and began to type:

Dear Dick Smith
My name is Ryan Campbell, I am 17 years old and live in Merimbula,
NSW. I am a licensed Private Pilot with 200 hours and by April 2012
I will be a Commercial Pilot…

I summarised my life, my experience within aviation and my ambitions. I told him about the jobs I had taken—at the supermarket, washing dishes and washing semitrailers on weekends—so I could afford flying lessons, and the scholarship I had won. I told him that my long-term goal was a job in the airlines, frequent aerobatic flying and an active role in Youth in Aviation, somehow promoting flying to young people around the world, something that had not been done in the way I felt it should. And then I got to the pitch:

I am writing to you regarding the history making flights you have made
throughout your life… I want to be the youngest pilot to fly solo around
the world. I have always wanted to do this but it seems so far out of
reach. For this reason I have kept quiet about my wish yet I am certain
staying quiet is one thing I will regret when I am older. We get one shot
at life and we are only young once, I have been blessed with an amaz-
ing start in aviation and I feel it is the best start I could have wished for
and the best building block to begin a flight of this magnitude.
I am unsure about where to begin, the cost, the aircraft, the planning
and even establishing the fact that this flight is possible. I feel I need
to establish a better view on what is involved in the various aspects of
this flight and the best way to begin thinking about it. I think by estab-
lishing a clear outline of what I am trying to achieve, partnered with
the support of several individuals such as yourself, I will have taken the
first step by setting a platform to build on, something I feel needs to
be done sooner rather than later. I want to be the youngest pilot to fly
around the world; I want to use that fact to illustrate the accessibility
of aviation to young Australians, and further abroad if possible. I hope

you can understand the importance of this to me and provide your professional opinion. I would love the opportunity to meet if possible or talk further, and hope to hear from you soon. Yours sincerely,
Ryan Campbell

I sat back and admired my handiwork, then scanned the letter carefully for spelling mistakes. It was only then I wondered what on earth I was doing. Did I really think I could just send Dick Smith an email? Part of me thought this was a ridiculous idea, but the other part overpowered that. After all, for years I had been saving page after page of information about aviation of any kind, I had found out whatever I could anywhere about flying solo around the world. So I hit the send button.

I didn't want just to sit back and wait for a reply I doubted I would ever receive; there was another possible avenue of approach. During my hours of Googling I had stumbled across the names of Ken Evers and Tim Pryse, Australian pilots who had flown around the world together in 2010. I had scoured their website with envy. They had circumnavigated the globe for Millions Against Malaria to increase awareness of malaria and raise funds for fighting it, and not only that, but they had done it in the first Australian-designed and locally manufactured aircraft to fly around the world. I had found Ken Evers's details online and sent him an email similar to the one I had sent Dick Smith.

When I had finished, I thought, well, that's that. I'd done my best. I tried to remain optimistic, I didn't let myself wonder what I would do if neither Dick nor Ken replied: I would worry about that when it happened, or rather didn't.

But early in 2012 I received two emails. This was the first.

Dear Ryan
It sounds like a great project to become the youngest pilot to fly around the world. However, it is fraught with some problems—which I am sure you are aware of.

One is that in the United States a special law was enacted by their Federal Government to prevent aviation records being undertaken by young people. This was after a young person with an instructor and from memory his father on board crashed, killing everyone.

Personally I have never supported this move to having someone doing it younger and younger, because I suppose the limit becomes when the person is so young that they lose their life on the flight. Having said that, when I originally heard of Jessica Watson's journey, I wasn't that supportive, however after I had learned what a capable young lady she was, I ended up putting in some money to improve safety.

In my own flights, I waited until I had earned enough money to pay for the flight myself. However, I have supported other young people who have needed to raise money from donors to complete their flight. Of course, as you understand aviation records are extremely expensive. So where do you go from here? Well I am not sure, but my suggestion is you try and get the hours up as much as possible and then see if you can get a wealthy company to support you. They could then get a return in publicity for your flight. Remember they will be of two minds in supporting you because they know that if something went wrong—and it can and even the best planned adventures can go wrong—they will be attacked and criticised by the media.

If you can get a major sponsor and your flight instructor, or people who know of your flying abilities, can verify to me that they believe you have a chance of safely completing the flight, I would certainly put in some money towards extra safety equipment. This would not be a large amount, as I don't own a major company like Dick Smith Electronics any more that has this type of money available for adventure.

All the best with your ideas, I hope you can go ahead. Regards
Dick Smith

Not too long afterwards I heard from Ken Evers. Ken's email was short as he had been delivering an aircraft to India. But he said that he would help me in any way he possibly could and would speak to me once he was home.

I couldn't believe it. Two of Australia's leading aviators, and the word "no" had never been mentioned, not once.

Ken was in contact as soon as he returned home. I don't think he realised he was one of only two people in the world who knew about my idea. For four weeks we emailed back and forth, each message becoming longer and more detailed. Every time I opened my inbox I would learn something further about the requirements of flying yourself around the globe. At the end of the four weeks, my crazy dream was becoming more focused, and I could see Ken had little hesitation in moving forward. At the end of the last email in our conversation was a single line: *Let's get this party started.* I sat back and took a breath. I couldn't believe that only four weeks after I had contacted him, Ken, who had done so much and was so busy, was willing to do all he could to help. Maybe, I thought, Ken would be my Don McIntire. (With his wife Margie, Don McIntire had supported Jessica Watson to the hilt. Don was a great adventurer who had done many amazing things: he and Margie had lived in Antarctica for a year in total isolation, he had sailed solo round the world, led sailing expeditions to Antarctica, flown round Australia in a gyrocopter and so much more.) Ken's support was as incredible as Dick Smith's. Now I had someone to back me. I had the support of Dick Smith. I had the basis for a team. What now? There was one easy answer to that. I had to tell people what I wanted to do, the secret I had kept hidden for so long. They needed to know how much time I had devoted to this, how serious I was. Starting with Mum and Dad.

My mum is a "text me when you get there" mum. If I ever forgot to do that, which I did just about anytime I went anywhere, I could be sure that the phone would ring three minutes after my predetermined and heavily documented arrival time. The "I drove slowly and just arrived" excuse could be stretched only so far.

I have given Mum lots of other opportunities to practise her communication skills. I was the kid who said he didn't need a list to remember four items to buy at the grocery store and returned home with three. The kid who left his school jumper at home, despite the best recommendations of the weather man and my entire neighborhood, and spent the day freezing. I was the kid who parked in a shopping center car park, spent thirty minutes in the shops and two hours trying to find my car. Knowing all this, I figured asking Mum and Dad whether I could fly around the world could only go well, right?

I pulled a folder from my cluttered drawer and emptied out the old schoolwork. The printer hummed away turning all my information-filled emails from Ken and the cherished reply from Dick into hard copy. All this was color-coded and in chronological order and placed back to back with all my previously accumulated information. The most important bits were highlighted. I had to make the information as simple and clear as possible. That way I figured Mum and Dad could read it faster, which in turn would reduce their chance of having heart attacks.

After dinner one night and making sure I dried the dishes—a strategic move, I might add—I asked Dad what he would say if I told him I wanted to fly around the world. Mum was sitting over at the dinner table listening in. Dad, who of course was a flyer himself, thought the idea was pretty cool. Mum joined the conversation with a similar view that it would be quite the adventure.

Okay. So here we go.

I handed them the folder and explained the story. They read through the emails and slowly realised what I was telling them; that this was no crazy out-there idea that would be gone next week. They asked me a lot of questions, where did this idea come from? What made me really want to do this? How do you take a single-engine plane around the world? What did I see as a next step? I answered each questions as best I could based on what I had learned from Ken. Despite the research I had done, there is no doubt that none of us had any idea what was involved in flying around the world. Mum and Dad recognised that for me this was not an opportunity to ignore, but one to follow up and see where it led, and that I had to find out myself. They knew I didn't want to regret not having done it in later years.

We decided that a good first step was to talk to my Uncle Andy, an experienced commercial pilot, and to my flying instructor, Alan. Folder in hand, I drove to the airport and my uncle's company, Merimbula Air Services, as I was due to work that day anyway, checking out a new aircraft with Alan. It wasn't the best time to give him my news, so I asked for a quick chat before the end of the day.

I flew north in the new aircraft, while a curious Al sat in the other front seat. Seeing no better time than the present, he asked what I wanted to talk to him about. Short of having an impromptu lesson in skydiving there was no way I could escape. And so, nervously at first, I told Al the same story I had told Mum and Dad.

His response was fantastic. He said he believed I could do it, and encouraged me to have a go. I got the same response from my Uncle Andy. They could see the magnitude of the challenge, yet because they both knew my flying and more importantly my attitude towards flight, they saw no issue in moving ahead. Their belief and encouragement were wonderful, they just meant so much. And now I had a team, a team of seven—me, Mum and Dad, Alan, Uncle Andy, Ken Evers and Dick Smith. A team that would go on and grow into something beyond a number.

4

SMALL STEPS

I loaded the Cessna with our overnight bags and strapped in. Mum hopped into the right seat while Dad and Uncle Andy stood by to see us off. Mum and I were off to Bendigo in Victoria, the home town of Ken Evers, my newly acquired mentor. My flight bag had a folder jam-packed with questions.

Still not being sure what flying around the world actually entailed, I looked forward to meeting Ken in person. I wanted to see the enthusiasm that had glowed from every email he had sent me, to find answers to the million questions now absorbing my every waking moment, and more than anything else, to add some certainty to what had occurred over the last few weeks. In terms of detailed planning, I was in limbo, eager to sit down with Ken and find out the next steps. I had sat down and laid out the research done to date, setting out what I thought I knew. The support team and I had all agreed that meeting Ken would give us some kind of initial direction to begin planning.

As we taxied to the end of the runway at Merimbula airport, I realised that we might have been heading to a meeting about flying around the world solo but this was the first time I had taken Mum flying outside the local area. We passed the familiar boundaries of the Sapphire

Coast and flew across the white peaks of the Snowy Mountains, chatting away as the land flattened to vast flat stretches of countryside. Two and a half hours after takeoff, we touched down in Bendigo, almost in the middle of Victoria—with a population of 83,000 - not exactly a little Aussie country town. We unpacked, tied the aircraft down and made our way to our motel and dinner.

The next morning we waited at the curb for Ken, who pulled up soon after to give us a lift out to his house. His number plates read "Avi8tor," he was smiling eagerly, and in an almost hyper manner he stretched out his hand and introduced himself. I was worried; even though we had spoken via email, the momentum that the flight would gather was dependent on Ken; more specifically it would depend on how our chat went throughout the day. Ken was a family man; he had a lovely wife and three young boys and was heavily involved in a career outside of aviation. The more I spoke with Ken the more I realised, regardless of where he was working, that his passion was purely within aviation; stories flowed and the more we spoke the more excited we became. Ken had experienced what I was hoping to do, he was one of the very few who understood what was involved and although this included the associated dangers, risks and hardship, more importantly he understood the feelings of accomplishment, achievement and satisfaction, and the rare feeling derived from successfully flying an aircraft around the world.

I had to keep an eye on the clock; still restricted to daytime flight I intended to fly back home after our chat with Ken and arrive back in Merimbula well before dark.

I explained to Ken that an American, Barrington Irving, had broken the world record in 2008. Barrington had flown around the world at the age of twenty-three; before that the youngest round-the-world flyer had been thirty-seven years old. I was seventeen, and I had six years to complete the journey and still break the record myself. My rough plan was to take on the flight in mid 2014 when I would be twenty. Ken saw no issue with the time frame. He pointed out that we would need to take the weather and route into account before finalising a date, but we ticked the "when" box and moved on.

There were so many questions. What would I fly? Would I fly east or west? What route would I fly? And, for a start, how was I going to get an airplane? It was evident I would need to raise the funds through sponsorship, but how? How much flying experience did I need? How do you deal with different languages? How does Customs work in each country? How do you stay awake? What do you eat? What do you wear? How do you fly for so long in a light aircraft? Where do you put all the fuel?

Ken spoke a mile a minute, I listened with eyes wide and ears open while Mum sat furiously writing notes. (She knew she had to do that: after all, I was the kid who couldn't remember four things to buy without a list.) Not only did Ken answer my marathon list of questions, but he told many stories of his own around-the-world flight, and I began to realise what I was getting myself into. Ken had no hesitation about my ability to fly safely around the world but he was also very frank about the dangers of such a trip.

He set out the risks of the journey in a very long list. Some would not be understood and overcome until much closer to the departure date, but Ken gave us an overall view. The greatest danger most people mentioned was flying a single-engine aircraft over water, where engine failure could mean ditching into the ocean over a thousand nautical miles from dry land, in the freezing waters of the North Atlantic or within reach of the pirates in the ocean close to India. There was the danger of flying a small ill-equipped aircraft over nearly every kind of terrain in any kind of weather. There were on-the-ground issues too, apart from dealing with different cultural differences and living standards: the legalities and logistics of landing in various countries, not to mention a young pilot's vulnerability to being ripped off in various ways. It was an eye-opening conversation. With the time zipping away, we scribbled a quick timeline, including rough estimates of the major elements of the flight, from planning to finding an aircraft. With a rough idea of the big picture we then put together a job list, things to get done as soon as possible.

Ken and I decided to meet again, next time with Dad, once these jobs were behind us and we could set out our next goals. That afternoon Mum and I flew home again, this time with even more to chat about. I was relieved and excited, just beginning to understand what I was in for. At the same time I was so happy to have Ken on board. He was beyond supportive, his positive attitude was all the inspiration I needed.

Over the next month, while I continued to fly with Merimbula Air Services, I began work on the job list. First things first, Ken had said. Before we could venture out and approach sponsors or aircraft manufacturers we needed an image, something material that would represent everything in my goal, from a world record to supporting youth in aviation.

We brainstormed a name for the adventure, discussed logos and began calling potential website designers. I would trundle to work daily with a laptop computer in the back seat of the car, working on my plans in between flying tourists up and down the Sapphire Coast.

Using Google as my friend, I found a long list of web designers, and with nothing to lose I began to call. Minutes in, I came up against the sort of reality that was to become all too familiar. A young guy who lived not too far from my home town was very interested in the flight and offered a discounted rate as partial sponsorship. $9000. Sweet. I could sell my car and carry the computer to work.

I declined his offer and tried someone else. But every call ended up the same way. With my phone in hand, I wandered around the airport car park chatting with Ken about my frustrations. It was so hard to find someone to sponsor the website, maybe this was something I could somehow pay for. "If I can get a cheap site up and running, maybe potential sponsors could be directed to it," I said.

'No way," said Ken. "You have to present this in a way that's going to make companies and organisations want to support you, okay? You need proper sponsorship. Getting a good website, a properly designed one, is critical—it's not a question of money at all. It's the first step." He meant, of course, that I shouldn't pay for the website, even though I could; convincing a company to sponsor the website would show other, potential sponsors that this was a good idea with serious possibilities.

After I had agreed to try and find someone professional to support the website, no matter what it took, Ken told me he had another idea. "You've been saying you want to fly round the world at twenty," he said. "But why not aim to complete the flight in 2013, when you'll be nineteen, and become the first teenager to fly solo around the world?'

This was something I hadn't even considered. The more Ken expanded on this idea, the clearer it was that he had put an immense amount of thought into it, and the more I thought about it, the better it seemed. Of course it meant an accelerated timetable, but I was prepared to consider that.

Two years before, as a budding schoolboy aviator boasting a full seven hours of flying time, I had attended the 2009 Australian International Air Show with my family. This is held every two years at Avalon outside Melbourne and regularly features planes from the RAAF, the US Navy and the US Air Force. For most of that weekend I had gazed skyward, dreaming of throwing an aircraft around the sky with the same precision as every air show performer. Between performances we had escaped the sun and strolled through the exhibition pavilions, trying to show some kind of genuine interest in purchasing the state-of-the-art missile on display while we filled our bags with free stuff.

It was at Avalon that I came upon the Swamp Comics character Ding the Duck and his creator Gary Clark. Ding, unlike his fellow duck companions, has yet to learn to become airborne, even though he has taken many, many flying lessons. Each attempt brings with it a laugh and almost every outcome possible. As I skimmed through the comic book on display I chuckled, knowing I needed to take this home. Gary said a quick hello and signed inside the cover before I ventured back outside to look skyward once again. That afternoon I sat in our holiday cabin with a pencil and paper and drew Ding, scribbling away to pass the time.

When I got home I started to draw Ding everywhere, at school, at home, on the bus. Ding became our Year 12 class mascot. We drew a six-foot-high version across the wall of the English classroom with chalk. (I recommend doing this when the teacher is not present.) On our "muck up" day, just before graduation, my friend Izzy and I used pink line marking paint to draw Ding on our school oval, then flew over the school to admire the artistic ability that thirteen years of education had given us.

Now, two years later, I was mulling over a catchy title and logo. The name came first, and it was supplied by none other than my mum. "You want to do this round-the-world flight while you're still a teenager," she said. "So why not call it Teen World Flight?'

Perfect, we thought; the name represented everything we stood for, including youth in aviation. Now we needed a logo—and almost immediately I thought of Ding. What better way to capture the interest of kids than with a bright cartoon duck? A phone call later and Ding's creator Gary, a fellow pilot who was delighted to be part of the adventure, was at the drawing board. Gary and Ding were well on their way to joining the Teen World Flight team.

With a name and a logo in the making, we made countless calls to web designers across the countryside. Finally we scored a meeting at Snap Franchising in Sydney. With my shirt tucked in and paperwork in hand I travelled to what would be the first of many meetings with potential sponsors. The team at Snap was fantastic. Their excitement about the flight was evident from the very beginning and they did even more than we expected of them. Lots of travelling, multiple meetings, phone calls, and emails later I had my first corporate sponsor, not only for a website, but for everything we needed in the way of web design and printing.

After one meeting with Snap, I packed my paperwork and extra notes into the folder and headed through Sydney's dense traffic towards

North Sydney. I had a meeting with Dick Smith. As I parked in the driveway of his house then rang the doorbell, I realised how nervous I was. Corresponding with someone of Dick's eminence and reputation was one thing: meeting and talking to him face to face might be quite another.

Dick opened the door and I was greeted with a "g'day" and a handshake. We went inside and sat at the kitchen table while Dick peppered me with questions. We spoke about my plans and work completed so far, how I would raise the money required for the venture—at the time we estimated it would cost between $220,000 and $600,000—and the planned outcomes of the flight. I sat and listened as Dick shared stories from his own flights. He felt very strongly that the trip should be planned so I could see and experience as much as possible. He said it should be an experience that stretched further than aviation and become an adventure in discovery and learning. I began to realise that Dick Smith was just a normal Aussie bloke, though one with aspirations and clear goals he had worked very hard to achieve. He must have thought I was okay because he offered formal support then and there, not only in contributing to the safety of the flight, but in formally joining my team as a safety advisor. To have Dick Smith acknowledge the dream, efforts and commitment alone was fantastic.

Just before I left, Dick asked whether I had ever tried OzEmite, a spread for sandwiches or toast produced by his company Dick Smith Foods. On our way out, Dick grabbed an opened jar of OzEmite from a kitchen cupboard and invited me to try it. I couldn't believe Dick was actually doing this, especially as this was the first time we had met. While I was licking the OzEmite from my finger, I looked up to see Dick Smith, the entrepreneur, accomplished aviator and businessman, doing exactly the same thing. It was a ridiculous, surreal moment, and I couldn't help inwardly smiling. After complimenting him on just how good his product was, I took the now gifted half full jar of OzEmite and hopped in the car.

It was now time to tell the rest of my family and my friends about the project. I had imagined doing this almost since detailed planning began. It wasn't that I was being secretive, we just wanted the project to have a little more certainty before sending it through the grapevine. The last few months had been productive, jobs were being ticked off slowly and we knew what image we were projecting. We had set a date to announce the flight to the public; it was all happening.

My brother Adam's twenty-first birthday party looked like the perfect opportunity to tell the family. And so I stood next to him as he gave his thank-you speech, turning over what I would say in my mind. We're a large, close-knit bunch and twenty-firsts are really big deals. I was facing members of both sides of the family: grandparents, uncles, aunties, a small herd of cousins, Mum and Dad, brothers, a future sister-in-law and friends, all listening in.

Adam finally said, "I've only got one more thing to say, and I'm going to hand over to Ryan, who would like to say a few words." My carefully rehearsed speech lingered on the tip of my tongue and then disappeared completely, leaving me a blabbering mess. Now I think back on it, I could have started with a better choice of words than: "I have been wanting to tell everyone something for nine months...'

Then I lost it. No matter how hard I tried, I could not produce any kind of structured sentence. This was the first time I had announced my plans to a crowd, the fact that it was family made it even harder. Everyone sat nervously wanting to know what I had done nine months ago that was worth crying about and when I finally managed to say that I was planning to become the youngest pilot in history to fly an aircraft solo around the world, I think quite a few people were relieved. Everybody in the family was beyond supportive, and that was wonderful.

I now had to tell my mates, many of whom had flown with me at various times. This was a bit harder than I had thought. In fact, a couple took a while to understand just what it was I wanted to achieve. No cabin crew? So no peanuts, right? How long would it take? But basically everybody was cheering me on. Well, nearly everybody. There were a couple who said, "Oh yeah, mate, keep going, great idea," but I could tell that they thought I was a nutter. Two other blokes my age said pretty average things about the flight, and I knew they were just talking out of jealousy. I had a bit of flak on social media, too. Only to be expected I guess.

Two mates of mine, both slightly older than myself, had found themselves in Merimbula in the pursuit of aviation. Matt was working for my uncle flying scenic flights, while Jonno was finishing off his licence with Big Al, my flight instructor. We had all become good friends, spending way too much time at the airport, mostly on the ground unless funds permitted. We were aware of each other's strengths and weaknesses and carefully studied each other's landings; if there were the slightest bounce, the one responsible wouldn't stop hearing about that near crash landing for a week. I had learned a lot from Matt that helped when passing my commercial pilot's licence.

I told both Jonno and Matt about my plans, a bit worried about they would say, being about my age, knowing my ability and with similar experience. At first they didn't believe me but after I gave them some details, such as what Dick Smith had to say about the idea, they were convinced. Only days later Jonno, a musician, wrote about our chat in his blog:

I've never met someone so passionate and dedicated to flying. He is a thorough and confident pilot whom I have learned a lot from and have every confidence that he will achieve his goal and leave quite an impression in doing so. If there is any one nineteen-year-old on the planet who can put in all of the work and fly solo around the world, it's Ryan Campbell. —Jonno Zilber

That meant a great deal to me.

5

STARTING TO SHARPEN THE AXE

Give me six hours to chop down a tree
and I will spend the first four sharpening the axe.
—Abraham Lincoln

The local newspaper ran a story on the flight and the local radio station called for the first interview. AOPA, the Aircraft Owners and Pilots Association, who had awarded me the aviation scholarship in 2010, ran a story in their national magazine. The word was now getting out there. This was no longer just *my* dream.

Mum, Dad and I packed our bags and took off for Narromine in central New South Wales, the location for the inaugural AusFly fly-in, a celebration that brought all areas of Australian aviation to one central hub. I had been invited to AusFly by its organiser, a guy who heard about my plans on the grapevine. It was a pretty small air show, but as a practice run for public speaking and a place to officially announce the flight to the public, there was nowhere better.

We arrived in Narromine in Dad's tiny 1965 Cessna 172 on a Saturday morning, parked the plane and tied it down. That night well over two hundred people gathered in a hangar for dinner and the doors were open with two show-winning aircraft nosed in towards the stage. As the sun went down, the aircraft created silhouettes against the dusky sky while the hangar slowly filled with aviators of all kinds.

Public speaking was still not my strong point. I sat at our table eating dinner and feeling incredibly nervous as I looked forward to when this would all be over. The night went on with formalities and awards, then finally David from the Sports Aircraft Association of Australia stood up to introduce me.

I laid out the colour-coded speech on the lectern and began to speak, my voice shaking and my hands holding the wooden stand in a death grip. Slowly I told the story of the journey so far, what had been achieved, and what was in store for the future. David stood to the left of me with outstretched arms holding a humungous blow-up globe that Mum had found on Ebay with the intended flight path joining thirty-odd destinations in a single line. The globe created significant interest as I used it to explain the flight path: departing the east coast of Australia, tracking through Norfolk Island, American Samoa, Kiribati, Hawaii and into mainland USA. Once across the USA, the flight path headed north towards the top of the world, across the North Atlantic via Canada, Iceland and then into Scotland. The marker pen had divided Europe, a flight path from Scotland to England, France and Greece before Egypt, Oman, Sri Lanka and Indonesia. A fine line connected Indonesia to the west coast of Australia and across the continent, back to where I had started.

At the end, after asking for help in any form, I thanked the crowd for listening. As I backed away, eager to find some form of strong alcoholic beverage, people started to stand up. "We will sponsor you," one said, "And so will we," said another. The representative at Bose, the electronics company who had a booth at the show, offered me a headset worth $1200. "Take it and see if you like it," he said, "and if you do I'll give you a couple to use on your flight." The support, the belief and the encouragement were phenomenal. I stood by my table, hardly able to believe my eyes as dozens of people lined up to say hello and to ask about join-ing Teen World Flight as a sponsor. It was great.

Now we had to harness this support, as well as learning everything else we needed to. I would go to bed every evening knowing a little more about circumnavigating the globe than I had done that morning, whether from someone I had spoken to, something I read or a lesson learned through trial and error. I spent a lot of time every day stress-ing about the job list that seemed to grow every day and the looming deadlines forever clouded by the chance of failure. Not enough time was spent looking back.

I soon learned some serious life lessons about the differences between knowing how something should go and the reality involved in making it happen. I had to do so much every day that I forgot just how much we had all learned about the ins and outs of the flight. There was no better time to realise this than when complete strangers started asking ques-tions. "What will you eat?" "Will you sleep while you're on autopilot?" "How will you go to the toilet?" And even, "Are you going to stop?" It took a while to get used to some of these, even though we heard them over and over again. Some questions made me smile, some made me think. Others caused me to stand there wondering what on earth I had gotten myself into.

Ken's support was phenomenal. Flying around the world was any-thing but a documented step-by-step process, not even on Google, and he had information that was vital to the flight; information not read-ily available in books or online. Seeing how much effect Ken had on the flight in the early stages made me realise that I would need to find more people with particular areas of knowledge, with expertise in areas I didn't know about, whether flying itself or aspects of the planning stage. I put myself out there, admitting my own lack of knowledge and asking for help, and gradually the team grew. Little did I know then how large it would become. Some people were prominent from beginning to end, others would play one-off parts that were all vital to the success of the flight. And they joined the team in unexpected ways, too.

We knew we had the big picture, a broad understanding of where to go and what to look for, what the best case would be and what could possibly be the worst.

More than anything else at this stage, we needed funds. This was an expensive adventure far beyond anything the average family could afford, including mine, but this where the challenge lay. Mum and Dad offered all they could, as did family and friends. They helped wherever possible, including backing me financially to go to the first meetings with potential sponsors, meetings for the website and image and to visit experienced pilots so I could gain further knowledge. These were the meetings where I had nothing behind me except the dream, my family, Ken and Dick Smith. My brother Adam bought the laptop we used to put together the sponsorship proposals and my other brother Chris spent hours on the end of a phone and typing hundreds of personalised letters to potential sponsors.

We wrote letters to every company we could think of, whether to do with aircraft or not, asking for funds or goods and services. We thought the direct approach would work; we'd just sit down with any company that showed an interest or looked promising, we'd tell them what we wanted, they would tell us what they could give and we would sort things out from there. But after we talked to Snap, who had designed our website, we realised we had to be much more structured than that. We needed to have levels of sponsorship—gold, silver, bronze—and outlines of specific costs involved. We had to be able to say exactly what sponsorship money would be used for, how much everything would cost, and outline every return. We thought $2000 was about right as the minimum figure for having a logo on the airplane. With no expe-rience, we tossed various ideas around and got as many opinions as possible. And then one day I was walking across the bridge near home and I looked down and saw a brick with a company name etched into it. Great advertising, I thought, what a good idea, and I bet it didn't cost much either. I mulled this over for a while. I guessed that many of the people who wanted to support my venture probably weren't especially well off—maybe not wealthy enough, for example, to fork out $2000 for a logo. But what about asking potential sponsors for less money? What could we give them? How could we offer thanks and appreciation to those who wanted to be a part of the flight?

That's how I came up with the idea for the 500 Club. We said it would cost $500 to have a short message, signature or the name of a school or business written on the flaps of the airplane, and also mentioned on the website. This turned out to be a great idea; heaps of people wanted to do this. The first time I spoke to the public at AusFly in Narromine in September 2012, we had people standing up and wanting to contribute straightaway. The first people who bought a 500 sponsorship, apart from my grandparents, was a company called Avplan. They have an iPad app for aircraft navigation. It turned out that Bevan from AvPlan had always wanted to fly around the world but had never been able to proceed past the planning stage. Having Avplan on the plane was his way of fulfilling his dream.

We worked very hard on the sponsorship proposal, we must have refined it about a million times. Snap printed it up for us, completely changing what we had written. We went from a one-page document to a thirty-page proposal in a folio printed on glossy paper, and tried it out on different people. If someone like, say, the head of an engineering firm said bluntly, "Nope, I wouldn't read that," we would go through it all again and change it. We had to learn how to appeal to as many different groups as possible.

I learned a lot about the media at this stage, too. The first story about me, as I said, had been in the local paper. It wasn't what I expected; it had things in it that I hadn't said and information that was incorrect. But as a result, a bloke from a town on the Sapphire Coast contacted me and asked what he could do to help. He said he could do PR. When we met he was persuasive. He told me he could guarantee eighty grand in sponsorship in the first month. He was successful, he'd done well, so I believed him. But for months it was all promises and nothing was happening. This taught me a very important lesson that was verified time and time again: nothing is confirmed until it is in your hand or signed away. We soon parted ways and I continued to look ahead. and I could just see this wasn't going to work. We spent quite a lot on this guy and ended up with very little in return. It took a while before I managed to find someone who knew media.

It was okay to stand up in front of an audience in Narromine with a globe and explain what route I wanted to follow, but that was the easy bit. Actually plotting the flight path took a long time, and a million things had to be considered. The path had to have legs shorter than the aircraft's maximum range, it had to take into account political situations in the countries I was planning to visit, questions of Customs and immigration, "ports of entry" into each country, costs to transit each stopover, visas and legal requirements for a visiting pilot and much, much more. We knew that after we had chosen the route we had to find out whether every country, whether on a stopover or being overflown, would issue us a landing clearance. Some countries demanded less paperwork than others although some, such as the USA, wanted you to fill out your name, address, passport number and flight details about 487 times. Ken had recommended a company in the United Kingdom that could take care of organising clearances. This was the only area of the flight planning that was outsourced and not completed within our team.

Sorting all this out took months, countless emails and a headache or seven. Each destination would need to be contacted, Customs organised at the entry and exit of many of the stopovers, fuel availability confirmed and reconfirmed on a regular basis. In some cases, fuel would have to be shipped and stored for my arrival. Accommodation and airport transfers would have to be organised; due to my age and lack of a steady income I couldn't hire a car or own a credit card. Routing would have to be chosen and put into flight logs for each and every leg around the world. Aircraft maintenance, with the accompanying paperwork and legal issues, needed to be confirmed well before departure.

I had to ensure I was ready to take off and fly east, over water, through endless changes in airspace, over mountains, through four diverse seasons and into situations I had never seen before. With safety paramount, this was one of the most important areas of planning. I would require an instrument rating to fly IFR, or instrument flight rules, a six-week course to teach a pilot to fly within cloud and weather where visual navigation with the ground is impossible. With such a diverse range of weather and so long being spent in the air it was essential to have the ability to fly through cloud and not have to navigate around it. This also allowed me to fly an aircraft at night, without which the entire plan was impossible. I would have to study for four weeks and pass an exam in order to get this instrument rating. Underwater escape training, emergency survival training and lengthy conversations with very experienced pilots were added to the pre-departure "musts."

Apart from the obvious—an aircraft—the amount of equipment required for the flight was huge. Ferry tank system. Sign writing. Oil. Oil funnel. Fuel filters. Fuel water testing paste. Spare HF radio aerials. Tool kit. Cleaning equipment. Gloves. Fuel water filtration funnel. Headset. Navigation equipment. Emergency location beacons. Life jacket. Cold water immersion suit. Life raft. Portable GPS. Portable VHF. Safety throw bag. Sea dye. Mirror. Strobe light. Emergency heat blanket. Rations. Handheld compass. Hivis clothing. First-aid kit. Survival kit. Sunblock. Insect repellent. Medicine. Tie down kit. Cowl plugs. Aircraft cover.

As the planning progressed, items were added to every list. Whether purchased, sponsored or on loan, each and every item was slowly and sometimes painstakingly gathered together.

The "big picture" was proving to be bigger than anything I had ever imagined.

6

IN THE GOOD OLD USA

Although every item on our equipment list was vital in some way, one stood out far beyond the rest. An aircraft.

Not just any aircraft, but one that met a long list of requirements, mostly concerned with safety. Speed, state-of-the-art avionics and navigation systems, aircraft and engine reliability were all absolutely necessary, too. One major and non-negotiable factor was the aircraft's ability to fly long distances over water. Although the route was not finalised until late in the planning phase, we had a rough idea of how I would cross the Pacific Ocean and therefore what the longest leg—Hawaii to the west coast of the United States—would be. With the longest leg spanning over 2000 nautical miles, the aircraft would require roughly three times the usual quantity of fuel. We would take a regular light aircraft—whatever we might choose it to be—and modify the interior to accommodate a large fuel tank and pump system, allowing extra fuel to be transferred to the engine during flight.

By working through our requirements, we came up with a list of suitable aircraft types. All were powered by a similar piston engine, all equipped with four seats, all outfitted with state-of-the-art avionics, all boasted a suitable cruise speed. Now we had to work out how to find our perfect plane, and then how to pay for it. The ideal way to source an aircraft would be for an aircraft manufacturer to lend it to us as their form of sponsorship in return for publicity during the flight. A second option would be to source an aircraft privately, whether purchased or on loan. Last but not least, we could hire an aircraft, which meant finding someone who was willing to see his or her machine venture on a flight that was nothing if not risky. This was a constant preoccupation for all of us—and it rarely left my mind while I was studying for my instrument rating at Port Macquarie, four hours north of Sydney.

The decision had been made early on to take on the flight as a teenager during 2013 and not in 2014 as originally planned. We then needed to decide on a date, but how? I began to look at an event called AirVenture, the world's biggest aviation celebration that takes place in the USA in late July. I had always dreamed of flying into AirVenture in the same way I had dreamed of flying around the world. I worked backwards from the show using the rough route we had decided on to determine the departure date from Australia. In the same way, I worked from the air show forward to see what date I would arrive back home. With a rough itinerary in hand, I went to Ken. We needed to study the weather for all the legs when I planned to undertake them; luckily the itinerary I had put together worked and each crossing of the oceans aligned well with the expected weather. It was decided then that I would plan to depart on 30 June 2013.

Every day that passed without an aircraft, every day that brought us closer to the takeoff date, caused a little more stress. We couldn't do any detailed flight planning, preparation for the installations of an extra ferry tank in the cockpit of the aircraft or paperwork until we knew what plane I would actually be flying.

We had sent our sponsorship proposals and information about the flight to aircraft manufacturers around the globe. One had gone to Cessna, one of the largest in the world. I happened to be in Townsville, north Queensland, visiting my brother and his partner, and one evening at dinner my phone rang. On the other end was an employee of Cessna in Wichita, Kansas.

It was early December 2012 and Cessna was due to shut down for Christmas, but they sounded really interested in supplying an aircraft for me, and quickly. We exchanged several emails and arranged to talk via Skype later that night, Australian time. The 2am Skype meeting gave the strong impression that they wanted something finalised as fast as possible before the end of their working year, less than forty-eight hours away.

If we managed to pull this off, it would change everything. The project would become a whole lot simpler.

Fighting to remain calm, I set up the computer, ironed a shirt and laid it across the back of the chair. With notes sitting neatly on the keyboard I set my alarm for 1:45am, 1:50am, 1:55am and 2:00am before climbing into bed. I hardly slept. As I silenced the alarm and ignored my brother who was asleep only meters away, I turned on every light in the room. I had a cold shower, cleaned my teeth and got dressed. The best thing about a Skype meeting is that although you require a neat and professionally ironed shirt, the pants are completely optional.

With my ironed shirt and pyjama shorts on I sat down, ready to chat with one of the biggest aircraft companies in the world. I stared at the computer screen willing it to ring, and at a little after 2am it finally did. After the team at Cessna was introduced we began to chat, covering all aspects of Teen World Flight. What? Where? When? Why? We spoke about the work completed so far, and where we had found support. The conversation was fantastic, they were great people who seemed to have a genuine interest in the flight, and also in seeing Cessna become a part of what Teen World Flight was trying to achieve. After a conversation lasting around an hour we parted and I pulled off the ironed shirt and crashed back into bed.

Cessna had implied that our partnership would be finalised quickly—we had spoken about all that at length—and so it was with great eagerness that we expected a reply the next day. We didn't hear from them. But that was okay. We had been too optimistic, thinking things could be resolved so fast. So we turned our attention to other matters connected with Teen World Flight and waited for the end of the Christmas and New Year break.

On the day Cessna began their 2013 working year I sent another email. There was no reply, so I set my alarm for 2am and called Wichita, leaving messages on several different Cessna numbers. Still no response. I was confused. How did we get here after such a positive conversation? Maybe they were all at a convention somewhere. Maybe messages were not getting through. January was slipping away and I decided to seek advice. I called Dick Smith, an owner of Cessna aircraft himself, to ask his opinion. I had told him about Cessna's reaction, and like everyone he had been very excited. What should I do now?

Dick's reply was far from what I had expected. He suggested I buy a suit, a tent, and a plane ticket to Kansas. I should set up the tent on the front lawn of one of the biggest aircraft manufacturers in the world, clamber inside wearing my suit and wait until somebody saw me.

My first reaction was: "Ha ha ha! Good one!" But Dick was serious. And as I mulled over what he had said I thought perhaps there was something in it. I floated the idea, and the general opinion was that if Cessna was really as interested as they had seemed, everything would be fine once I saw them. And I was convinced that face to face I stood a better chance of explaining Teen World Flight and making sure they supported us. And so I embarked on two days and nights of solid planning, checking passports, organising transfers and internal flights in the USA, booking accommodations - I had decided the tent probably wasn't necessary. And I had spoken with Dick on a Thursday. By Saturday morning I was standing in the departure lounge of Sydney's International Airport with an airline ticket in my hand and a new suit neatly folded in my carry-on luggage.

As I waited for the flight, the enormity of what I was actually doing struck home. Oh my. I was trying to stay calm, telling myself that in a few days I would return home with a partnership from Cessna, the flight would progress rapidly and we would be right on track for the departure. Because this plan had been Dick's idea, I headed to the bookshop intending to buy Dick's book to read on the plane. Reading his words seemed like a good way to understand more about this man who was doing so much for me and who had supported the flight since the very beginning. Unfortunately they didn't have a copy and so I looked for something else to read. I looked up and standing right in front of me was Dick Smith, the real Dick Smith, and his wife Pip. I just stood there, trying to convince myself that they were actually looking at me.

Dick, who was travelling overseas too, was just as surprised as I was. "Wow, hi!" he said. "You're actually going to Wichita? That's great!'

'Yep. I'm going," I said. "You told me to, remember?" We had a laugh and a quick chat, and wished each other well, and I promised to tell Dick how the trip went. Maybe, I thought, seeing Dick Smith at the airport was a good omen.

I clambered aboard a Boeing 777, laid my suit out flat and settled in.

Thirteen hours, several movies and some form of reheated sausage casserole later, the aircraft touched down in Los Angeles. I stood in the Customs line and put on my most emotion-free face for the security photo, collected my suitcase and headed for my first connection, a flight from Los Angeles to Atlanta in Georgia. However, somewhere between Los Angeles, Atlanta and the further connecting flight to Wichita, my bag took a vacation. No problem, I still had my suit and a complimentary "we lost your bag but there's absolutely no need to worry" free toothbrush.

Having never been to the United States in winter, I braved the cold as I ventured to the motel in Wichita, the aviation capital of the world. Other than a Cessna sign on a large white building behind the airport fence, Wichita seemed quiet, bleak and cold; it was a dull city, nothing like I had imagined. It was late Saturday night, and so I went straight to bed. Sunday was put aside for a day of paperwork, looking for other potential manufacturers and sponsors and contacts. I planned to make my way to Cessna first thing Monday morning.

I ironed my shirt, a lengthy and frustrating process, and that was before I even thought about the tie. I called for the motel shuttle to take me to Cessna headquarters and made my way downstairs. Not until then did I really start to think about just what I would say to Cessna, who still had no idea I was popping in to say hello. Who would I meet and what would they think? Next morning the motel shuttle driver and I found our way to Cessna's head office, but I was a bit worried to notice that the car park was strangely empty. Surely one of the largest aircraft manufacturers in the world would have a few more employees hanging around? We drove around for a little while looking for some kind of activity. Eventually, feeling this was a waste of the shuttle driver's time, I asked him to drop me off and pick me up later. This turned out not to be a good move.

I eventually found the front door and rang the bell. Nothing. I waited for a while and called a few numbers hoping to reach the employees I had spoken with on Skype from Australia. Still no answer. After an hour I spotted someone walking to one of the few cars parked outside, wandered over and introduced myself. After a quick chat it turned out it was Martin Luther King Day. No one works on Martin Luther King Day. Another hour later I was picked up and shuttled back to the motel. A whole day wasted and, worst of all, my shirt needed ironing again.

The following morning when I got there, I found the car park jam-packed with vehicles from end to end. This was more like it. I walked to the front desk and asked to speak with one of the contacts I had previously made. After a short wait, I shook hands with a wide-eyed and surprised-looking young man. I'm not sure what he expected or what he could do, but we chatted casually as we walked throughout the building to his office.

It turned out that many of the higher-ranked members of Cessna, including those with the authority to act on on our previous conversations, were away. While my new contact made a few phone calls I was taken around the Cessna Citation factory, the many hangars where some of the world's leading corporate and private jet aircraft are manufactured. At the end of our tour I was told there was not a lot more I could do apart from waiting. I said I would stay until I could talk to somebody who could act on my proposal and, full of hope, I headed back to the motel. While I waited for a call that afternoon I sent dozens of emails and called the people at home who were waiting to see how I went. I couldn't wait to get back to Cessna, just to sit down and talk.

That afternoon I received an email from the Cessna employee I had met that morning. It was short, one and a half lines. Cessna were "unable to provide support" in my venture but thanked me for my interest.

After I read that, I didn't know what to say. Here I was on the other side of the world and up until now I had used the positive meeting from Cessna in late December to justify everything—the plane ticket, the transfers, the accommodation, the time away from home. All gone now, money down the drain. I replied politely, asking whether there was anything else I could do. No reply. That was evidently the end of any connection with Cessna. As I sat in my motel room, I started to get angry. This wasn't because Cessna had declined any assistance in the way of sponsorship; I was more than used to that by now. It was just that I had come all this way, and here I was five minutes from their head office looking at a computer screen with a thirty-word email they could easily have sent me at home in Australia. That was hard.

I told everybody at home what had happened then sank back, wondering what else I could do. There was something. I contacted Beechcraft, an aircraft manufacturer also based in Wichita. No answer, but I caught a taxi to the front gate, hopped out and walked into the security booth. The security guy, who really wanted to help, made many phone calls over the next hour, but no joy: to get into the building, let alone to see anyone, I would need prior permission and passport clearances, all of which would take a week.

For the next two days I sat at the motel desk making phone calls. I spoke with just about every major aircraft manufacturer in the USA and with any aircraft company I thought might be interested in supporting my flight. After all I was in the USA, so I might as well take advantage of it, I thought. I wanted to make sure I didn't arrive back home and regret not looking at every option.

Eventually I left Wichita for San Francisco, where I landed after a short stopover in Texas and some dodgy Mexican food for breakfast. I was hoping to visit the world headquarters of GoPro in San Mateo just south of the San Francisco city center. This was a small bright spot. GoPro high-definition cameras are used in airplanes all over the world and it seemed like a great match for Teen World Flight. I had called GoPro from Wichita and felt the best chance of sponsorship would come from visiting them before heading home. I met with an employee, discovering that the two guys I had already contacted were based in southern California. Overall GoPro seemed interested although they could not give me an immediate answer. With nothing more I could do I decided to catch a plane home.

This had been the first real test of the attitude I had been developing over the previous few months. At the very beginning I had been faced with a decision—to fly around the world or not. I had been filled with doubt and had a million questions and I knew I could do one of two things: run away or jump into a deep black hole and give the plan everything I had. It was as basic, as simple as that, a yes or no decision. If I said "yes" I would give 150 percent until the day the plan fell over completely or the day I landed back in Australia after a successful flight. If I said "no" the whole adventure was over, I would walk away and move on. I would not look back, and I would never have another go. Every time I had a complicated decision to make, at all stages, I made it as simple as possible. So far I had said yes, and now I had a team, I had support and I was beginning to get significant sponsorship. We were getting closer.

The story was far from over, I knew. I boarded the 777 once again, sat in the window seat and settled in. It was time to relax, to have a drink and watch some movies.

A couple of hours off the coast of Los Angeles and just east of Hawaii I decided to take a break. The cabin was dimmed and nearly all the other passengers were fast asleep. I opened the window blind and to my consternation saw the pitch-black darkness catch fire. Lightning flashed all around, there was storm after storm. I had never seen storms that were so savage or widespread. I sat watching, my heart in my mouth, for over an hour. What if I got caught in that?

When I stepped off the aircraft in Sydney I had only one thing in mind. I wanted to ask the pilots about those thunderstorms. At the far end of the baggage claim I spotted the four members of the flight crew, in full uniform, waiting for their bags. I was wearing tracksuit pants, a shirt with a picture of the baby from the movie *Hangover* and runners with my headphones around my neck. I looked like a typical nineteen-year-old.

'Can you tell me if those storms just east of Hawaii were severe?" I asked the captain.

'No, they are always like that," he said, "Actually they were quite okay tonight. We hardly had to divert off track at all.'

'Oh, okay. Thanks." I grabbed my bag and walked away, with more than enough food for thought. I would be in that exact piece of airspace at night in only a few months" time. Was this the brightest idea I had ever had?

7

LOGISTICS

One of the greatest challenges a young pilot faces is increasing his flying time, and building mine was a necessary next step. To qualify for a commercial licence I had to have a minimum of 200 flying hours under different conditions and categories: in cloud, solo, dual or cross-country.

I didn't have my own plane, of course, so I had to find other ways of clocking up my hours. Through a connection with the Frogs Hollow Aeroclub while I was still in my final year at high school, I had met a man named Andrew who had bought a four-seat aircraft and was looking for someone to fly him around as he worked through his flight training. I got the job. My instructor Alan and I were flown to a nearby airport to pick up Andrew's aircraft. I was aiming to do a little flying around the local area to become comfortable with the new plane, then my brother Adam and I would pick up Andrew the following weekend and fly north to the Sunshine Coast.

It was a late-model Cessna 182, a high-wing four-seat aircraft. At that stage it was by far the newest and highestpowered machine I had flown, and a lot of fun. I sat and planned a flight from Merimbula north to the Sunshine Coast, a good seven hours of flying. Still being a low-time pilot I had my brother Adam come along for the ride, think-ing two heads are always better than one. We set off early one morning for what was a long but fun and rewarding day. We met Andrew and all became much more comfortable in the aircraft with a few more hours behind us.

That was the first of many flights in that aircraft and the beginning of a friendship with Andrew and his family. And as that friendship grew, I started to think out loud to Andrew, to tell him about my hopes and fears for my grand plan. I had nowhere near enough experience to fly around the world; even if I did have enough knowledge of actual flying, that was probably not all I would need to learn; I had no air-plane and no lost city of gold that would enable me to buy or hire one. There were so many things I didn't know or didn't have, and I was wor-ried about most of them. But each time I brought up an issue, Andrew raised me a solution. A successful businessman and a new pilot, he had seen and experienced a lot, and had overcome many difficulties. From him I began to learn one of the most important lessons of my impending adventure: regardless of the requirements, challenges and seemingly impossible mountains to climb, all I truly needed was the courage and commitment to pursue my dream. And when we were up against the biggest challenge of all—finding an aircraft—Andrew was there. He offered more than his support; he offered his own Cessna.

From the beginning, we had had a list of options in finding an aircraft, and taking away someone's private aircraft was right at the bottom of the list, a last resort. But now knowing that we had a plane available if all else failed was fantastic. It gave us peace of mind and a way to keep calm as we looked into the question.

Bit by bit we were running through and discarding possibilities, and at the same time we were ticking off the days before departure. There were so few left. In fact, we had reached a point when we had to know what aircraft I was taking. We needed a set registration to send on to each location, we needed figures and data to plan the flight. And we needed the aircraft itself so I could do training flights and to organise the internal fuel tanking and associated lengthy approvals. Not to mention that if you intend to fly around the world by yourself, it looks quite good if you actually have an aircraft.

After phone calls and meetings with Andrew, we decided to accept his more than generous offer and to take the Cessna. I arranged to pick up the aircraft and fly it to the Australian International Airshow at Avalon, where we had a booth to promote the flight and and to look for further sponsorship and supplies. After the show, the aircraft would return to Andrew in southern Queensland, where Andrew would continue flying, then five weeks before departure I would pick it up again. Having already spent a lot of time flying the Cessna, only the tanking, fit out of equipment and testing of the plane would have to be completed before my departure. Yes, these were all huge jobs but most of the preparation work could be done without the aircraft itself.

As the word spread, along with photos of the Cessna, many people wondered about the aircraft choice. Would it be able to complete the trip? I didn't know, and as I hadn't spent years evaluating different aircraft in trying situations, my way of finding out was to talk to those who had. I spent hours on the phone and had many meetings with a wide range of people.

Two, Jim Hazelton and Ray Clamback, stood out. Both were ferry pilots, professionals whose job it was to fly aircraft from A to B, either from the factory to their new home, or from their former location to a new one. A and B were almost always a very long way from each other.

My circumnavigation was in effect a long list of consecutive ferry flights, all joined to create a constant flight path that stretched around the world. Jim and Ray had flown aircraft to all corners of the globe and had crossed the Pacific Ocean hundreds of times. Ray had nerve-racking stories about ditching aircraft into the Pacific. As he gave tips I listened carefully and took many, many notes; after spending hours with both men I had an immense amount of new knowledge.

Originally we had looked for an aircraft with a high cruising airspeed in order to reduce the time taken for long hops. Jim assured me that Andrew's Cessna 182 would be one of the best aircraft for what I wanted to do. If I took Andrew's aircraft, it would be in a completely private deal and in no way affiliated with the Cessna aircraft company in the USA. Andrew's aircraft could be loaded with extra fuel and still easily stay in balance—an essential for safe flight—and it could fly the longest leg from Hawaii to California with relative ease. The Cessna's cruising airspeed was not particularly fast, but its ability to shine in other areas was a simple yet acceptable trade-off.

With Jim's advice in mind we began working on preparing the 182. We took photos of it, as well as measurements and notes. Although the plane stayed up north with its owner, we were able to plan the ferry tanking and begin the paperwork trail, the registration could now be passed to destinations abroad and flight routing could be finalised using the 182's cruise speed and fuel burns. We felt we were getting there at last.

As the Avalon air show neared we started to prepare for the event among all the other jobs. With our own booth for the five-day show between the end of February and the beginning of March, we planned to promote the flight both to the commercial sector of aviation and the general public. We had banners, stickers, small globes with the flight route marked, a giant globe, a donated headset to auction and all the forms and information on each level of sponsorship. I packed my bag, got a ticket to Brisbane, and went off to pick up the Cessna.

The five days at Avalon were fantastic; between talking to hundreds of people every day and managing quick runs outside to see the F22 Raptor fly, there was little time for rest. I took a handful of proposals and walked the aisles of each exhibition hall and within days I had most of the safety equipment sponsored. The interest in the flight, and people's generosity, was simply fantastic.

One important person I had to see was Matt Hall. Matt is one of Australia's leading pilots, with a phenomenal background in the Royal Australian Air Force, including flying combat in Iraq. He went on to become Australia's only competitor in the Red Bull Air Race series, a high-intensity, heart-stopping race revered around the world that makes pilots fly through pylons and go upside down while remaining very close to the ground. Matt is also a skilled and experienced air show performer. I had first met him at the Temora airport in central New South Wales during an aerobatics competition. I was a shy, quiet 14-year-old, too scared to go and say hello. Someone who knew him took me over and introduced me. I stuttered for a second while he added to the growing number of signatures inside the cover of my logbook.

Matt had just released a book in time for the 2013 Avalon show and I wanted him to sign my copy. As I waited in line, a guy in a Matt Hall Racing shirt introduced himself as Dave. He turned out to be Dave Lyall, Matt's operations and media manager. I explained about the around-the-world flight. Now that we had the plane, I knew I needed to focus on getting word about the flight out there, which meant learning more about media. I asked Dave a couple of questions and he asked whether I had a media manager. I explained that we had had some local help for a short while but I was now back to doing things myself. Immediately Dave seemed interested, we exchanged details and decided to chat once I was home. And then Dave took me over to say hello to Matt, which was even better.

Avalon wrapped up on a Sunday. We pulled down what had been our home for the last five days and packed it back into the ute before heading to bed. It had been a great show. The sponsorship drive had gone quite well with a number of new 500 Club members, a wide range of equipment sponsored including nearly all the safety equipment, and a pocketful of business cards representing people and companies who were all interested in having their logo on the aircraft. I had met some fantastic air show performers, one of whom, an American named Bob Carlton who flies a jet-powered sailplane, had shown a keen interest in the flight and promised to meet me at AirVenture in Oshkosh, Wisconsin, during the world's biggest air show. Bob and his wife Laurie were wonderful people. That was all great, and I had the feeling that meeting Dave would also turn into something quite exciting.

Early Monday morning I returned to what was now a deserted showground. A few workers were pulling down marquees while planes were moving slowly out to the runway and taking off. I went in search for help to move the 182; we pulled it to the apron where engine startup was allowed. I jumped in and taxied to a queue of aircraft, waiting patiently as a number of F-18 Hornet fighter jets took to the sky. It was a blue-sky day, perfect for a flight back to Brisbane.

As soon as I arrived back in Merimbula I made contact with Dave Lyall. With more time to chat I found out about him and his company, Sports Communication Australia, while at the same time giving him a much more detailed overview of Teen World Flight. I told him what we were aiming to do, what stage we had reached, what challenges lay ahead, how we hoped to use media and much more.

Soon afterwards I travelled to Sydney to meet with Dave. We discussed how he and his company could help. I soon learned just how complex the media would be; it was too easy to underestimate the level of work required to achieve a successful result. For a start, we would have to contend with constantly differing time zones. That by itself was a major headache, and there were so many other things to consider.

After a few meetings and a lot of emails, plus supplying an overall plan of action, Dave and Sports Communication Australia joined the team. They were offering help in a large number of areas: sponsorship, media, social media and more. From this point on Dave became a huge part of Teen World Flight. Getting him and his team on board was one of the best decisions I made.

8

CAUGHT IN THE HYPE

It's so easy to sit back and dream of an adventure. You can sit and play out endless amazing moments in your head, imagining the achievement of great things you might once have thought were out of your reach. Your mind brushes off the challenges, the hurdles that lie between dreaming and achieving. You are so caught up in the hype of your dream that you fixate on the goal, not the journey.

If I had known what was ahead, I might have given up before I started.

We had to face up to problems right from the beginning: problems that ranged from a misdirected email to the unending need for sponsorship. With Dick Smith I spent a lot of time discussing the challenges of flying around the world. There was a long, long list of aviation-related issues, all of which would need to be resolved before departure. But there was one overriding issue that could not be ignored.

Money.

The team had drawn up a budget, pages and pages of estimated costings that stretched right across our the kitchen table. I added up each and every item, including the value of equipment that could most likely be borrowed or obtained through sponsorship. Then I looked at the final amount. It was sobering. Had I added an extra zero some-where? No. I was facing yet another brush with reality. The amount required to carry out my plan was $250,000, which we had estimated was the total, including goods and services.

Mum and Dad had helped out wherever possible but they could not possibly back me to that extent. The funds would have to be raised through sponsorship. My personal challenge lay in not only raising the funds and successfully completing the flight, but making sure I could return the money Mum and Dad had given me.

I was learning that actually piloting a light aircraft around the globe was only one part of the challenge facing me. Flying around the world as a teenager involved a sponsorship drive beyond anything I had imagined. I was about to embark on some non-aviation-related life lessons.

I sat in the office at Merimbula Air Services and carefully put together cover pages for dozens upon dozens of sponsorship propos-als. My oldest brother Chris sat for hours writing personalised letters explaining just why various companies would benefit from partnering with Teen World Flight and I would read through each letter before adding it to the ever-growing pile. We had endless lists of companies we thought might be interested. Every day I received several "Why don't you ask…" calls and after each call the list grew longer. We had a lot of work ahead but if you asked us, we were all over it.

While we worked away on our carefully constructed production line of proposals, we had partnered with our first major sponsor—Snap Franchising. Snap agreed to take over all "web, design and print," responsibilities, which included a professional approach to potential sponsors. Within weeks we had drafted a sponsorship proposal the size of a small novel. It was fancy, professional and even had its own cardboard folio. We had four levels of corporate sponsorship. The 500 Club, the lowest, was extremely successful. After my grandparents became the first to join, membership spread to friends, my old Year 12 high school class, pilots, aviation-related businesses and groups.

There were even messages from families on behalf of pilots who are no longer alive, pilots who had a dream to fly around the world.

The office in my brother's bedroom began to look like Australia Post's mail sorting facilities. We had envelopes, stickers, business cards, contact details and proposals going everywhere. We all sat around the kitchen table carefully constructing proposals, folding the flat pack folios and inserting the dozens of information filled pages. We had cardboard boxes filled with envelopes addressed to potential sponsors, all of which had to be taken to the post office. I would struggle through the door with each box, becoming very aware that the expression of the woman behind the counter was changing with every box: from surprise to astonishment to downright hostility as she realised how many letters she would have to process before the sun went down.

A few companies replied by letter with variations on "Thank you for your proposal but unfortunately at this time…" but in most cases we heard nothing. Maybe we hadn't told people enough, we thought. And so we sent more and more information-filled envelopes but the response was far less positive than I had hoped. I asked the advice of people who had experience in seeking sponsorship; after a great deal of discussion we decided that maybe the proposals were too big and we would benefit if they were simplified.

We tested various methods depending on whom we were approaching. Some companies were targeted with a written proposal while with others we made personal contact, including face-to-face meetings and phone calls. The "nos" were frequent but the joy and relief when someone jumped on board to support the flight were phenomenal, and we took great pleasure in ticking off sponsored equipment from the lengthy list of required items.

I went to many meetings, talking to a range of people and sharing the story of Teen World Flight and what we hoped to achieve in the coming months. Media interest and coverage were increasing, thanks to the work of Dave Lyall, and this was helping in securing funds. I travelled to aviation events to speak face to face with the representatives of different companies, hoping they would express at least a desire to support the trip. One in nine or ten companies we approached ended up supporting the flight in some way. It was interesting to see which companies provided support; often they were those we least expected, such as Dale and Hitchcock, an earthmoving company based in Canberra, who joined the list of sponsors even though neither owner was fond of light aircraft. I think people were attracted to the spirit of adventure that the whole flight represented, and personal contact also played its part.

One Sunday, while we were watching aircraft zoom on and off the grass airstrip at Frogs Hollow, one of the members asked to have a chat. It turned out that the Frogs Hollow Aeroclub were thinking of running a fundraiser event for my flight and they wanted to know whether I would have any issues if they went ahead. Of course I had absolutely no problem with such an event and I was humbled that they wanted to help out.

As the weeks went on I rarely heard anything of the fundraiser, just a few questions here and there. Knowing firsthand how much was going on for me at the time, the Frogs Hollow members made it a priority to plan their event without me having to worry about anything.

Four months before I was planning to leave, we gathered at the function room of the local bowling club for the Frogs Hollow Aeroclub "Your Ticket to a World Record" fundraising dinner. I walked in the door and was blown away: 227 people sat at a series of round tables, filling the room. Globes were spread everywhere, each showing the proposed route for the flight and complete with a toy aircraft hanging above them. Frankie J. Holden from the band Ol' 55 was the master of ceremonies, and there were not just friends, family and locals, but pilots who had made a special trip just to be there. What happened that night was amazing. It was so much more than an event that provided a significant proportion of the flight's funding—a whopping $24,000—it was 227 people showing their support and belief in what

I was trying to achieve. I had no idea that a solo flight around the world meant so much to so many people, and I was humble and grateful.

Taped to the fridge door at home was a calendar that outlined our lives for the near future. It had always been there, covered in day-to-day jobs, important reminders and regular birthdays, thanks to a family big enough to populate a small village. It had been a great way to keep track of meetings and deadlines during the planning of the flight but what began as a scribbled note here and there had now become a constant flow of things to do and places to be.

One morning I wandered into the kitchen and stared into the open fridge hoping breakfast would jump out at me. It didn't. I closed the fridge door, accepting my misfortune, and was blinded by highlighted yellow boxes on a newly printed calendar. June 30—Ryan departs.

The flight had made the calendar, there was six weeks remaining and there was a lot to do. What I didn't know was just what these six weeks would bring.

I had meetings left, right and center, always finding myself on a plane or sipping a Red Bull, adhering to my restricted "P plate" speed limit en route to Sydney. There were lunches where I had to don a tie and tell the story of what I was about to attempt, knowing I should have been at home attending to the small mountain of jobs and paperwork.

The phone was ringing constantly. Often the caller was Ken and we discussed flight planning, preparation and the last minute requirements; if it was Dave we talked about media, sponsorship, public speaking or—yet again—further preparations to have everything in order for departure.

We continued the sponsorship drive, gathering more and more support as the time went on. I began to speak with sign writers, defining the way we would display the sponsors on the aircraft itself to acknowledge their generous support.

We finalised the route, convinced after nine months of adjustments that we had taken each and every comment and recommendation into account and created one of the safest and most sensible around-the-world flight routes. Our departure point had changed several times, from Sydney to Canberra and elsewhere and back again. Finally, after taking in a long list of aviation and non-aviation related factors, we chose Wollongong because it was just south of Sydney and had a thriving small airport.

An issue soon arose about the date when we would return to Wollongong. Initially we had decided on 14 September, but soon afterwards Prime Minister Julia Gillard announced that the federal election would be held that very day. We altered the flight route over the following weeks, working to take out days and move the arrival date back one week to the weekend of 7 September. The schedule was tight but it was possible—always bearing in mind that safety was the number one priority and that with any number of unknown delays this arrival time might not be met anyway.

I heard about a course called HUET—Helicopter Underwater Escape Training—otherwise known as "learn to swim upside down out of a helicopter without sinking." Overseen by Westpac Life Saving, the course was held in a small classroom close to the Westpac Life Saver hangars that overlooked the Pacific Ocean. A small class including pilots and members of a television crew sat and listened to the theory of how to survive an aircraft ditching into the water. We had the common goal of not drowning in the practical pool assessment later that afternoon.

After successfully escaping a replica of an overturned helicopter cockpit, both visually and while blindfolded, we clambered from the pool to learn about the life raft. I was last to undertake the practical task—pulling myself from the water into an inflated raft wearing a cumbersome life jacket. I felt like I was back in P.E. in primary school, once more a highly undertrained and far from malnourished kid with a poor physique being asked to do something way beyond my capabilities.

I hung on the edge of the life raft, with five or six classmates waiting inside for me to haul myself in. Not wishing to try this more than once

I gave it everything I had. I turned out to be a little physically fitter than I had been in primary school and I literally flew out of the water and into the life raft, clearing the first guy before landing in the lap of the blonde TV presenter. Safe to say I took my HUET certificate home with pride.

We continued work on preparing the Cessna 182, using measurements of the cabin to source additional aluminum fuel tanks that would be mounted inside the aircraft. Not being able to find exactly what we wanted, we designed a tank from scratch, one that would be manufactured and approved specifically for the flight. We looked at all aspects of the aircraft—speed, range, overall performance in varying configurations and much more, including reading the avionics pilot manuals from cover to cover. We estimated the flight times so we could pinpoint where aircraft maintenance would be required, and once that had been done we started working through the legalities of international maintenance on an Australian registered aircraft.

Ken travelled across to Merimbula for a weekend. We spent the whole time planning the flight—hardly anyone's idea of a relaxing few days on the beaches of the Sapphire Coast. We had planned, fundraised, worked through countless problems and finalised the route but not once had I picked up a detailed map, and it felt wrong.

Ken had assured me that putting together the flight logs—the actual paper flight plans that defined each leg's finer details and times that would be carried in the aircraft—was not a huge job in comparison to the others still to be completed. I had trusted him, but with a nine-kilogram box of maps known as charts sitting on the kitchen floor I soon wanted very much to have this particular task behind us.

Fortified by a constant flow of coffee and hot chocolate, we spent over twenty-four hours unravelling maps and almost literally joining the dots, picking flight routes that would comply with international airspace regulations while also acknowledging the limitations of the aircraft. We started at Wollongong, my departure point, and finished the first leg at Norfolk Island in the Pacific Ocean east of Australia.

The world is covered in aviation "waypoints," precise positions in the sky specifically for use within aviation navigation, all labelled with three- or five-letter designators that form a combination of letters that aren't actual meaningful words, but that can be pronounced: for example, "DODUX." The list of waypoints grew as the night went on and every leg of flight planning was completed. There were literally thousands.

I ventured to my doctor with a list of countries in hand and after an hour we had a pile of prescriptions for the required immunisations. My now pincushion-like self went for the tablet option wherever possible.

The lounge room floor began to disappear under the equipment laid across it, from clothes to an immersion suit and emergency equipment. The lounges were covered with paperwork: copies of my passport, proof of immunisations, countless bundles of visa paperwork, bank account statements, aircraft maintenance documents, flight plans. There was even a letter of support from our local MP, Andrew Constance, which he said might be used if I ever found myself in a sticky situation and needed some form of official-looking written support.

Dave, his colleague Lloyd and I met regularly to discuss media issues. How would we share the flight with the thousands of interested onlookers, who would be in charge of what, what I would need to do while I was away, how publicity for sponsors could be organised. We also needed to work out the chain of command, and what would happen in the event of an emergency, which involved setting up and thoroughly exploring a crisis action plan with family and involved team members. We didn't share these crisis meetings with our wider team group, which by now seemed to measure in dozens, if not hundreds, but kept them to the original seven or so members: sharing that information around would only have created more stress. There were also at least two exciting sponsorship and media possibilities to be explored. Telstra were showing interest in coming on board as sponsors: having one of Australia's premier telecommunications companies would be enormously useful. We had several meetings and things were looking very promising. We were also talking to the Channel 9 current affairs program *60 Minutes*.

Finally everything seemed to be coming together. The Cessna 182 was living in Redcliffe just north of Brisbane where Andrew its owner was undertaking his flying training. We had travelled to Brisbane a number of times to talk about the 182 and what would be involved in using it for the world flight. We had decided not to pick up the aircraft until the last possible minute so that Andrew could get the most out of his training; after all, he would be without it for nearly three months. We needed to find several items before we could pick up the plane, too: not impossible, just time consuming.

My aim, over and above the goal of a circumnavigation, getting a world record and promoting youth in aviation, was to make sure this was an enjoyable experience for everyone. I didn't want anyone to be put in an uncomfortable position just to see Teen World Flight become a success. This included family, friends and of course Andrew, who after all had been more than generous in lending us his plane.

On a Monday morning six weeks before departure, Andrew sent us through the final aircraft hire agreement. I printed off the document, sat with Mum and Dad at the kitchen table and read through each section. I soon realised that there was a major problem.

One clause in the agreement dealt with the requirement that nobody should be at financial risk due to the nature of the flight. It was not at all unreasonable, but I could not guarantee it. Andrew, the owner of the aircraft, was clearly at risk; so were my backers, and so were Mum and Dad. We had talked about the issue of fiscal security, of course, but the difference between a theoretical possibility and a legal requirement was now all too evident. Having planned the flight and even written a risk mitigation report for the Civil Aviation Safety Authority, I should probably have known better.

We didn't give up. I didn't sleep that night, just lay awake thinking how this latest hurdle could be overcome. The next morning I called everyone I knew, beginning with Dick Smith, seeking answers. I spoke with successful businessmen and accomplished pilots, the same people who had offered wisdom and support over the previous months. They could all see the issue, but the problem appeared to be insoluble. What was asked was not unreasonable; the clause did meet the stipulation that the flight should be seen as a positive experience, not one that involved widespread risk or liability for its supporters. However, in the rush to get ready for the flight, with so many other issues demanding attention, I had not considered what its finer details implied. What I thought it would be and what it was turned out to be completely different.

Now I had to face facts. Six weeks to the day before departure, we no longer had an airplane.

I sat at the kitchen table like a zombie. I felt sick. I called Ken and told him the whole story, from the reasons behind losing the aircraft to what each individual person had said about the issue. My voice was shaking and even though I thought I was doing okay he could easily tell I wasn't. We had worked through so much to find ourselves so close to the departure, everything was coming together in only the last week, yet all of a sudden the most vital puzzle piece had gone missing. Everything else remained, yet without an aircraft it was all useless.

At the very beginning I had made a "yes or no" decision based on whether I would attempt to fly around the world or not, whether I would take on the endless challenges that came up along the way. I had said yes. As part of that deal, whenever there was an issue I could never say no and just give up, not until we had tried absolutely every avenue and there was no way the issue could be fixed. With this in mind giving up was simply not an option. The only thing to do now was to find another aircraft, one we could secure without the requirements faced with the previous Cessna, one that could be covered solely by our fantastic insurance sponsor Julian and the team at QBE Insurance.

I called everyone I could think of, from team members to aircraft companies. We sat as a family and looked at the options; several people I called were also thinking of potential possibilities. One or two even

offered their own aircraft and, while this was a phenomenally generous gesture of support I couldn't accept, mostly because their aircraft
were not suitable. With pages of notes piling up in front of me I called
an aviation company from Melbourne, one of several listed down the
page. I explained the issue once more, the guy on the other end of the
line was very interested and more than that, he had an idea. He told
me that he knew of a fairly new model four-seat Cirrus, very similar to
the aircraft in which I had completed the section of my training that
allowed me to fly through clouds and weather solely using the instruments. This plane had been sitting in a hangar near Melbourne for
quite a while and needed to be flown.

A session of phone tag later I was in contact with the aircraft owner,
a warm and friendly woman, Tina, who had previously flown the aircraft herself. I explained the issue again—I was good at it by now—and
her response was fantastic. She saw absolutely no issue in the aircraft
being hired for the flight. There were a few conversations to be had in
regards to the journey, preparations and the team behind me, but the
flight itself was not an issue. The aircraft had been affiliated with QBE
Insurance before and neither Tina nor her husband saw any problem
with the coverage on offer.

Two days later Mum, Dad and I set off towards Melbourne to have a
look through the aircraft and to meet Tina. We stopped at the airport,
not only to have a look at the Cirrus but to speak with the aircraft engineer who had been completing all the maintenance. Then we drove
into the Melbourne CBD and met Tina and her husband. We sat and
chatted away for hours as if we were all long-lost friends. They were
keenly interested in the flight and asked lots of questions, and were
happy to be a part of the adventure.

We finally said goodbye as we were all facing a long drive home, and
after pulling out of the car park I immediately called everyone I could
think of to update them. Only three days after losing the aircraft, after
sitting at the kitchen table wishing I was anywhere but there, wondering whether it was all over and whom that would affect, we had

another aircraft. What was more it was fast, and new, and though we would have to work hard to make necessary changes such as tanking, changing the sign writing, registration and the flight plan itself, things could not have been better.

I needed to apply for a permit allowing the aircraft to fly, even though it required scheduled maintenance. I wanted to take it back to Merimbula where it would be serviced at Merimbula Aircraft Maintenance. Rex, who ran it, and his colleagues Eddie and Glynn had already given us an enormous amount of support, and over the next few weeks they would become even more closely involved. Through a friend I contacted an airline pilot who owned and flew his own Cirrus and asked whether he would travel with me to Melbourne and fly back in the Cirrus to Merimbula. I figured that the time in the air was best spent learning as much as possible from someone who knew the machine well. He had absolutely no problem with this and I agreed to contact him again once I had the permit to fly the plane back to Merimbula in my hands.

It was Monday morning, seven days after we had lost the Cessna, only two days before we planned to pick up the Cirrus and five weeks to the day before departure. I was sitting in the lunchroom of Merimbula Aircraft Maintenance and morning tea, which is always full of laughs, had just finished, leaving me peace and quiet to work on the permit application form. If we submitted it that day we would have it back in time for our flight from Melbourne. As I filled in the details my phone rang, it was the engineer who maintained the Cirrus. He had decided to undertake a "bore scope," an inspection of all the internal parts of the engine using a camera on a long and flexible arm. The aircraft had been sitting for quite a while and although the engine had been turned over it was rarely flown. With the long overwater stretches in mind he thought it would be best to have a look. What he found was devastating. Corrosion on a gear tooth embedded well inside the jungle of moving parts rendered the aircraft unserviceable. Heartbreak. I was gutted. What now?

We brainstormed, we phoned people, we thought of every option possible. Underneath the determination to get this right was a sense of panic, almost hopelessness. How many second chances would I get? How long could we play this game before time ran out and safety became compromised? Was this a sign?

With safety as the number one priority and the inability to move the departure date further away, any compromise would mean the flight was over for good. The flight had always been marketed as Teen World Flight; the record was to become not only the youngest but also the first teenager to fly solo around the world, which would become a little more complicated if I turned twenty before finishing the flight. Along with my age, the flight planning including accommodation, fuel, customs and immigration requirements among a hundred other preplanned items were now set in stone, trying to move them all would be an absolute nightmare, if not almost impossible.

We had two courses of action we could take. One was to source another aircraft, the other was to ask a team of volunteers to completely rebuild the engine of the Cirrus. Both looked out of the question.

I made a few more phone calls, including one to a pilot named David who lived in northern New South Wales. I had borrowed an aircraft from him for the Wings Over Illawarra air show in Wollongong earlier in the year; without the 182 this had been a way of having an aircraft on our stand to create further interest in Teen World Flight. At the time David had had a very new model Cirrus for sale, and we had considered this as an early possibility. However, once we knew that buying a plane was not possible we had moved on. But now with catastrophe looming I called David and told him the story, explaining what had happened with the last two aircraft and what that meant for the flight. Although I couldn't purchase his Cirrus outright I asked whether he would be willing to hire it to me for the duration of the trip. David said he would have to think it over. That afternoon David called back. He was willing to hire out the aircraft although we would have to tick a few boxes before the deal was finalised. These were items we had already faced, including insurance and hire agreements, as well as providing David with a general overview of the flight. We worked flat out for days juggling paperwork and phone calls, trying to make everyone comfortable with the situation.

We were finished within a week. Now we had an aircraft, an aircraft that had recently been flown, tried and tested. The perfect airplane for the trip.

9

NEARLY THERE

At last we had a plane, and a good one, a four-seat low-wing Cirrus that was a leader in its class. A very safe aircraft, too: its composite moulded fuselage included a full-sized parachute for use in dire emergencies.

The day after finalising the Cirrus I packed my bags to go to Sydney where my manager Dave and I had meetings with both *60 Minutes* and Telstra. *60 Minutes* was doing a story on the adventure and Telstra had agreed to become the principal partner. Not only was Telstra a sponsor offering a financial contribution—much needed at the time—but they were also offering their telecommunication resources. These, from a mobile phone to the installation of a satellite phone and tracker in the Cirrus, were absolutely vital. Meetings with the *60 Minutes* producers and Telstra were aimed at giving each organisation a deeper and better understanding of Teen World Flight, exactly what a solo around-the-world flight would entail.

After seeing Telstra and *60 Minutes*, I flew to Tamworth in central New South Wales to meet David, the owner of the Cirrus. Dave was a great guy with a solid background in flying Cirrus aircraft, and we wandered into the hangar where I met my new best friend—A 2009 Cirrus SR22 with the registration VH-OLS, or Victor Hotel Oscar Lima Sierra.

It was white with black and grey decals splitting the blank fuselage into a work of art. It was sleek, without rivets, struts or wires: a machine that the Wright Brothers could have only dreamed about. The thick composite propeller sat still, seen easily from the interior, equipped with very advanced avionics and everything else that was needed for a young pilot to travel the world alone. It was beautiful.

It was also sitting high on jacks because it was halfway through its major inspection, the one that was undertaken every 100 flying hours. While it was being finished off David and I went flying in another Cirrus, talking over the main points of the aircraft. We got in, pushed the throttle forward and took to the sky. For me a Cirrus was an absolute rocket ship, capable of speeds around the circuit that were faster than anything I had experienced to date. It was also comfortable. The stick sat off to one side and with the door closed, my arm comfortably rested in a natural position. With little more than a thought, the plane would dart about the sky. I was hooked. One short flight in the now ready VH-OLS with an instructor the next day and I was ready to go. I fuelled up, we shook hands and I thanked David yet again, waved goodbye and took off.

I flew to Caboolture, north of Brisbane, where I was to take part in an Advanced Pilot Seminar or APS. Most of the time I was trying to work out the intricacies of the new plane and taking note of such things as its cruise speed, fuel burn and overall performance. I touched down, very narrowly missing a flock of birds, tied the aircraft down, covered it up and headed to a motel. The Advanced Pilot Seminar focused on correct engine management techniques. With one engine and a lot of ocean to cross I listened carefully and took notes. The course was being run by David Brown, who had organised my initial talk at the AusFly air show and the APS crew. Advanced Pilot Seminars had just been introduced into Australia, and David had help from John Deakin and Walter Atkinson who had run these seminars in the USA. John had near on 40,000 flying hours and a lot of very good stories, many of which were hilarious. The knowledge he and Walter had about the aviation industry was simply phenomenal.

David, John, Walter and the crew looked after me extremely well. They knew what I was up against and offered as much advice as they could, including some one-on-one conversations when the weekend was over. They came to the airport with me to look at the Cirrus, we said our goodbyes and promised to keep in touch. I took off with my head crammed with information, knowing that I was much better informed than I had been before coming to Caboolture.

I flew south to Port Macquarie on the mid north coast of New South Wales where I had completed my instrument rating training; I needed to spend a couple of days refreshing these skills and applying them to the new aircraft. We flew a few navigation exercises and covered the skills I had learned not so long before. The Port Macquarie stopover was important; not only did I brush up my skills but it boosted my confidence as a pilot when I was under so much other pressure.

From Port Macquarie I headed home, flying the Cirrus through the clouds to Merimbula. Landing there after all the stress, doubt and worry was a triumphant moment. I now had a beautiful and very advanced aircraft which I would fly from Wollongong in just over a month's time. It represented the perfect end to the two hardest weeks of my life.

The biggest issue we now faced was altering the already completed planning to suit the Cirrus. This involved changing such things as registration numbers and speeds on a flight plan. These were challenging enough, but storing and carrying fuel inside the aircraft proved an even bigger issue.

A week of calculations and phone calls led us to a solution that we felt would work. We would remove the rear seat and install a 600-liter fuel "bladder," a soft baglike tank that would lie deflated and flat when empty. When full it would be secured by a carefully structured and designed network of ratchet straps. We began on the paperwork, organising the EOs, or engineering orders, to have the modifications on the certified aircraft approved. We had weight and balance figures calculated—the maximum weight with which the Cirrus was allowed to take off—but would have to increase that by 20 per cent because of the extra fuel and equipment we were carrying. We measured the aircraft and sent the figures through to the sign-writer to allow the sizing of the sponsor decals; although we continued to seek sponsorship we needed to begin printing decals for the plane. The addition of Telstra to the list of sponsors had been fantastic and a phenomenal help, but we were still far behind our allocated budget, a sum of money that had only ever been based on estimates and educated opinions. We were lucky that through a friend at Merimbula airport, Bruce, we were able to have the sign-writing organised and applied by Bruce himself. We had to get the Cirrus as ready as possible for what would be a very important media day.

I flew the Cirrus to Wollongong to meet Dave. We were about to embark on some filming with *60 Minutes* as well as flying beside the Channel 9 news helicopter to gather some air-to-air shots of the plane that had now been christened the *Spirit of the Sapphire Coast*.

The night before we started filming with *60 Minutes* we had dinner with the crew; I would meet them in several places as I flew around the world. My story had been assigned to Charles Woolley, a long-serving member of the *60 Minutes* family. Although seen regularly reporting on serious stories and current affairs, Charles Woolley was just a normal friendly guy. He had opinions on different things, spoke about family and friends, liked to have a beer, expressed his hatred and frustration towards leaf blowers. If I could somehow retell his jokes about them I would, but I can't.

We met at the airport the next morning early enough for *60 Minutes* to take a shot of the hangar doors opening as the sun rose. I flew the Cirrus alongside the news chopper, with senior news reporter Mark Burrows in the right-hand seat, to gather some footage for the evening bulletin. The whole morning was a constant rush, not only because of the filming—we also had to kit out the Cirrus with several cameras so *60 Minutes* could capture the entire solo journey. Dave's amazing organisation saw interviews with television, newspapers, magazines and radio all crammed into one day. That afternoon Charles Woolley, or Uncle Charles as he suggested I could call him, climbed into the Cirrus and we flew south to Merimbula. The rest of the crew drove by road, all meeting the next morning for a final day of pre-flight filming.

Within a few hours we had visited my old school, Sapphire Coast Anglican College, and filmed a talk with the kids. We then travelled home where Mum and Dad were waiting. With Mum being a clean freak at the best of times, the fact that Charles Woolley was popping over to say hi made things interesting. Any family gathering meant that the house had to be spotless, let alone having a 60 Minutes TV presenter come and visit. There was not a speck of dust in that house.

I stood back after finishing my filming and watched as Mum and Dad were interviewed; it hit me suddenly that Charles Woolley from 60 Minutes was sitting at our kitchen table. Wow. He was genuinely interested in the flight and we all responded to his warmth and curiosity.

And now, after so much practice, once again we packed my bags, carefully checking and double-checking everything. The last of the equipment was gathered and piled at the door. Some of the remaining decals were applied to the aircraft. Emails were sent, good wishes were received and the days on the calendar were disappearing.

Further talks with our new partner Telstra, with their goal to connect me in every way possible, saw the installation of a satellite phone into the aircraft. This allowed long-distance communication when the HF radio did not work or when other means of contacting family and team members failed.

I had only one job left to do—to install the fuel tank into the aircraft. The regulations in relation to fitting additional tanking into the Cirrus were very strict, and the operation had to be carried out very close to departure. With only days left I flew north to Kempsey in central New South Wales, where Darren and the crew at Macleay Aircraft Maintenance began fitting the tank into the aircraft. I watched every move, learning where each fitting went and why it was there. There was a good chance I would need to understand this if something happened to go wrong during the trip, so now was the time to learn. Along with the tank, a HF radio used for long-distance communication was fitted for use over water when the normal aircraft radios were out of range. To service the radio inside the cabin a long wire aerial was fitted to the exterior of the aircraft, running from nose to tail underneath the belly of the plane before extending at waist height to the right wing tip, where it was secured.

From the front seats rearward the aircraft was stripped, the trim and seats were taken out, leaving room for the tank. The ratchets, all six brightly coloured straps, lay across the tank like netting. A selection of fuel lines ran under the seat and into the right foot well where they joined an array of fuel and hand pumps. These would take fuel from the bladder tank inside the cockpit and let it transfer via a fuel line running under the wing into the right-wing fuel tank. When the switches were turned on, the right tank would fill with fuel, increasing the aircraft endurance from five hours to a whopping seventeen without stopping.

We filled the tank with a small amount of fuel, I clambered into an aircraft that now smelt like fuel and took off. I circled over Kempsey to test the system. From what I could tell the tank worked okay with a reduced fuel load, but the real test would come when the tank was full. Unfortunately that was not an option at this time due to Australian aviation regulations defining when and where the tank could be used, so I packed up, said goodbye and flew the aircraft home.

With the Merimbula airport undergoing maintenance, the Cirrus was put into a hangar at Frogs Hollow. I worked between home and the airport, finishing up the final jobs at home while I zipped back and forth to the plane. We installed cameras into the aircraft and spent an afternoon with Rex, Eddie and the maintenance boys changing the oil and learning a few more skills. With the engine covered up and wiped down, the last equipment fitted and tested, we closed up the hangar.

The next time I would see the aircraft would be the day I departed for Wollongong.

The clock was ticking away, rushing by a little too quickly. I had packed all I could, we had checked everything over and over again and now I was left with little to do except go to bed. Finally, after years of work, I was nearing my comfort zone, sort of. I checked the weather and planned to depart Merimbula the next morning. It might have been the beginning of an unknown adventure, a type of flying that I had never experienced before, over water and through outrageously different environments, cultures and situations, but it was flying. That was all that mattered.

I woke up early after a night of little sleep and a lot of thinking. Showered, dressed in the flight suit, packed toothbrush and bags in the ute.

The plan was to fly the aircraft from the little Frogs Hollow grass airstrip to Merimbula early that morning. The Merimbula runway was opening just in time for my planned departure celebration. Constant rain had been battering the Sapphire Coast so a quick check of the runway at Merimbula would be required before attempting a landing in the Cirrus. This was not the day for taking chances and mine would be one of the first aircraft landing on the newly upgraded runway.

Dad and I set off for Frogs Hollow while everyone else planned to meet us at Merimbula. As we drove past home, I spun around and wondered: "Will I ever see this place again?" I knew from a mathematical and logical point of view, considering our planning and priority towards safety, that I would. But my mind was playing games; there were times when it took absolutely no notice of common sense.

I opened the hangar and Dad and I wheeled the Cirrus out into the open air. It was a cloudy, dreary day with skies threatening another downpour. One by one other pilots arrived at Frogs, all members of the aeroclub who would be flying to Merimbula to see me off. I completed my thorough pre-flight inspection and packed the aircraft in the quiet surrounds of the little grass airstrip, knowing Merimbula was beginning to fill with locals. I started up and taxied away.

It was a short flight but an enjoyable one, leaving Frogs with a quick look over the shoulder at an airstrip and aeroclub that had played such a huge part in my flying life. I headed through a gap in the surrounding hills before descending into Merimbula. Normally it was a sunny coastal town but today it was overcast, and a glance to the north confirmed low-lying cloud in the direction of Wollongong. I touched down at Merimbula and taxied straight to the bowser; all that was left to do was to refuel and apply some of the last stickers before departure. The aircraft was wheeled into Rex's hangar at Merimbula Aircraft Maintenance and Bruce, who had organised much of the sign writing, was on hand to apply the last decals. I zipped away to put in a flight plan, an official notification to air traffic control as to who you are, where and when you are flying, and to check the weather. As I walked back I spotted the ever-growing crowd pushed up against a makeshift fence, all squinting for a look into the hangar and the Cirrus.

It was vital to me, however long it took, to have the last of the sponsors" logos added to the aircraft, including the aircraft's name—*The Spirit of the Sapphire Coast*, encompassing the hard work put in by both the Frogs Hollow Aeroclub and the local area. Without the support of each and every sponsor: the individuals who passed on small amounts including international currency for food; the clubs and organisations teaming together to raise funds; the hundreds of members of the 500 Club; the shops that fundraised through a "loose change jar'; up to the large organisations such as Telstra and our other corporate sponsors including Snap, Dick Smith Foods, Jeppesen, QBE, Dale and Hitchcock and many others, the flight would have simply not gone ahead. This support showed the world that a young person with a dream, courage and commitment, can and will find support within the community to help their objective become a reality. All of us represented that it was possible to leave Merimbula with a common dream to conquer the world.

We disconnected the fence, parted the crowd like the Red Sea in the Bible and had the aircraft towed to the taxiway. We had a quick chat standing on a makeshift stage and with a thank you to all involved, I said goodbye and hopped into the Cirrus. I started up and as soon as the aircraft was firing, both Mum and Dad cut a ribbon—evidently a structurally sound device keeping me within the confines of Merimbula airport—then I was free. As I began my checks, a lengthy process, everyone began cheering and a stream of water shot from the fire truck. I have no idea whether everyone was excited or they just wanted to get rid of me so they could go and grab breakfast. However, finally I was finished and taxied towards the end of the runway.

I lifted off, turning immediately to come back around over the airfield once more, and with a pass overhead I rocked my wings to wave goodbye and focused on climbing ahead through a low cloud base en route to Wollongong.

Although I would officially depart from Wollongong early the following morning, it was safe to say I had truly left home. The familiar coastline and surrounding areas where I learned to fly were behind me, the cloud that engulfed the aircraft made things a little easier as, with no sight of the ground or water, I could have been anywhere. Each memory, whether a first solo, my first navigation flight or the fun times flying the coast with family and friends were all based around this area. Hopefully the next memory, the successful end to a solo circumnavigation, would happen in these skies in just a few months' time.

I touched down in Wollongong after an approach through the rain-filled clouds from the south and taxied to a large hangar. The doors were only just cracked open, sheltering the contents of the building from the pouring rain, yet within that small crack was a bunch of media personnel and cameras filming my arrival. I climbed out, said hello and for the next twenty minutes proceeded to walk back and forth to the aircraft in the rain for the benefit of the cameras.

We filmed that afternoon with a number of people, ticking off the media for the evening news stories. Again Dave took control and told me where to go and what to do. Without that I would have been lost. Telstra filmed for a few hours, calmly holding an umbrella as I stuttered my way through various interviews. As I worked away I received a text message from Dick Smith. He wanted to know whether I would be in Wollongong that afternoon. He would be off overseas early the following morning and therefore miss my departure.

Months earlier Dad and I had visited Dick at his property in Canberra; in a fast low-wing wooden Falco we had borrowed from a friend, Ian Newman, we had touched down on Dick's airstrip only two hours after he called to invite us over for lunch. We parked the aircraft and climbed aboard a nearby train, a real train, and rode through Dick's property to the front door of his house. At lunch Dick had asked whether I was superstitious. I bluffed through the moment wondering what he meant, and then he offered something amazing.

Dick explained that he had an original piece of fabric from Sir Charles Kingsford Smith's plane, the *Southern Cross*, which he had acquired many years before. Dick had taken it with him on five around-the-world flights, it had gone with Gaby Kennard when she became the first Australian woman to circumnavigate the globe solo and it was given to Jessica Watson, the youngest person to sail solo around the world. Other adventurers had also had it as their good luck charm. It had always come home. That day Dick asked whether I too would like to take the fabric with me, and I was naturally honoured to accept.

However, a little later Dick had called to let me know that the fabric, which he had taken with him on a recent helicopter trip, had been left with the helicopter in an inland town. It was a major disappointment: the symbolic value of that piece of cloth, reminding me of my grandfather and the stories of him flying in this very airplane, the Southern Cross, with Kingsford Smith himself, was immense.

At Wollongong we kept filming in the wind and rain. We then heard a whine of a jet engine and walked outside to see that a Cessna Citation business jet had just touched down. The jet taxied up to the hangar and parked only meters away. Behind the window was Dick

Smith, smiling from ear to ear and waving something in his hand. Dick jumped from the jet and ran across the tarmac towards me. In his hand was the fabric from the *Southern Cross*.

He said he had woken up that morning and driven to the Bankstown airport just south of Sydney. With a member of his crew he had climbed into his jet and flown out west to the helicopter, solely to bring the fabric back to Wollongong. He explained that he did not want to see me leave without it even if that took "the most expensive retrieval mission I have ever been on" to make it happen.

It was a small grey square of fabric two or three inches across, and I secured it to the cockpit dashboard where I would always be able to see it. It joined Granddad's pilot logbook which I had hidden away in the aircraft.

Dick wished me well and flew off, we finished filming and then with the help of friends we filled the aircraft's ferry tank with enough fuel for the first leg of the flight, to Norfolk Island. It was a challenging task, one I hadn't completed before and I was grateful for sets of extra hands, especially in the rain. I strapped in the tank, covered it with sheets of foam ready for my bags to be put in the next morning. We pushed the Cirrus back into the hangar, took the bags to the car and headed to the motel. That night, after checking the forecast weather several times, we dressed up and set off for dinner with a huge number of family and friends. We relaxed and chatted but called it an early night. Everyone was leaving very early the following morning for the Illawarra Regional Airport for something that had sometimes seemed impossible—the beginning of a 24,000 nautical mile, 45,000 kilometer journey that would take me, hopefully, solo around the world.

10

ON THE WAY

The next morning the alarm went off at 4am. I climbed out of bed and headed for a cold shower. My mind was racing with a feeling that overpowered everything else, a feeling that I would come to know well in the months to come. It was fear: hesitation in moving ahead into the unknown while at the same time realising there is no other choice.

I pulled on the flight suit, a grey full-body fireproof Nomex suit tailor-made by Sisley Workwear. It was covered in epaulettes, name patches, security cards and the Australian flag, all meant to convince the authorities in different countries of my position, professionalism and rank. I rolled my other clothes—bare minimum casual gear to see me through my non-flying days—and crammed them into a small duffel bag. I had to strain the zipper shut while squishing the bag with one knee—a series of actions that became very familiar in the weeks to come. Before heading outside I sat with the computer one more time, looking at the weather forecasts for the overwater trip to Norfolk Island. They were far from great, but not bad enough to delay my departure. I packed up my laptop and headed to the car.

We arrived at a large hangar at the Illawarra Regional Airport, which was filled with vintage aircraft being displayed, restored, maintained and flown by the Historical Aircraft Restoration Society. At the very front was the Cirrus, the latest in small single-engine aircraft, equipped and ready to set off around the world.

As I ran around flustered, completing the most thorough pre-flight inspection of my life and packing the aircraft, family and friends started to arrive. It was still dark and the hangar doors were closed, yet dozens of people surrounded the aircraft in matching Teen World Flight shirts. Charles Woolley and the *60 Minutes* crew were there, and Nan and Pa stood by with a "Good Luck Ryan" banner, patiently waiting while the last preparations were completed.

Two men from Australian Customs arrived at the hangar and issued me the paperwork required to fly out of Australia. After I had signed the General Declaration, or Gen Dec, a Customs form I would use every time I entered or left a country, we opened the hangar doors. The Customs officer handed me a card to fill out just before I re-entered Australia. It felt strange to think about returning to Australia before I had gone anywhere.

We swung the aircraft around and I glanced at my watch: nearly time to go. With nothing left to do, I started to say goodbye. With each goodbye the realisation of what was just about to happen hit me. As the farewells became harder to say I moved more quickly, finally reaching Mum, Dad, my brothers and sister-in-law. All of them, with Mum leading the charge, were in tears. I was doing all I could to keep it together myself, and so I needed to keep moving as quickly as possible. When I had finished I clambered up the step and into the Cirrus.

I strapped in and made myself comfortable, telling myself to relax, go slow and move through each step as if I was going flying on any other day. As I flicked switches the aircraft's avionics came to life, but so did my mobile phone. I was used to constant phone calls and now I wonder why on earth I chose to answer it at that delicate, nerve-racking point in time when everyone was watching me with bated breath. But I did.

'Hi Ryan, it's Tony Abbott here,"—it was the man widely tipped to be the next Australian Prime Minister. He was calling to wish me well on the trip. Just the fact that he had taken the time to acknowledge Teen World Flight was a great feeling. I slipped my phone back into my pocket and with a "clear prop" call out the open door, ensuring the area was clear, the Cirrus came to life in the cool morning air. I worked through the checks and slowly taxied the aircraft a little further away from the surrounding crowd. And with my run ups complete— the routine checks of the aircraft's engine undertaken before each and every flight—I turned and waved goodbye for the last time.

I was extremely nervous, yet I felt that this wasn't really happening. At the same time I knew I had to go, I had to take off, whatever might happen. I had to trust that the last two years had given me the experience and knowledge to take on the trip, along with the unknown challenges it would provide, that I as a solo pilot had the ability to make crucial decisions without the input of another crew member. I would just have to take it step by step, leg by leg, or it would all just become too much.

I taxied to the end of the runway, realising that the power needed just for that showed how heavy the aircraft was. I also knew that the ferry fuel tank was only half full and at some point in the coming month I would be taxiing with the tank full at 120 per cent of the normal maximum takeoff weight. I stopped just prior to the runway, checking and double checking everything once again. I lined up and pushed the throttle forwards, the engine roared to life.

I was airborne. Only 24,000 nautical miles to go.

I climbed 500 feet and slowly banked to the right; the dry land that had filled the front windshield became the Pacific Ocean and the coastline edged closer. The Cirrus began to skim through the first layers of the low-lying cloud, giving me a little relief from the unknown and unnatural feeling of nervously tracking towards the water. If I couldn't see it, I thought, maybe it wasn't there.

I asked air traffic control how far from the mainland I could go before expecting to lose contact with the standard aircraft radios; at that point I would have to use the high-frequency long-distance radio for the first time. I was surprised at just how far I could fly from the Australian coastline before needing to use the HF. This was good. I could settle in and concentrate on completing the first ferry fuel transfer without worrying too much about other jobs.

As I skimmed in and out of cloud I looked back. The coastline was a distant smudge of green grass, the grey skyline and the rocky cliff faces blurring into the horizon. I tried not to think about being over water in a single-engine airplane—the one thing most pilots said they had thought about constantly during their own journeys.

I levelled off at 9000 feet above sea level, still zooming in and out of cloud. It was time to start transferring fuel from the ferry tank for the first time. The aircraft had three fuel tanks, one in each wing and the ferry tank in the rear cockpit. This 600-liter soft tank strapped in place of the back seat was connected with a fuel line to a contraption of pumps in the right-hand front foot well. Two electric pumps, along with a backup hand pump, would propel the fuel through a pipe running from the cabin to the outside of the aircraft, under the wing and into the right-hand tank. When the pumps were switched on the fuel would transfer and the right-wing fuel gauge indication would slowly climb.

With the plane settled I checked the valves and taps on the fuel system; everything was in the correct position. I then switched on both electric pumps, and heard a loud harsh rattle coming from the foot well. During testing I had been able to tell the difference between the sound made by the transfer of fuel and the noise when the lines were full of air, which meant the pumps were running dry. I knew that this rattling sound meant that fuel was not being transferred from the tank.

I waited, thinking that the fuel might take a minute to run through the lines, but the sound persisted. This was far from what I needed. We had tested the ferry system with a very light fuel load but regulations had not allowed for a full test with the aircraft operating over weight. My heart began racing. What if there was something wrong?

With the aircraft now on autopilot I unbuckled my belts and turned to kneel backwards in my seat. I knew that air could become trapped in the top of the bladder, not allowing fuel to reach the lines. As the pumps rattled I removed the filler cap for the tank and shuffled the bags that were sitting on top; I could hear a burbling sound as air escaped the tank. I twisted back around with the filler cap secured once again, adjusted the air vents to push the fumes and smell of avgas to the rear and waited, praying that the pumps would now pick up the fuel.

No luck. I crunched a few numbers and worked out just how far I could fly with the fuel I had in the wing tanks alone. I wouldn't be able to get as far as Norfolk Island, but I could reach Lord Howe Island. I had chosen my flight route to track directly over the top of Lord Howe, as it was a secondary landing destination in the case of engine trouble or average weather at Norfolk Island. I decided that if I could not manage to get the fuel to transfer I would land at Lord Howe instead.

Not wanting to give up and change my first destination just yet, I decided to use the hand pump. If I could get it started manually I hoped the electric pumps would then do their job. With the correct valves and levers turned, I pumped the fuel by hand for ten minutes or so. I put the hand pump away and flicked the switches that brought the electric pumps to life. There was an immediate and familiar loud rattle but only moments later it became muffled. The fuel gauge indication increased, it took a little encouragement but the fuel was now transferring. The relief was instant. Destination: Norfolk Island. As the flight continued I carefully monitored the fuel gauge, switching on the pumps from time to time to ensure that the right wing always had sufficient fuel. I began working on trend sheets, taking note of all the engine's figures and indications in detail every fifteen minutes; a change in one would be easily noticeable on paper. Coming close to the distance from the Australian coast where I was expecting to lose radio coverage, I switched on and attempted to tune the HF radio.

This was an external radio fitted purposely for the flight and the controls and screen sat on my knee with an attached handheld microphone. I had been warned by ferry pilots that the HF was not a nice piece of equipment to use. Even with the long and cumbersome aerial attached to the outside of the aircraft it was still unbelievably difficult to get a good signal.

It made hearing others and being heard quite frustrating. I had to have the radio on and to be in contact with air traffic control at all times, never more important than when crossing between the airspace of different countries.

The sky above Australia is simply Australian airspace that extends a certain distance from the mainland in all directions. At the point where it ceases, known as an FIA, or Flight Information Areas boundary, the airspace changes to that of the neighbouring country. On my leg to Norfolk Island I would be crossing into New Zealand's airspace and therefore I needed to contact Auckland on the HF radio that was now switched on and tuned.

I said goodbye to the Australian controller, wondering when I would hear another Aussie accent under the same circumstances, grabbed the handheld microphone for the HF and attempted to call Auckland. "Auckland radio, Auckland radio, Victor Hotel Oscar Lima Sierra..." Almost instantaneously a voice with a Kiwi accent replied with my clearance through their airspace. Another new task was out of the way and I sat back to take a breath. As I crossed into New Zealand's airspace I smiled: I was now an international pilot.

All seemed well, but in the rush of the morning I had made an important mistake. My lunch box, filled with dozens of muesli bars, was in the aircraft but sitting well behind the ferry tank at the rear of the plane. I was hungry. I promised myself I would never, ever do that again.

What with the business of the fuel supply and the HF radio, time had sped past and I was more than halfway to Norfolk Island. Still suffering from nerves I was eager to get the aircraft on the ground, to have some time to myself to forget the hype of the day and to prepare for the next leg. As I approached my destination I tuned the radio for Norfolk Island and made an inbound call to let any other aircraft know of my whereabouts and intentions. It seemed an odd thing to do, I thought; who on earth would be flying out here? A woman at the airport responded, providing an update on the weather in return for an updated arrival time.

Before I could descend I had one last job. Ken had explained that some countries required an insecticide spray to be used inside aircraft before landing. The "top of descent" spray, which he had organised, was a can of insecticide to be used before commencing descent towards the destination. By the time you touched down any potentially living organism would be dead. I grabbed the can from my bag, had another quick read of the instructions and removed the lid. I started to spray the insecticide around the cabin. Ken had provided a few cans and we had agreed I would top up in the USA if required. With this in mind I continued spraying until the can was empty. I can assure you that every living thing inside that aircraft was dead and that nearly included me. I pushed the nose of the Cirrus towards the ocean and began my descent.

In the distance I spotted a small green island protruding from an ocean that seemed endless. When I had reached gliding distance of the island I felt a combination of excitement and relief: the realisation that I had reached my first goal, one that had seemed so distant for years. I turned overhead to have a look at the airstrip and windsock before joining the approach to the runway. It was a rough approach; the wind that flowed across the ocean unobstructed was now streaming over this elevated rock sitting in the middle of nowhere. I closed the throttles and touched down, taking a deep and well earned breath.

As I rolled out on landing and the aircraft slowed I completed my after-landing checks, then glanced around to see what Norfolk Island had to offer. There were either some very poorly placed car parks and no one in Norfolk Island knew how to drive, or the dozens upon dozens of cars scattered randomly across the hills surrounding the airport were all there to see me and the Cirrus arrive.

I parked the aircraft on the corner of the main apron and waved hello to the two young women who had come out to the aircraft. I knew I was to keep the door shut until Customs and Immigration had acknowledged the correct use of the insecticide, I was then given the okay and raised the door to an enthusiastic welcome. I handed the used can to one of the women, who took note of the batch number on the label and handed it back. When I asked whether I needed to keep it she queried whether, being only my first stop, I would use it for the next few destinations. Turns out you only spray the insecticide for a few seconds before putting it away, and when they found out I had emptied the entire can they nearly cried with laughter. If there are any foreign insects or bugs now living on Norfolk Island, you can be assured they did not arrive there with me.

I unloaded my bags and followed the Customs officer inside.

I was tired and had just completed the longest non-stop leg of my life. After signing the Gen Dec from Wollongong along with another for my next leg, I was taken out through the arrival gate of the terminal. As the doors opened a sea of people let out an almighty cheer, they had watched me land and now stood patiently waiting to welcome me to their home.

I had landed in Norfolk Island. Leg number one was complete, and although there were many more to come, I was simply proud of the day's achievement, shattered and ready for bed.

The last conversation before departure with flying instructor Alan Lindsay

Gathering invaluable insight from an Australian aviation legend, Jim Hazelton

Dick Smith and I, next to his Cessna Caravan. He travelled around the world twice in this plane!

A postcard view of Christmas Island

The Christmas Island international terminal

Volcanic molten lava enters the sea in Hawaii

Next to the tree planted by Amelia Earhart herself in Hilo, Hawaii

US Customs and Border Protection — it made all the forms worthwhile

The plane has its 100 hourly major service with Corporate Flight Management in Smyrna, Tennessee

I met up with my mentor Ken Evers in Tennessee. He was on holiday with his family and dropped by for a few hours of uplifting conversation.

Niagara Falls from far above

The office before departing for Iceland — should have paid for Premium Economy

Rekyavik Airport, hiding behind the iconic Icelandic architecture

An Icelandic glacier

11

PACIFIC INTERLUDE

After saying hello to the locals I walked back onto the tarmac to cover up the aircraft. I was really surprised by their interest in the flight; the fact that they had taken the time and effort to welcome me to Norfolk Island was fantastic. After the six hour flight, the ferry tank had collapsed after having nearly all the fuel transferred to the main wing tanks, the bags and equipment that sat on top now lay in a heap looking as if I had stood twenty meters away and hurled them through the door. After deciding to clean up and organise everything the following day and with the aircraft secured for the night, I headed across the airport grounds, through the terminal and out to the car park.

A local business, the Heritage Hill motel, had decided to support my journey. The owners drove me from the airport to the motel; I was shown to my room, the place where I could drop my bags on the bed and collapse on the couch in sheer relief. A local club had organised a dinner for that night and I had been given a car. I agreed to meet the organisers by the water in a few hours, but first I had to tell everyone I had arrived. Norfolk ran on a completely different network, including the internet, but I got online and emailed the first of many updates to the team back home, knowing they would receive it when the stars aligned and the Telstra mobile beamed into action. I had most of the next day to discuss things in detail with the team, but right then all I needed was a quick feed, chat and bed.

Dinner was great, and I was humbled to see how many people were fascinated by what I was doing. There was a quick speech, I thanked the club, and then had an hour or two of casual chatter, all the while looking at sunset over the Pacific Ocean. It was an enjoyable evening but it wasn't long before I headed for bed and a good night's sleep.

The next morning I woke up and had breakfast while crunching some numbers about the fuel load required to get me to Pago Pago in American Samoa, my next destination. I arrived at the airport and met the crew I had organised to help refuel the plane, and we pulled the Cirrus next to the bowser. It was only the second time I had filled the ferry tank and this time I needed a significantly greater quantity than I had used on the last leg. We started with the wing tanks before unstrapping the ferry tank and everything around it and placing it on the ground; there was equipment everywhere. As the tank was inside the cabin there was a risk of spilling fuel inside the aircraft, not a good idea. With this in mind I inserted a length of plastic PVC pipe into the filler cap, allowing the pipe to extend outside the open door of the plane. The guys switched on the pump and I started filling. It was a long process, requiring a keen eye to make sure the fuel didn't splash back up the filler tube and not-so-conveniently offer a complimentary shower.

We reached the final required amount of fuel and I handed the hose down off the wing. I then tried to remove the plastic pipe, only to discover that it was stuck. Really stuck. The tank was so full that it had pressed the pipe up against the side of the cabin, denying it any movement whatsoever. After a little thinking we decided the only way to remove the pipe was to remove some fuel.

I took a breath as the refueller set off to find a forty-fourgallon drum to transfer fuel into from the ferry tank. This wasn't quite how I had imagined the first refuel away from home would go, but it was a lesson learned. Fortunately it was a problem that could be fixed within half an hour.

As I waited, I wandered around casually checking the aircraft. A few stickers had been tattered in the heavy rain I had encountered en route to Norfolk; the thick cloud had produced occasional heavy showers. I casually ran my hand down the leading edge of the propeller to ensure that it was undamaged. As I did I felt something strange, and a closer look revealed the biggest chip in a propeller I had ever seen. Although nearly every propeller suffers some form of damage from stones or similar, this was far from minor and definitely something to look at before setting off the next day.

Now the priority had changed. There was no point in putting the fuel back into the tank after we had removed it. The aircraft would then be very heavy, not ideal if the damaged propeller needed any work. If we could fix the propeller we would refill the ferry tank with the fuel that was removed.

I called Rex in Merimbula Aircraft Maintenance and explained about the propeller; he said that the procedure for fixing it would depend on how deep the chip was. Norfolk Island had no certified aircraft mechanic and I spent three hours trying to get useful pictures of the prop back to Rex in Merimbula. This was successful up to a point but Rex, who had contacted the manufacturer of the propeller, said the damage looked so bad that it might need to be replaced. If so, the flight would come to a screaming halt and the budget would be blown out too.

I was sure the damage was not that bad, so with limited mechanical knowledge and the burning desire to set off to Pago Pago the next morning, I took more detailed photos with a ruler showing the dimensions of the damage and sent them back to Merimbula. Hartzell, the propeller manufacturer, said the damage was within limits and after sealing the chip I would be able to continue the flight.

In just a few hours, with the locals all pulling together, we had the damaged area of the propeller as watertight as it had been when new.

Now we had only to put the fuel back into the ferry tank before the sun went down. We pulled the aircraft back to the bowser and a bunch of people guessed how much fuel had been removed—the hand pump used when removing the fuel had given no indication of how much was pumped into the drum.

I had barely begun pumping when one of the young guys called out that there was a leak in the tank. You have to be kidding, I thought. We had a quick look and realised there was a loose fitting, luckily not a hole in the tank itself. One of the guys quickly squeezed through the baggage door with a shifter to tighten up the culprit before fuel found its way onto the floor. As he clambered through the small opening near the rear of the aircraft, the already tail-heavy plane decided to sit down. The nose rose high and the tail neared the ground; I yelled something that resembled English and we all froze, carefully letting the weight move forward and the nose wheel meet with the earth once again.

It was over. The aircraft was refuelled and sat ready to take off for Pago Pago early the following morning. All that remained to do was to submit the flight plan that night. I must admit I was a little worried; what had supposedly been a day off had become an absolute mess, with problem after problem rearing its head all day. Was it going to be as hard as this all the way around the world?

I set off to the motel to get ready for dinner at the home of a local couple. It was a welcome gesture and left me with nothing to worry about apart from preparing for the next flight. I had submitted the flight plan via fax, something I thought only old people still used, yet had a call from the New Zealand air traffic control soon after. There were a few issues with my plan, requirements I had no idea about at all. I altered the plan and sent it through. Once I knew it was approved I kept a copy to use as a template as the trip went on.

Again dinner was fantastic, it seemed to me that the people on Norfolk Island couldn't do enough. This was a tightly knit community, I discovered. I had been given a rental car and as I drove the streets throughout my stressful day, every person passing in the other direction waved. I had no idea who they were, but after the first few the awkwardness passed and I waved back as if we had exchanged gossip at bingo only that morning. I set the alarm for early the next morning, packed everything and set it by the door of my motel room. It was now time to forget the day I had just endured and to focus on the flight to Pago Pago, the next stepping-stone across the vast Pacific Ocean.

Next morning I woke up to howling winds, which did not surprise me greatly. A quick visit to the meteorology office the evening before had told me that the wind would not only be strong but moving in the opposite direction from where I would be heading. This meant that the flying time would be longer and the groundspeed slower. The officer on duty told me that the winds were forecast to become even stronger over the next few days. I had to decide whether to leave immediately or wait out the worsening weather conditions over the next few days. However, I had calculated that even with the winds I would have enough fuel to land in Pago Pago, so I decided to leave as planned.

I left the motel while it was still dark, parked the car and carried the bags to the plane. Having signed off the Customs paperwork on my arrival, all I needed to do now was to print off the latest weather reports, do pre-flight checks and take off. Glen, one of the airport managers, met me at the office and we printed off the weather information.

I said goodbye, clambered into the airplane and sorted everything out, making sure not only that the equipment was in the right place, and worked, but that my lunch box was within reach this time. I started the engine and entered the extremely long list of navigational waypoints into the GPS while the engine warmed up.

After pulling the HF radio from its side pocket, I dialled the frequency for air traffic control, the same Auckland-based frequency I had successfully contacted just before my arrival two days before. This was standard procedure: it was a requirement to let air traffic control know you were ready to depart so they could provide any clearances into various airspace. For over ten minutes I called, but there was simply no response. After trying a number of different frequencies I sometimes heard a faint voice in reply, but it was of little use.

I called Glen, who had only just finished wishing me a safe journey over the radio, and asked him to contact Auckland over the landline telephone, letting them know I was taxiing and would be airborne soon. After waiting for a while, Glen had a response. Auckland required that I make contact with them using the HF radio, and I had to do that as soon as possible. If I didn't they would file a non-compliance report against me. I had no idea how serious this was, but it definitely didn't sound like a certificate of appreciation.

There seemed nothing for it but to take off and chance it. If I stayed on the ground I still probably wouldn't be able to contact Auckland; if I took off and climbed away from terrain, the chances of getting a suitable signal were far greater. The only problem was that if I took off, failed to contact air traffic control and decided to return to Norfolk Island, I would be unable to land because with so much fuel on board I was way over the maximum landing weight. I would have to circle over the airport for a number of hours to burn a significant amount of fuel. Without clearance I taxied along the runway, noticing once again how heavy the aircraft felt. I turned at the end of the runway and immediately realised how strong the winds were. In a few minutes the Cirrus was airborne, and I held the nose level with the ground to build up a little more speed. No sooner did the ground drop away than I was flying over the ocean, a sea covered in huge breaking waves. The wind was hitting the aircraft at a speed of 44 knots: I was only flying at around 100 knots.

As I climbed over the Pacific Ocean I tried to get in touch with Auckland again. After a few more tries I heard the reply in a welcome Kiwi accent; I was relieved that I would not be receiving a grumpy letter in the mail. I set my course for Pago Pago.

Remembering the lessons I had learned from the first leg of the trip, I took the plane up to 9000 feet above sea level, a cruising speed, and began to transfer fuel, once more removing excess air from the tank by clambering into the back and using the hand pump. With that complete I began to monitor the outside temperature: it had been six degrees Celsius just north of Norfolk, but I was tracking towards the equator and the temperature was climbing.

Every hour I called through a position report on the HF, indicating my altitude and position in degrees of latitude and longitude. The pilots who told me about the HF had been right: it was intensely irritating to use, so when I was told to contact a nearby island using the standard aircraft radio I was only too pleased. The problem was that I could not make out the island's call sign. It sounded like "Fa-some-thingsomething-cracklecrackle." I asked the person who had given me the information to repeat it, which she did several times. This made no difference. I frantically searched the charts to find something that sounded like "Fa-somethingsomething-cracklecrackle." Luckily I found it—obviously "Faleleo."

I called Faleleo, pronouncing it to rhyme with "Galileo." The man on the end had no idea I was talking to him; I might just as well have stuck to my original pronunciation. I started to mush the word together, pronouncing it every way possible. Fortunately, the man on the other end was polite and he finally understood what I was trying to say. If you ever find yourself in a light aircraft in the middle of the Pacific Ocean, "Faleleo" is pronounced "Fa-lay-lee-oh."

I was flying away from the sun, in and out of cloud, and after eight hours in the air I watched it set behind the left wing. I descended over the water then, as I broke through a fluffy cloud, I noticed a large black mass in the middle of the ocean, speckled with lights. I was approaching Pago Pago.

However, I couldn't see the airfield, as the lights were still dim. I checked the charts again and took a closer look, then I realised that the lights were not on. I tried to activate them but there was no success, and no reply from anyone on the ground. And so, with daylight fading fast, and being in the middle of the ocean without any other choice, I decided to land without runway lights.

I touched down with the very last lingering glow of the setting sun—I discovered it was an extremely large runway—and approached the big Samoan who was holding two glowing orange batons and waving directions to the Cirrus. I shut down and opened the door to be greeted by a Samoan hello from a man who introduced himself as Arthur, and a swift punch in the face from the humidity. The temperature was well above thirty degrees Celsius, even so late in the day.

I was tired. I took the bags from the plane and locked it up, accompanied by a shower of rain. Arthur and I walked via Customs to sign the arrival documentation and continued to an office where we organised a time the following day to prepare the Cirrus for its onward flight. Arthur was my handler in American Samoa, the person designated to help in clearing Customs, organising, refuelling, parking the aircraft, accommodation, transfers and anything else I needed. I had handlers for most of my stops. They were a godsend in most cases and some of them I will remember for the rest of my life.

I checked into a local motel, thankful to escape the humidity, and had a brief chat with someone from the local newspaper in the bar, sipping a Coke under the sign that said you had to be twenty-one before imbibing alcohol. Then I called it a day. Throughout the trip, my aim was to fly early in the day in order to escape the late afternoon weather, especially around the equator with its tropical thunderstorms that gradually built up during the day. Then after landing I would pack up and head off to somewhere I could rest, spending the following day in refuelling, packing up and preparing the aircraft to set off again.

My day in Pago Pago, American Samoa, was interesting. In the morning I duly refuelled the aircraft, even though the rain (which I had come to know as the Pago Pago Sideways Rain thanks to the gusting wind) was doing all it could to delay the process. A further complication was that the refueller spoke no English whatever, though he smiled enthusiastically. Arthur stood by to translate such phrases as "A little more," "It's not my airplane, please do not spill the fuel" and "Whooaah." I stood in the rain and wind counting out $100 US bills and feeling somewhat conspicuous. After talking to a local TV crew under the open-air terminal, I paid the fees at the Customs office, got into a taxi, dropped some things at the motel and set off to drive around the local area, a trip organised by the newspaper reporter I had met the evening before.

On Norfolk Island I had mistakenly left behind an emergency personal locator that I could activate in the event of an emergency to transmit my exact position. I needed to replace it, so I got into a taxi and went into town looking for an electronics store. Pago Pago was quite a place. Damage from the 2004 tsunami that swept across the Pacific Ocean was still obvious, with the ruins of buildings sitting next to the rebuilt and renewed city. There were wild dogs roaming everywhere and taxis apparently made from a combination of different car parts. I had been told that deceased family members were often buried in the front yard of their descendants" homes, and I did see a number of these graves. The taxi driver was particularly keen on showing me the local fish canning factory, an important economic center for the town. The smell was almost deafening. Needless to say, I couldn't find a replacement for my personal locator.

I put in the afternoon checking the plane and writing a blog, studying for the next leg and washing my flight suit. (It's always a good idea to press "start" after you have put clothes into a dryer, I have found.) I set the alarm for three the next morning, with the weather promising to be wet and windy.

I woke the next morning knowing one thing for sure: three in the morning is too early for anything except sleep. After showering and dressing I met Arthur and we headed for the airport. I pre-flighted the plane by torchlight in the sprinkling rain, and after a quick photo with Arthur and a farewell handshake I prepared to leave Pago Pago for my next stop, the coral atoll of Kiritimati, or Christmas Island, part of the republic of Kiribati around 1300 nautical miles away, with a flight time of approximately eight hours.

The runway lights were working but the rain and wind were steadily increasing and my nervousness grew. The charts showed a very large and troublesomely placed mountain hidden in the inconveniently unlit sky. I realised I would have to undertake what is known as a standard instrument departure; just after takeoff I would turn right away from the mountain, then, once I had reached a comfortable height I could turn towards Kiritimati.

As I taxied down the runway I realised again just how large it was; the painted centerline was as wide as the Cirrus's cabin and I nearly needed to refuel once I reached the other end. The wind was strong and gusting straight across the runway, directly towards that inconveniently located mountain. I gave the aircraft full power and we lifted into the pitch-black sky.

Now for the really hard bit. I could see absolutely nothing, a feeling that reminded me of trying to find my way back to my bedroom at midnight after closing the brightly lit fridge door. My palms were sweaty, my hands shaking as I climbed through 500 feet and turned right onto my assigned track. I stared at the instruments, checking and rechecking my flight direction, making sure everything was as it should have been. Suddenly I realised I had been making life more difficult for myself than necessary. The Cirrus was equipped with synthetic vision. On the screen in front of me was a visualisation of what lay ahead, but I had been so focused on the instruments that I had completely disregarded this. I could see the bright blue sky and the slightly darker ocean ahead, and on the left edge of the screen was the mountain, gradually sliding out of view. I took a deep breath of relief and calmed down. This was, I knew, a perfect example of being caught up in a moment and being overrun by nerves: a lesson learned and something I could apply during the rest of the trip.

Gradually I climbed to 9000 feet, methodically moving through standard procedures. These were becoming more familiar, but they were still far from routine for me. Then I tried to contact air traffic control via the HF radio. No luck. For two and a half hours I yelled slowly and clearly into the microphone, making sure my vowels were rounded and concentrating on not swearing. Eventually I gave up and decided to try something else.

The satellite phone provided by Telstra was installed in the right foot well; I knew reception was intermittent, as one would expect, but a call could get through provided you were patient. The phone did not actually ring when a call was coming in; this was not really an issue because so few people had the number. I leaned over and dialled. My brother Adam answered. It is safe to say that he did not expect a call at three in the morning from anyone, and definitely not from me. I told him everything was fine, and asked him to call air traffic control for me using his Australian landline. I needed to make a few calls to get the full message through to Adam, but it worked.

Once Adam had made contact with air traffic control and passed on my position and intentions he gave me a call back. Without the phone ringing, he just started talking. Here I was, flying across the Pacific and all of a sudden my brother was just talking to me as if we were chatting at home in Merimbula. I'm guessing that's what it's like to lose your mind.

I finally let Adam go back to bed and switched the navigation page to show the aircraft's longitude and latitude. Countdown to the equator. The Cirrus was flying well and the weather had cleared up; for the first time in a while I was simply enjoying the flight. As the aircraft crossed the equator and entered the northern hemisphere, shown extremely accurately by modern avionics, I let out a cheer. I didn't really know what else to do. It was hard not to have anyone to share such moments with.

Shortly afterwards I descended towards Kiritimati. The sky was clear and for the first time during the flight I could see the horizon clearly in all directions. It gave a very good indication of where I was: right in the middle of nowhere. It's difficult to understand the size of the Pacific Ocean until you see it from a single-engine airplane with the "nearest airports" function on the GPS displaying "Nil."

An atoll suddenly appeared, glistening swirls of green and blue water surrounding flat sand, looking like something from a cruise brochure. I flew to the left side of the island and came down to 500 feet. By now I was in contact with a woman at the airport, and although I was tired I just had to fly low around the coastline before I touched down. At last, I thought, I would be able to stretch out and relax on the beach, and I could hardly wait.

I landed on a nice, smooth runway and taxied to a large tarmac apron. The airport seemed deserted, I was the only aircraft in sight. I radioed the airport lady, who was also nowhere in sight, and asked where I could park. She replied: "Pick a spot. You're the only aircraft here until next week." Wow. Glad I missed peak hour.

I parked up next to the terminal, a rickety structure that looked as if it was about to crumble to the ground, hopped out and stretched my legs. I had just completed three legs in a row, lasting seven to ten hours each, and was beginning to feel it.

A man named John, who was my handler, walked towards me. I knew about him from my mentor Ken, who had also stopped here on his own round-the-world flight. John was the only white man on the island. He owned a general store that provided all the necessities required for life, from food to tools and medical equipment and a few luxury items such as small laptops and pushbikes for those who could afford them, all sourced from Australia or the USA before being shipped to Kiribati. Planning to refuel the next day, I hurled my bags into the tray of his little green truck and climbed in.

As we drove along the gravel roads I realised something very forcefully. This was no island paradise, but a Third World country. Houses were makeshift lean-tos, men, women and children were barely clothed. Dinner was tied to a post to stop it running away. So much for the tourist brochures: it was a real eye-opener.

John dropped me at the Captain Cook Motel, the only one on the island. It made the Formula One budget motels—the ones where you stretch out and your hand pokes through the window on the other side of the room—look like the White House. I think I was the only guest in the building. I hauled my bags into my room and looked longingly at the rickety bed.

I was exhausted, but I needed to send updates to the team to let them know everything was okay, then grab dinner and an early night.

I woke up at eight the next morning with my laptop and paperwork scattered around me. I had fallen asleep at 4:30 the previous afternoon and not moved an inch for fifteen and a half hours.

12

ONE LEG AT A TIME

I looked at my phone and lay still, dazed and confused, trying to work out whether it was 8:30 at night or 8:30 in the morning. I had never slept for so long in my life, but there was no doubt I needed it.

I had a shower; although what came out of the showerhead barely existed, I am fairly sure it was water. I was very hungry, but had passed the kitchen on the way to my room and decided it would be better just to eat the muesli bars I had in my lunch box. With a few hours to waste before fuelling the aircraft I sat back and compiled another blog. Then, with backpack and sat phone at the ready, I set off for a walk.

John lived just around the corner and would be helping me refuel. Due to the nature of the island, the tiny amount of light aircraft traffic that passes through and the use-by date on aviation fuel, I had needed my own avgas shipped to Kiritimati from Hawaii by boat. John had picked up the three drums of fuel and placed them in storage until my arrival.

I found the drums of avgas in John's warehouse; he had them loaded onto the little green truck and his two sons took me out to the Cirrus. One of the boys drove and I rode with the other in the back, both of us holding the drums steady as we bumped along the gravel roads.

Although the drums were new they were far from pristine. Each was covered in rust, not only having made the journey from Hawaii but having sat on Kiritimati waiting for my arrival. One of the first things you learn in flight training is the vital importance of having clean fuel. Any contaminants can cause rough running or even a complete engine failure. We had known what the drums at Kiritimati would probably be like and I had worked out a number of strategies for testing the fuel before filling the aircraft. I knew it would be a long process.

After checking that the drums were sealed and within the use-by date we opened the caps. I then used a large wooden stick with a water-detecting paste to test for water in the drum itself; if there was anything other than fuel in the drum the paste would change colour. So far so good. We filled the wing tanks, passing the fuel through two filters. This made the process painfully slow but a quick glance to the right gave me all the patience I needed—there was an awful lot of water out there. After the wings were full we filled the ferry tank, adding every drop of avgas from all three drums. I was becoming quite good at strapping the ferry tank down and each time I found a better place to store something. Within another half an hour we were finished.

I then spent some time with John, who showed me around the warehouse and parts of the island close to his home. I was offered some dried tuna freshly baked from the sun, which I declined, and returned to my motel room. After finishing off a few jobs I read through the flight plan for the next leg.

This would take me north to Hilo in Hawaii and directly through the inter-tropical convergence zone or ITCZ. The ITCZ is a band of bad weather that moves up and down around the equator depending on the time of year, producing thunderstorms and weather phenomena that are far from inviting. Ferry pilots had mentioned the ITCZ during the planning of the trip. They told me that sometimes it would be non-existent, giving you a blue-sky day, but more often that not it produced amazing storms. Either way it was something to plan for and keep a keen eye on.

I walked outside and down to the beach with the satellite phone. With a little time up my sleeve I made a call to Ken to update him on progress, but really just to have a chat with a familiar voice. He was very happy with the flight so far and we spoke about a common goal: to land on the mainland of the USA, having completed both the longest leg and the longest overwater section of the entire flight.

Having successfully completed three legs I was growing used to the discipline of planning while flying. The idea was to take the flight just one leg at a time. When one leg had been completed the next leg became the focus, not the one after, just the next leg alone. Continuing with this idea, I decided to split up the entire route into six sections.

1. **Crossing the Pacific Ocean**—From Australia to the mainland of the United States of America
2. **Crossing the United States**—From the west coast to the east coast then north to Canada via the world's biggest airshow in Wisconsin
3. **Crossing the North Atlantic**—From Canada to Scotland via Iceland
4. **Crossing Europe**—From Scotland to Greece
5. **The Middle East and Asia**—From Greece through to Indonesia
6. **Australia**—From Indonesia to the west coast of Australia and east to Wollongong

Taking this into account, I had only two legs to go before the first section to the USA mainland was completed. I knew that those after the USA would be hard and relatively risky, but peace of mind came from knowing that the flight across America would be a well earned break and much less stressful than the Pacific had been.

I packed my bags little by little, making sure that my dinner of muesli bars was left loose. I would pack a few items and then pause to step on several large ants that wandered across the floor, pack a little more only to find more ants welcoming themselves into my room.

When I was finished I sat on the edge of the bed and took off my socks, now covered in ants, before spotting a small crab scuttling from door to door. What sort of place was this? And what other creatures lurked in the room, including beneath the bed? I tried to go to sleep slowly, convincing myself that nothing could scale the bed legs. If I stayed up there and my socks stayed down there I was sure I would see the next morning.

It was dark when I the alarm woke me, really dark. At around 2am I got up, dressed and prepared as well as I could, then went down to the front desk and asked whether my flight plan could be faxed through to Hawaii. But the phone lines, or rather lack thereof, would not permit that. I called San Francisco air traffic control on the satellite phone, explained who I was and that I needed to submit my flight plan. With perfect timing, the satellite phone lost reception and contact so I redi-alled and started again. The air traffic controllers soon worked out what was going on, and five or six phone calls later they had jotted down the details and submitted the plan.

John drove me to the airport and we said goodbye. I started up the Cirrus and taxied towards the runway, still the lone aircraft on the island. I dialled the HF radio frequency for San Francisco and made a radio call to let them know I was taxiing for takeoff. As I completed the final checks and prepared for departure, one of the controllers told me that my flight plan route had me tracking through something called a SIGMET, which meant "significant weather." Today's SIGMET was for embedded thunderstorms towering from sea level to 60,000 feet, around twice the height a domestic airliner would fly.

Before I had a chance to panic the controller offered a solution: alter-native tracking that would take me to the edge of the storm, around it and onto "the Big Island" of Hawaii. I asked for the alternative details and sat ready with a pen but what I received were a bunch of latitudes and longitudes from the controller's radar, not the GPS waypoints I had been expecting. I sat at the end of the runway with the engine running and absolutely no idea how to enter latitude and longitude figures into the avionics. Could I possibly take off? The alternative, I decided, was muesli bars for dinner and being attacked by the island's crab population. I decided I'd give it a go.

But twenty minutes later the map showed that the newly entered waypoints derived from the provided latitude and longitude figures had seemed to work, taking me nearly 100 nautical miles to the right of my original course. That was okay with me. The airstrip ran parallel to the coast, and as soon as I was airborne I slowly banked the Cirrus to the left in order to pick up the track to Hawaii. The aircraft's instruments were showing towering figures, it was a hot and humid thirty-two degrees Celsius outside and the engine temperature had risen significantly. I had been told from the very beginning to keep that temperature within certain limits so I lowered the nose and let the aircraft speed up. Although the climb slowed down, the engine was now receiving more air and therefore, I hoped, cooling a little.

However, the oil temperature exceeded the limit. I was extremely worried but saw no other way of cooling it down. I reached behind me and pulled out the pilot's operating handbook, the instructions for the aircraft. I looked through to confirm the maximum temperatures in which the Cirrus could operate. The owner's original limits set were lower than the actual maximum temperatures, a good idea for a safety buffer but not so great just then. I continued the climb to 9000 feet above the sea, knowing that as I climbed the air would become cooler and therefore bring the aircraft's temperatures and pressures back to normal.

I sat in cruise for a little while; the skies ahead were blue and everything seemed calm as I began my list of duties. Then, as I transferred fuel and argued with the HF radio, the sky ahead turned gray. To the right there was bright blue sky, yet to the left it was as dark as night. Large grey clouds had formed at a low level, above them the weather continued into the atmosphere but rain showers hindered the view. It looked okay for now so I continued.

I soon realised the weather to the left was definitely the storm cell I had discussed with air traffic control earlier that morning. The darkness and cloud were beyond anything I had ever seen. Although the edges were crisp and definite, allowing differentiation between the storm and the clear blue sky, the center remained a murky grey mess that gave no indication of just where I could fly in order to remain clear and therefore safe. Although the air traffic controllers had sent me nearly 200 kilometers to the right I was still going to fly straight through it, a massive no-no. I called San Francisco and requested to fly a further 50 nautical miles to the right, and tracked across to the right visually. Although this took me away from the center of the storm, I soon realised there were smaller storm cells that were unavoidable unless I tracked via Mexico. The aircraft was already being shaken up and down and side-to-side; I disconnected the unhappy autopilot and weaved my way through towering cumulonimbus clouds. Each time I could see where I was going I had to decide whether to fly left or right, depending on which direction I thought would be the smoothest and where the next cell sat. It was like playing chess while trying to cross a river on stepping stones. I only took a wrong turn once, choosing left when I should have gone right, and realised the error almost immediately as the plane began shaking again. After what seemed like days, I weaved around a storm cell to see continuous blue sky ahead. I turned and looked back to see an angry wall of storms and a very dark sky, and I could not have been happier to be heading in the direction I was. I couldn't believe just how suddenly the weather had cleared. I took a breath and focused on the few hours left before touching down in Hawaii.

I switched from the HF radio to the standard aircraft radios when told to contact "Honolulu Approach," and just prior to letting them know where I was I tuned in the "ATIS" frequency. The ATIS is an automated rotational message that gives weather and airport information for your arrival. Part of the message was: "Caution: volcanic ash in vicinity of Hilo International airport."

No way! How cool was that? I had never been anywhere near a volcano, let alone flown past actual volcanic ash. I was really pleased, then I decided it might be a good idea to look out for the ash itself; it was after all the last thing I needed to fly through. In the distance I could see a layer of what looked like a dark cloud, it sat at my current height and stretched out over the water where it dissipated.

I called Honolulu approach, requested descent under the ash cloud and then switched across to the Hilo control tower. As I flew towards Hilo I began to skirt the coastline. In some places the ground was a pitch-black colour with no signs of life anywhere nearby. This I gathered was dry lava; the tracks it had formed in around houses and over roads were easily visible.

I was slotted in in front of a Hawaiian Airlines jet, and just to be flying in the same airspace as a Hawaiian aircraft was exciting. I touched down in Hilo and taxied in, guided by air traffic control to Air Services Hawaii, the company looking after me during my stay. Ken, who had stopped in Hawaii with fellow pilot Tim, had told me a lot about Air Services Hawaii and my handler Shanna. It was good to know that someone who had been approved was waiting for me, but I was too focused on other things to be excited about meeting anyone.

I nosed the aircraft towards the marshal before bringing it to a stop and shutting down, sat quietly and waited for the US Customs officials to walk over to the aircraft. As Hawaii is a state of the USA I would pass through Customs here and not have to worry again until I left the US on my way to Canada. I had been told just how strict US Customs were and had seen the amount of paperwork and prior approvals involved in transiting the country. I was fairly sure I had it all, including a small hard-to-get sticker attached to the outside of the aircraft. The only problem was that half the sticker was now missing, thanks to the battering the Cirrus had taken in the storms.

The Customs guys were fine. I waved my can of insecticide, showing that I had again sprayed the cabin prior to descent—just a few sprays and not the entire can this time—and only then was I allowed to open the door. I hopped out and waved to Shanna, whom I guessed correctly was a young woman holding a lei and smiling broadly, and then waved to the gathering of welcoming media before leaning on the wing and answering the Customs questions. Once the guys knew I was not smuggling people, drugs, food of various sorts or anything else illegal, I was good to go.

I spent another half an hour chatting away to the newspaper and radio. We then packed up the aircraft and headed for the motel. My stop in Hilo was scheduled to be one of the longest because of the scheduled aircraft maintenance; the plane needed a minor service every 50 hours and a major service every 100 hours. Finding a company permitted to carry out the service while I was there had been a logistical nightmare. Any country I visited when those hours ticked over had to have an organisation permitted to legally carry out the service. But we had finally found one who would do the 50-hour inspection, which included a minor oil change.

I threw my bags on the floor of another motel, turned on the air conditioning and decided to use my skills as a sleuth to find somewhere to eat. My diet of muesli bars had become quite old and I needed real food and I couldn't drive anywhere so it needed to be close by. A large neon sign was glowing outside my window announcing "Ken's 24-hour Pancake Parlour." This detective work was too easy. I pulled on some shorts and a shirt and wandered over to Ken's. I was barefoot, though not by choice; my shoes were still locked inside the aircraft.

I spent the next hour breaking down the world's longest menu. It was something I could have studied for English in high school, and not a salad or muesli bar was in sight. As I sat at the long bar on a red speckled stool, peering through the mustard and ketchup, a waitress popped over to voice her opinion about my lack of footwear. I told her I actually didn't have any shoes and although I promised to buy some from Wal-Mart later, food was my current priority.

I eventually shuffled from the diner to hail a cab, weighed down not only with a greasy American hamburger but the guilt of eating four days" worth of calories, including a lifetime supply of fries. I stocked up on snacks to replenish my lunchbox as well as buying some thongs. (Note to self: They are called "flip flops" in the USA. Thongs are a type of underwear that I have no desire to possess.)

As usual before bed I gave a quick update of the day's flight to the team back home. With a few days off I had time to supply a little more detail. But first I needed a good night's sleep—and that's exactly what I had.

13

THE LONGEST LEG

After a very welcome sleep-in I called to confirm the 50-hourly service then I caught a cab to the airport. I started the Cirrus and warmed up the engine, readying it for an oil change, then taxied from Air Services Hawaii to Awesome Aircraft Maintenance on the far side of the airport. Immediately the guys began work, removing the engine cowls, draining the now blackened oil and inspecting each piece of the aircraft. I decided to hang around. The thought of 2200-odd nautical miles of ocean ahead of me was well and truly on my mind, and even with my limited mechanical knowledge I felt it was important to stare into the engine bay, hoping I was helping. If I thought it would be useful, I would have talked to the engine.

Everything went well, except maybe the lunchtime jaunt to Taco Bell, a Mexican diner where regret quickly overcame the short-lived pleasure of eating the food. I started the aircraft with the cowls, the covers to the aircraft's engine, still removed for a quick test run. Everything seemed okay until something caught the mechanic's eye. A pulley running near the rear of the engine bay was shaking vigorously, not something that should be ignored, so we shut the engine down and had a closer look. It turned out the air conditioning pulley had worn severely. We could have left it alone—air conditioning, though desirable, was not vital by any means—but it was intertwined with other systems in a way that meant it needed to be fixed.

After another call to Rex at Merimbula Aircraft Maintenance and a call to Cirrus on the USA mainland, we had a solution: to remove the complete air conditioning attachment now and have it seen to during the Cirrus's major service which was scheduled to take place in Tennessee. This removed any risk that the issue could cause further problems on the long leg to California.

With the aircraft packed away for the night and after saying goodbye to the maintenance crew I headed back to bed. Bravely deciding to take on Ken's Pancake Parlor once again I headed to dinner, this time in footwear: my not so cool pair of thongs purchased at Wal-Mart. I walked in and sat down in the same spot as the night before, and no sooner had I done so than the lady who had questioned my lack of footwear appeared, excited and very apologetic. It seemed the local newspaper had my face emblazoned across the front page that day. Not a lot happens in Hilo and the flight had become big news. This ensured that eating at Ken's Pancake Parlor that evening was very different from the night before. I spent less time eating and more time talking, which was probably better for my long-term health.

After dinner I spent some time updating everyone with another blog. Thanks to Facebook and various other platforms, along with a live tracker on my web page, we were able to share the events of the flight with thousands of people from all over the world. A local from Hilo, Cam, had spotted the article in the newspaper and then discovered our Facebook page. He understood that I was not old enough to hold a US driver's licence and offered to show me around the next day. With two more full days in Hilo and with the weather looking good, I was happy to take him up on his offer.

The next day I became a tourist, sort of. This turned out to be one of only four days on the entire trip when I set off purely with the intention of discovering a new place and seeing new things. All other days seemed to be riddled with jobs, phone calls, emails, flight planning, aircraft preparation or actually flying. Cam was a young university student who also worked in an observatory. We spent most of the day travelling around the Big Island together, walking through lava tubes and across the fields of dry lava I had seen from the air when I arrived. We found lava streaming into the ocean causing billowing steam to rise into the air, I was shown the volcano itself as we sat among tourists looking into the top of the crater and we watched the steam begin to glow orange as the sun went down.

Although I had a few phone calls it was a restful, casual day and I was grateful for that: I well and truly needed to relax before a final day of preparation and then the longest leg of them all.

I arrived at the motel late, climbed into bed and tried to get some sleep, a semi-successful undertaking. Next morning Shanna picked me up and we drove back to the airport to refuel and pack the Cirrus. Once again we took everything out of the plane and carefully stacked the equipment under the fuselage in the hope it wouldn't blow away. The tank was nearly empty, but not completely drained. It was hard to pump absolutely all the fuel from the bladder while in flight; there was always a little fuel left in the bottom of the tank. As usual, when I arrived at the airport I had a page of fuel calculations in hand with exactly how much fuel I would like to have pumped into the bladder. Basically it would be filled completely this time.

Our calculations, standards and requirements of aircraft for the entire Teen World Flight had been based on the leg from Hawaii to the west coast of the United States, the longest part of the trip. If the aircraft could complete this leg safely it would have no issue with the others. It was a total of 2139 nautical miles or just short of 4000 kilometers, all over water. There was no dry land between Hawaii and California.

With the facts in mind and months and months of thinking about this one leg behind me, I started to refuel. I filled the main wing tanks to the brim before starting on the ferry tank. At the best of times filling the bladder required patience, filling too quickly caused the fuel to shoot up the filler pipe and make a ridiculous mess. Even when it was nearing three-quarters full only a trickle of fuel could be added at a time.

For nearly two hours I persevered with the refuelling, though I don't think the guy waiting for me had the same level of motivation. Each time I was ready to decide the tank was full, I remembered the size of the ocean, shut up and kept filling.

I never did reach the final number of liters listed on my page of calculations; the fuel just wouldn't fit no matter what I tried. I knew this was the case due to the fuel left behind in the ferry tank from the last leg, but as I could only guess how much had remained, I never had a firm final calculation of the amount of fuel on board. I strapped the tank in. The plane sat low and by only slightly pushing the tail towards the ground I could make the nose rise towards the sky. This was legally the heaviest the Cirrus could possible be.

I closed the doors and locked up. I had an organised time of departure and a harsh-sounding 2am start. With Customs sorted, I was ready to go. I returned to the motel via Wal-Mart and bought a few snacks, an ice brick and some cans of Red Bull. I placed them in the motel fridge and laid the lunch box by the door. There was no way I was forgetting those.

I did final jobs, spoke to a few people on the phone, including various newspapers and radio stations, and settled into my room to prepare myself as well as possible for this challenge. I had paperwork and charts spread from one side of the bed to the other, I studied away and thought of what to expect during the long leg. I had already checked with the guys in the meteorological office and had been told the weather was fine and that I could expect very little if not absolutely no cloud, along with nil winds. Cloud I could handle, but headwinds would slow the aircraft down and create a longer flying time. Because this leg was so long the Cirrus could handle very little in the way of headwinds before running out of fuel.

I packed as much as I could, stacked the bags by the door and climbed into bed, setting four alarms for 2am. Originally the departure time had been slightly later in the morning, but after finding out the Van Nuys airport in the San Fernando Valley would be closing at 9pm on the night of my arrival, we moved everything forward a few hours to ensure I would make it to California before Van Nuys closed. I tossed and turned, just staring at the roof, I fell asleep around 11pm. But before I did, I found myself thinking: whose bright idea was this again?

The clock told me it was 2am and the four alarms confirmed it as they sang me the song of their people. I have no idea how far the noise travelled but I decided that from now on I would stagger the alarms just a little. I was a heavy sleeper but four going off at once was maybe a little excessive.

I showered, checked the weather, packed the bags and kept an eye on the time. This ritual had happened a few times by this point and I began to think, regardless of the unknown adventures the day would bring, it was just a matter of taking one step at a time. Once I was at the airport I would focus on the legalities of Customs, then preparing the aircraft, then actually departing—all the while I would tell myself to stay calm, as everything had been planned so well.

Shanna picked me up from the motel. The look on her face matched mine: why are we doing this? We drove to the airport and out to the aircraft. It was dark and I began to pre-flight and pack by torchlight, something I was becoming very used to by now. A Customs vehicle pulled up and a guy wandered over in full and very official US Customs uniform. He also looked far from thrilled to be up so early as he pushed a form across for me to sign, and after wishing me good luck he went back home to bed.

The Hilo International airport was dull and quiet yet a large vintage Convair sat on the tarmac only meters from the Cirrus. It was being loaded with freight for what would be a run around the islands delivering supplies and equipment before Hawaii woke. An elderly pilot in a perfectly ironed uniform and with neatly combed grey hair walked by the Cirrus on his way to the Convair. With a smile from ear to ear he asked whether I was the kid from the newspaper. After I had introduced myself he went on to tell me how amazing and intriguing he found my flight. After I told him how cool the Convair was, he offered to give me a look inside. Hard as it was, I had to decline after I looked at my watch. He asked me dozens more questions, wished me luck and made sure I knew I was absolutely crazy. I found this surprising, considering how much flying experience this guy must have had.

Just before clambering into the Cirrus I dialled the number for my weather brief. During the planning stage I had been told to call 1800-WX-BRIEF for all my flight planning and weather related needs within the United States. The previous evening I had given them a call and asked to submit a flight plan. I had the form in front of me with all the details laid out, as I wasn't sure how this system worked. The guy on the other end of the line had been great, he asked for each detail of my plan in a structured order, just as it was on the form. He queried a few things, such as the peculiar Australian registration of the aircraft. When we were finished he asked whether I would like a brief of the weather, and when I said yes he told me to call back at 3am the next morning and it would be ready. So cool. The guy was great, they had a detailed weather report ready to go and as he began to read it to me I realised it was all in layman's terms, everyday English that was easy to understand and yet so different to the type of weather reports I was used to. Everything seemed similar to the report received from the Met office in Hilo—nil cloud and casual winds.

I said goodbye to Shanna and hopped into the Cirrus. The weight of the fuel meant that I had to climb up from the front of the wing and into the cockpit; if I had used the normal step the aircraft would have been sitting on its tail very quickly. I left the door open, hoping to have the humid air escape, started the engine and began to program the avionics. With all the waypoints entered into the GPS, I zoomed out with the hope of seeing the flight path extend from a little island to the hard-to-miss west coast of the USA. It didn't. The avionics were only designed to zoom to a maximum of 1000 nautical miles and my flight was well over twice that distance.

I taxied behind the Convair as it made its way to the runway, lined up on the center line and took a good look ahead. It was pitch-black, the runway's end sat on the coast meaning a departure would take you immediately over water and therefore into the darkness. I was worried about the takeoff; having to taxi so slowly had made me realise yet again how heavy the plane really was.

With the winds calm I pushed the throttle forward. I had to hold a little forward pressure to keep the nose down and let the plane build speed. With my heart in my mouth and after a big long breath I felt it accelerate well and calmly lift into the sky. Although the climb performance was far from impressive, it was a much more uneventful takeoff than the lighter departure from Pago in gusting strong winds.

I held runway heading and followed the instructions from Honolulu air traffic control. As I made a call to signify my departure there was a friendly, "Goodbye and good luck, young fella," from a couple of experienced Convair pilots. I was soon instructed to intercept my planned track to California, and with another goodbye from ATC I programmed the HF radio. With very little cloud potential, problems were simply a matter of the winds. With nil winds I was fine, with a tailwind I was better than fine, with a headwind I was not so fine. The nature of the flight, from A to B with no options in between, meant that my new best friend was a PNR, or point of no return. This is just as it sounds, the point at which you are committed to continuing with the flight because you do not have enough fuel to return to your departure destination. I had a nautical mile figure, say 1300 nautical miles from Hawaii, which became my decision point. When I reached my PNR I needed to be sure that I would be able to make California. If I had any doubts it was time to turn back to Hawaii.

It was still dark yet the avionics gave a very accurate indication of the winds, with a little digital figure and an arrow signifying whether I was facing headwinds or tailwinds. As I settled into the climb I noticed a headwind of around fifteen knots, which although not ideal meant very little forty-five minutes into a thirteen-hour flight when I was still creeping slowly towards the cruise altitude of 9000 feet.

With the very heavy Cirrus chugging away through the morning air I kept the autopilot disconnected and flew by hand. A few people had told me about autopilots doing strange things when the aircraft has a heavy load and I didn't want any unnecessary stress. After what seemed like forever I levelled off at 9000 feet, and although I kept looking at the winds I told myself to stay calm until the plane had built up some speed and settled into the cruise.

I began the gymnast-like act of twisting around to encourage fuel to flow from the ferry tank and out to the right-hand wing. There was so much fuel on board that the bladder and equipment on top of the tank actually pressed against the roof and I had only just enough room to slip down into my seat. The fuel began to transfer, I jotted down the times on my trend sheets more eagerly than ever to keep an accurate eye on my fuel burn. With the first transfer complete I called San Francisco on the HF radio, beginning what would be hourly position reports.

With the first jobs completed I had a little time to breathe. The night sky had gone and a sliver of the sun appeared directly in front of the Cirrus. It couldn't have been more centered if it tried. I watched the sun rise, so quickly that it grew right before my eyes. Yes the winds were not ideal, yes there was a long flight ahead full of uncertainty and yes I was scared, but maybe that's why this was the greatest sunrise I had ever seen. Just then I didn't want to be anywhere else in the world.

The sky was now light. From time to time I chatted to San Francisco, updating them on my position, altitude and the next waypoint I was tracking towards. I had been completing my "aircraft trends" every hour but with this leg being so long, and the supply of fuel being so critical, I decided to keep myself busy and do this every half an hour. I would jot down all the temperatures and pressures of the engine given by the avionics then work out the fuel burn so far, the fuel remaining, how far that fuel would take me and how much I expected to have when I touched down in California. The fuel remaining on touchdown was most important, a figure that rose and fell depending on the exact groundspeed at the time.

A casual few hours passed. I was comfortable with the rhythm of jobs that seemed to endlessly circle and that left me to concentrate solely on the wind. During the first few hours I told myself to forget about it. I had a long way to go before the PNR and so much could change within that time. The problem was that it didn't. The arrow still pointed towards the tail of the aircraft and the winds were constant.

I decided to think of some other options. I called air traffic control on the HF radio and asked for the "winds aloft," a meteorological report that indicates where the best winds would be for your desired outcome. The problem was that these reports are used mostly by airlines at an altitude of around four times mine. Few aircraft cross the Pacific at 9000 feet and air traffic control soon let me know that they couldn't provide the information I needed.

I decided to climb to 11,000 feet. It would use more fuel and upset the aircraft that was now set up in a cruise but there was a chance the winds would be more co-operative a little higher up. I set up the oxygen bottle, turned it on and slid the cannula over my nose. I had never used oxygen before but imagined it to be no different than breathing normally. It wasn't: the oxygen shot through the cannula at the speed of sound in short and completely sporadic bursts. However, it definitely helped me stay awake. The Cirrus crept to 11,000 feet, I levelled off and let the aircraft settle. I gave it time but twenty minutes later I had gained one less knot of headwind. One measly knot. I punched yet more figures into the calculator, deciding whether to try 13,000 feet. If it was no better, there then I should have saved the climb fuel and maintained my original 9000 feet.

I was getting frustrated and nervous; I was five hours from the coast of Hawaii and at this speed a good ten hours from California. I was in the middle of nowhere and for the first time felt very alone.

I kept thinking: Why can't there be tailwinds? Why should this flight depend on such minute figures, requiring risky decisions based on factors I have absolutely no control over? Why on earth would returning to Hawaii take so long?

I repeated the process and took the aircraft to 13,000 feet, let it settle and hoped for the best. I was rewarded with another knot, one solitary damn knot less headwind. At this rate if I continued my climb into orbit I might just have the groundspeed I was looking for. But clearly the wind speed was not favourable at any level I had tried, so I saw no reason to change altitude again. I maintained my flight path and re-calculated the point of no return.

I wouldn't say I was feeling desperate by now, but I was probably at the notch below. I decided to try something else. At the point closest to the PNR, I sent a text message through the sat phone to a guy named Chris whom I had met just before I left Australia. Now an airline pilot, Chris had experience ferrying aircraft all over the world. During the previous week he had helped me with weather and a few questions I had along the way. I sent a short message, one that took a long time to write as I bent around the passenger seat trying to reach the phone: "Winds not favourable as forecast, nearing PNR, need tailwinds."

Within minutes Chris had messaged back. My heart raced. After a look at the winds aloft and the latest forecast from home, he told me that there should be a change to a tailwind five hours from California. I did another series of calculations based on that. If what Chris told me was correct I wouldn't have an issue with fuel; if not I would arrive running on fumes, but would make it. There was one other option. If the winds didn't change I could divert to the San Francisco area, which sat a little closer to my current position than Van Nuys.

The upshot was that I felt comfortable about flying on. By the time I had finally made the decision I was only miles away from the PNR. As the nautical mile figure ticked by on the avionics, the last chance to head back to Hawaii passed.

I knew then that I would either be sleeping in California or spending a night bonding with Bob the life raft. Bob seemed like a good guy but I was leaning towards a night in the Howard Johnson motel in Van Nuys.

I passed the PNR and felt somewhat relieved: the option of turning back was gone, meaning I had one less thing to think about. I continued my rotational duties and decided to have something to eat.

You don't need to be a genius in the operation of the human body to understand that spending fourteen hours in a one-meter by one-meter confined space is not ideal. Fourteen hours is a long time, and Ken's Pancake Parlor in Hilo had not really provided a sustainable source of nutrients. Knowing this, I had altered my meal plan completely; I had breakfast the day before departure, but only a snack for lunch, and dinner was sacrificed completely. Throughout the planning stage everybody's favorite question had been, "How do you go to the toilet?" My mentor Ken had kindly passed on "travel-loos," which were nothing more than glorified sick bags with some kind of special, fancy "granules" inside them. I don't know what they did but I do know there was no button with "flush" written on them, and I was determined not to use them if at all possible. Their chief advantage was that the box they were in was a great place to hide anything I wanted to keep safe.

The estimated time to destination had whittled away from over seventeen hours in the climb to now only six remaining. I had stressed over the winds for eight hours, I had trend sheets coming out of my ears. I was over it. I was, for the first time in a very long time, legitimately scared.

As I neared the five-hour mark the little arrow changed direction; with five hours and twenty-six minutes to run the winds turned completely. It was almost as if a switch had been flicked with an instantaneous change to tailwinds of ten to twenty knots. I was excited, so unbelievably excited and relieved. I began to calculate the fuel remaining based on the new speeds. It was all good news.

The sky began to darken as I counted down the final hours. I wasn't in the clear yet: although the winds had turned the fuel remaining was nowhere near as much as I had imagined. I spent a long time facing backwards pulling and pushing the ferry tank, ensuring that every drop had been pumped into the wing. The bags and equipment had slumped in a heap as the tank shrunk in size, I moved the bags and found that the tank was bone dry, now a cryovacked bag void of liquid or air.

Absolutely shattered, I reached for my lunch box. I had already eaten the snacks but decided it was time for the now not so ice-cold Red Bull. But when I pulled the can from the bag it was rock solid. My mind flashed back to the first time I had opened a bottle of ginger beer at 9000 feet. I had bought it from the Merimbula Airport coffee shop along with one of their famous brownies before setting off north in the then newly acquired Cirrus. I pulled off the cap with absolutely no thought of air pressure, and for the rest of the flight I wore the contents of the bottle with only a woollen pilot jumper to mop up the mess. The reduced air pressure had caused the can of Red Bull to expand and I knew that if I opened the can it would explode. I was so sad and even thought of placing it in a ziplock bag and giving it a go but decided that might not be such a good idea either. Instead I put it back in the lunch box. The sun that had risen over ten hours ago was now setting. The sky was becoming dark and a low-lying endless sheet of cloud was forming over the ocean. Having the sun set behind me made me realise just how long I had been flying.

I neared the coast and was told to contact Los Angeles approach. Cool! Things were starting to become more of a happy reality and less of a mind-numbing stress. I chatted away using the aircraft's standard radios and after so long using the HF it was a welcome treat to not have to yell. Finally, in the far distance I spotted a sliver of darkness on the horizon. It was the mainland of the United States.

I was still watching the fuel gauges as the sky darkened very quickly. Both now sat in the yellow zone and although I knew I still had sufficient fuel it was enough to play with my mind. I was switched to "So-Cal" or "Southern California" approach as I neared the coast. I watched the solid block of low-lying cloud dissipate when it reached the land, something I had never seen before. The hills of California neared and the coast zipped under the nose. I was the happiest kid on the face of the planet. So-Cal approach called me up—"Victor Hotel Oscar Lima Sierra, we have you tracking via Santa Barbara on your flight plan but if you would like direct to Van Nuys that would be available. Please note though, that will take you over water. Are you okay with that?'

For the first time in fourteen hours I laughed out loud. Was I okay with flying over water? I tracked direct and watched the lights of Santa Barbara pass by the left wing tip. Traffic was a "Southwest 737 crossing right to left and 1000 feet above." Sweet.

I dialled up the automated airport weather and information frequency for Van Nuys airport, hoping Runway 16 Right was operational, as it had been a dream of mine since the very beginning to land on that runway. As I listened in, I heard them broadcast that the "Runway in use" was 16 Right. I was beyond excited.

I tracked towards the airport above the lights of Los Angeles and I had never seen so many lights in my life. I was told to report the airport in sight, looked ahead towards where the avionics were telling me the airport was located and thought I spotted it. I let the controller know I had the airport sighted and he cleared me for a visual approach. I pushed the nose down and squinted harder, but what I had thought was the airport actually wasn't. I didn't need to be on the news for landing on a highway.

The controller queried my lack of descent. I admitted I couldn't see the field, and he asked whether I would like to conduct an instrument approach to bring me right down to the runway. However, I didn't think I had sufficient fuel to start something like that, nor the energy if it wasn't really required. He radar vectored me around to the right, I nosed down once again and there, ahead in the mass of lights, was a runway. It was a moment of utter relief, a familiar sight of runway lights, the exact spot where this flight would safely come to an end and the hours of decisions, stress and calculations would all be proved correct. I was beyond relieved, I was proud.

I touched down without event after fifteen hours in the air.

I had flown around 2150 nautical miles and completed the longest leg of the flight. I swung the Cirrus around and lined up with the marshal, just missing Jim Carrey's private jet. As I shut down I could see a bunch of people waiting alongside the plane, including both Mum and Dad. This was the first time I had seen a familiar face since leaving home.

I climbed from the airplane and carefully stepped down off the wing. With legs like jelly I said hello to Mum and Dad and took a deep breath. Mum was a mess, simply overrun with relief that this leg, about which she had heard so much, was over. Dad was much like myself, proud and relieved yet stunned and overwhelmed by the moment. I hadn't seen Mum or Dad since leaving Australia and to now catch up was fantastic. But regardless of how many stories I had to tell the day had been too long and the stories would have to wait.

I hopped into the back seat of the rental car and stared silently out the window as we drove to the motel. I wasn't tired, in fact wide awake with pure adrenaline running through my body. What I did have was a wonderful sense of accomplishment. We wandered from the motel room and at 1am sat in McDonalds for food and a debrief of the flight across the Pacific. It was strange to live in a moment that had been scrutinised for so long. Every detail had been broken down, thousands of people had contributed to the fact that here I was, sitting in the USA, having crossed the Pacific Ocean in a single-engine airplane.

14

THE ROMANCE OF VAN NUYS

Van Nuys airport sits inside the city limits of Los Angeles, within the San Fernando Valley. Even though it is free of airline traffic, it is one of the busiest general aviation or GA airports in the world. The Los Angeles International Airport (LAX) sees airliners arrive and leave, a hub for transporting millions of people all over the world, but smaller private aircraft need somewhere to go. That place is Van Nuys. It is home to all sorts of aircraft, from small two-seat training machines to private business jets as large as any airliner. The rich and famous use it as their home airport, taking charter flights and private jets to places throughout the USA and across the world. News and firefighting helicopters who work around the Los Angeles area are based at Van Nuys, and it is also the place were students do flight training. Surviving war aircraft as well as enthusiasts' planes of all shapes and sizes fill the endless lines of hangars, the diversity of flying machines at Van Nuys is far greater than the usual collection seen at a local Australian airport.

Van Nuys is the subject of the movie-length documentary *16 Right* (*One-Six Right*), named after the main runway: it is the story of Van Nuys airport from its beginning in the pioneering days of aviation through to the present. That documentary is very special to me. During my training, my mate Jonno insisted that I watch it. "How can you call yourself a pilot if you haven't watched *One-Six Right*?" he asked me.

He gave me the DVD and I settled down to watch it: I was captivated immediately. *One Six Right* took the magic of flight and turned it into an awe-inspiring, unforgettable visual story, with fabulous pictures of planes from pioneering biplanes to state-of-the-art private jets, all with the accompaniment of great music. There were pics of aviation icons, people who had followed their passion and achieved something great, owners of world-renowned aviation companies, actors, stunt pilots, racing pilots, pilots who had flown around the world. It made me long more than anything to get into a plane and fly off, I didn't care where, just as long I was in the air. As the credits rolled at the end I wished there was more. There wasn't, so to compensate I watched it again. And again. I can practically recite the commentary now, and the faces of the aviation figures and their aircraft are etched in my memory. And when we were planning the route I knew that top of the list of places to visit was Van Nuys airport.

After the adrenaline-filled McDonalds debrief upon my arrival into Van Nuys, I ventured to a welcome bed. I set the alarm for a few hours later, but crashed immediately; the adrenaline had worn off and the previous day had caught up with me. When the alarm woke me I rolled over to check the time and went straight back to sleep for a bit longer. It was not yet afternoon, and I thought it was okay still to be in bed. But before too long I was up and dressed and set off for Van Nuys once again; I had to be there mid-morning to film a short piece for Australian television covering the flight across the Pacific. On the way to the airport, I could really take in the landscape in daylight. The mountains in the Los Angeles area were large, dry and red, looking just as if they were from a western. As we headed towards the city of Los Angeles, I thought about the last few weeks. I had left Australia in the winter, with the cold mornings leaving dew on the aircraft. I had flown into thicker and more humid air, seeing the cold temperatures give way to the thick atmosphere of the Pacific islands. Already I had seen beaches, islands of all shapes and sizes, more water than Noah and his ark, thunderstorms, rain that was sideways, up and down, light and heavy, volcanoes, lava formations and now the red, dry mountains as seen by John Wayne. It was not easy to take all this in.

When the rental car arrived, the Cirrus was already outside the hangar. Signature Flight Support, a well-known Fixed Based Operator (FBO), has a huge base of aviation clients and takes care of the travel needs of the rich and famous. With Signature now taking care of me during my stopover, it was a new level of service that I could really get used to.

After an hour or so of filming I said good bye to US correspondent for Channel 9 Denham Hitchcock and the crew. Mum, Dad and I were then taken on a tour of the airport. We poked our heads into various hangars, with a quick sneak peek at a P51 Mustang from World War II that belonged to Tom Cruise. Could things get any better?

With Mum and Dad, I zipped off to Wal-Mart where we bought a large doona cover, then returned to the aircraft which I started to pre-pare for the trip across the States. I could say goodbye to the HF radio and the ferry tank; I would use only the standard aircraft radios and was flying short legs that required only the standard fuel tanks in the wings. I covered the fuel tank with the doona cover, making sure all the taps and pumps were turned off and out of harm's way. After a quick clean of the windows, we were ready to go. I had one more day in Van Nuys before starting the trek east.

That evening in the motel I wrote a blog, sent some emails and updated everybody at home. Then the guys at Signature emailed me to ask whether I would like to have lunch with Clay Lacy, one of the iconic figures from *One Six Right* and the current business owner of Van Nuys airport. *Would* I?

We arranged to meet at the Squadron Restaurant, a small café that faces onto the tarmac of Van Nuys. I got there early and wandered around the room for half an hour, just discovering the items that hung from the walls: pieces of aircraft shot up during the war, photos of young men my age having returned from combat, story after story of fear, determination and bravery that widened my eyes. On every table was a headset, just in case you wanted to listen to air traffic control while you were munching on your burger. I was in heaven.

Clay Lacy arrived, a big bear of a man in his eighties, wearing a sharp suit. He shook my hand and apologised for being late. He had an aura about him that seemed to captivate everyone in the room. Clay had been born in Wichita, Kansas, the city that some consider the heart of aviation. Beginning flight training in his teens, he had notched up around 2000 hours by the time he was nineteen. He started flying for United Airlines as a copilot on the DC-3, went on to fly the Convair 340, the DC-4, DC-6, DC-7, DC-8, DC-10, the Boeing 727 and the Boeing 747-400. His time with United, then, saw him move from a propeller-driven plane to a four-engine jet airliner, one of the largest aircraft in the world.

Mid career he took time off from United Airlines to join the California Air National Guard, where he flew the F-86 Sabre jet, a single-seat fighter. His time in the National Guard included active duty in Berlin, flying the C-97 Stratofreighter to Japan and Vietnam. And then in 1964 he took on something that would become a key element in the modern Van Nuys airport: he flew a Learjet, the first business jet, into Van Nuys. A few years later he founded Clay Lacy Aviation, which focused on corporate aviation and business jets, and he went on to create one of the largest corporate aviation companies in the world. He flew a P51 fighter in the Reno Air Races alongside fellow aviation legend Bob Hoover, he has helped revolutionise air-to-air filming and he holds nearly thirty world speed records. He retired in 1992 after nearly forty-two years of accident-free aviation.

With more than 50,000 flying hours, Clay Lacy is a hero whose career has spanned one of the most important periods in modern aviation, and he is still going strong. And he was having lunch with me!

Clay and I started to chat. I was blown away by his interest in Teen World Flight; he said he was impressed by what we had achieved so far and wanted to know where it would go from here. I couldn't believe that someone with so much experience was so interested in something I was doing. I tried to limit the number of questions I was throwing at him, without much success.

When we finished lunch Clay asked whether I would like to look around his hangars. Aaaah, yes please. I got into his car and we headed to his office, zipping through the security gate and out onto the tarmac. For the next little while we strolled in and out of hangars, looking at everything from business jets to a DC3; Clay has some very cool aircraft. I sat in the DC3, the P51 that he raced at Reno and the first Learjet to arrive at Van Nuys. It was unreal: I was touring the airport I had known so well from *One Six Right* with Clay Lacy himself.

Clay signed my pilot's logbook and we said goodbye. I went back to the Cirrus, the happiest kid on earth.

The rest of the day passed in checking the plane for takeoff, and so did the following day. It was ready to go and I had checked over the next few flights. I dropped into Channel 9 just across from Sunset Boulevard. It felt very odd to be standing looking over Los Angeles but surrounded by pictures of Australian TV presenters, including Charles Woolley.

I had seen and experienced Van Nuys in a way that was unique, I thought. It was something I knew I would never forget.

Today was the day to discover just what flying in the United States was really like. I was going from Van Nuys to Ryan Airport in Tucson, Arizona, the first leg towards the east coast.

As I was finishing off the pre-take-off checks, the last thing I expected was to see someone I knew. But I looked up to see a familiar figure coming towards the Cirrus. It was John Deakin, one of the American pilots who had given me a real helping hand during my Advanced Pilot Seminar engine management course back in Queensland. John is a pilot with over 40,000 hours in every type of aircraft you can imagine. I had read many of his frequent blogs online and his stories were phenomenal. John had taken a keen interest in the flight and now driven from his home in Camarillo, an hour's drive away, to see me off on my way to Tucson and to wish me well. It was great to see him again, and we more or less picked up where we left off.

I called my new buddies on the 1800-WX-BRIEF phone line and had a flight plan in the system and a departure time in hand. After taking a few photos to mark the occasion I said goodbye for a while to John, Mum, Dad and the crew from Signature Flight Support. I wasn't scared about flying through airspace that was unfamiliar to me; I was intrigued and eager to take on what I thought would be a challenge.

I started the plane as normal and began to prepare for a departure as the engine warmed, not that it needed much help during mid July in California. I called up Van Nuys air traffic control and requested my clearance and was told to stand by. For nearly half an hour my clearance was pushed back little by little. I just sat there while everyone awkwardly stood by; I could see they were thinking it was a long way back to Australia at this breakneck speed.

Finally, thirty minutes later I was given a clearance. The clearance is an approval to enter controlled airspace, restricted areas and different sections of sky; with a longer leg they can be quite lengthy. The controller warned me that it was "a long one." As he spoke I wrote, ending up with something the length of a short novel but I read back each word one by one and somehow I had the information correct on the first go. It was going to be a good day.

I taxied to the holding point just short of Runway 16 Right and because my flight plan had been filed to fly within clouds I was taken to the front of the queue. I waited for a Gulfstream business jet to touch down and at the same time heard a broad American voice from a nearby aircraft ask the control tower, regarding my registration, "Where does a *Victor-Hotel* aircraft come from?" A very long pause followed the tower's response of, "Uhhh um, Australia." I guess it was a bit of a novelty, even at a place like Van Nuys.

I rolled down the runway and flew into the skies of the USA for the first time in daylight. I looked down and waved goodbye to a small group of very patient bystanders before turning left and climbing up, up and away. The city was dense, the surrounding mountains were huge. It was amazing just to look down and imagine which famous person lived where. As I crossed over the Colorado River only an hour after my departure, the same river that flows through the Grand Canyon, I also caught a glimpse of Palm Springs, the home of a phenomenal air museum full of warbirds and a ridiculous number of geographically disoriented desert-bound palm trees.

I levelled off at 11,000 feet in order to clear the mountains that sat only just below the Cirrus. The city had become desert with the only sign of life being the little tinge of green that lined the banks of the Colorado River. I was being pleasantly surprised at the ease of flying in the US. Every now and then I would be passed off to another air traffic control center, just like home, but things were much more relaxed. The controllers were really nice and laid back as they vectored me towards Ryan Airport in Tucson, Arizona and gave instructions about when to descend. After a short, easy three hour flight I was lined up for the approach to the runway based solely on instruments from inside the cockpit and then transferred over to the tower. I was cleared to land but due to the winds was given a last-minute runway change. It was no big deal, they were telling me to fly to the right as I wished and that I was cleared to land on the new runway. I remember banking the aircraft around but spending most of the time looking at the desert floor. Hey look, a cactus!

I touched down and taxied to parking. Ryan Airport, I was sure, would be a great place. I had experienced so much freedom when flight planning across the USA, freedom I doubted I would have anywhere else, so I had decided to make the most of it. For this reason I had done some research on cool places to stop over. I had just arrived at one, included on my cool list because of Todd's Restaurant: it was almost on the runway.

It was phenomenally hot outside, the heat made even worse because of my flying suit and the lack of air moving through the plane. I chose the parking spot closest to the restaurant; the front door sat against the tarmac only meters from my wing. I clambered out, grabbed the essential bags and walked inside.

I sat down to have lunch in a typical American aviation themed diner. As I finished up a few fellow diners started to ask questions. I don't think they see many sign-written Cirruses in Tucson. One couple was so interested that we walked back out to the plane and I removed the cover so they could hop in and press buttons. It made their day, and they became my Tucson buddies.

I explained I was staying over in Tucson on my own and they were so intrigued that they decided to look after me. They dropped me off at the nearby motel for a quick freshen up then took me out to dinner and showed me around the little desert town. It happened to be the second Saturday night of the month, when Tucson came alive with markets and people everywhere. My new friends explained the difference between summer and winter in Arizona—basically too hot and then too cold. For that reason people referred to as "snowbirds" leave Tucson in the summer and move to a second house away from the heat, and so the town becomes deserted.

The next day was full of the usual jobs, a blog, catch-up emails, answering questions on social media and keeping on top of the continuous emails and jobs required for flight planning. With all that behind me, I found myself knocking on the door of the Pima Air and Space Museum, a very well-known aviation attraction. After a phone call to Australian radio presenter Alan Jones, I wandered inside for a TV interview. I laughed when the reporter introduced himself as Ryan. Here I was, Ryan being interviewed by Ryan after landing at Ryan Airport. I could sense a pattern in there somewhere.

I chatted away into a microphone that resembled something off the *Anchorman* movies, a colourful cover with the station's channel number printed across the front in bold. I continued on to have a look around the museum, blown away at the aviation history hidden away in each corner. I was then dropped at the gates of the Boneyard, more formally known as the Davis Monthan Air Force Base and home to the 309th Aerospace Maintenance and Regeneration Group (AMARG). The AMARG is an organisation that takes aircraft and preserves them within storage, some for re-use, some for parts and some for scrap.

The Boneyard sits in the desert for a reason; the atmosphere is perfect for the preservation of aircraft. Each plane is covered in a particular and meticulous way, the windshields are blanked out and the plane is placed in a line of similar type aircraft. We zipped around in a van, thankful for the air conditioning, as 4500 aircraft passed by the windows. It was a private tour so we stopped here and there when I spotted something exciting, such as President Eisenhower's old helicopter. The frequent warnings to watch for rattlesnakes hiding in the sand meant a plane had to be pretty special for me to get out of the van.

It was an eye-opening experience seeing fighter jets, cargo planes, bombers and so much more just sitting in the desert, some ready to fly again, others marked with a large red "D" for destroy. I took a heap of photos but nothing I could snap could do this place justice. It really was an aircraft graveyard. To see the Boneyard was phenomenal, but the visit was complete after meeting some of the high-ranking officials in the defence wing of AMARG. They were all amazing and successful people with a keen interest in Teen World Flight.

As I was packing my bags back at the motel, with the TV on in the background, a severe emergency weather warning took over the program and flashed upon the screen, just like in a movie. A little map showed a storm tracking towards Ryan Airport, with severe wind shear, hail and lightning.

The Cirrus was sitting outside, right in the path of the oncoming storm, so I called a cab and asked them to take me to the airport thirty minutes away. As we drove I phoned all the airport businesses I could in the hope of finding hangar space so late in the day. We could see a huge black storm sitting just off the highway and I taught the driver the Australian way of saying "drive a little quicker please."

I was in luck; a nice guy was on his way to meet me and open up his hangar. I grabbed the Cirrus, which had already moved slightly in the wind, untied it and carefully taxied to the hangar. We opened the doors and pushed it back inside; only then did I take photos of the phenomenal storm developing in the middle of the desert. I could see a dark and isolated cloud full of water, with the rain tearing down in a severe downdraft situated directly under the storm itself.

As I hitched a ride back to town with the hangar owner I took a breath and organised a time to retrieve the plane in the morning. I would be on the move again, this time to Texas.

Standing on the plane after completing the 9-hour journey from Goose Bay in Canada to Reykjavik in Iceland. That was approximately 8 hours and 55 minutes too long in the immersion suit.

The white cliffs of Dover. World War 2 aviators knew they were home when they saw these cliffs and many were the same age as me. A humbling experience.

The hotel owner translates the local Greek newspaper article on Teen World Flight — a lengthy process

Enjoying the sights of Cannes, France, on two wheels

The outer walls of the 'old town', Rhodes, Greece

The hills of Jordan

The peculiar crop circles in barren Saudi Arabia

The bustle and chaos of a Sri Lankan street

With previous world record-holder, James Tan, in Kuala Lumpur, Malaysia

One of the many great handlers, Jeff, in Kuala Lumpur

Low-lying weather before departure from Malaysia

William Creek, Australia, population 2. The only place where I ordered avgas through the pub

A g'day for Pa on my return to Wollongong, Australia. No doubt many stories to tell. (Photo by Dylan Robinson)

A humbling experience — from a wide-eyed young dreamer to sharing my adventure with Prince William at the Governor General's reception, Canberra. (Photo by Andrew Taylor/Commonwealth of Australia, Government House)

15

SOUTHERN HOSPITALITY

We pulled the aircraft from the hangar, I thanked the man for his help and hopped in the plane to venture to the fuel bowser. I said good-bye to my Tucson buddies, two lovely people who had gone out of their way to make me feel welcome, took a few photos and was ready to leave. I tried to obtain a clearance but for some reason it had not shown up in the system. Instead, I departed "VFR," or visually and clear of cloud. Once I was airborne I would contact air traffic control again and pick up my IFR flight plan. From that point on they would help me out wherever necessary and I could pass through cloud.

As I became airborne I was given a direction to fly and I was lucky: it was just off to one side of the Boneyard, allowing me to see its sheer size from the air. I picked up my original flight plan and climbed to 12,000 feet, another high altitude required to clear the mountains that zipped only just below.

After fifteen minutes on the ground entering dozens of navigational waypoints into the GPS I took to the sky and was immediately given clearance to go direct to El Paso in Texas.

I tracked along my flight path, edging closer and closer to the west Texas town of El Paso, and for a short while just off my right wing I saw the Mexican border. I was excited to be flying along "the fence" and had been looking forward to it for some while. However, my friends from Tucson had told me horrific stories of illegal immigrants attempting to find a new life over that very fence, and so my enthusiasm had become a bit dimmed. I was heading for Fredericksburg in Texas. Originally I had planned to go through a little town called Dalhart on the recommendation of a ferry pilot, but when John Deakin and his American counterparts had heard that I intended to go to Dalhart they nearly cried. Apparently it was a silage town with an aroma of its own, one that should be avoided if at all possible. That sounded like very good advice. After a little research I found Fredericksburg, an airport with the Hangar Hotel and an airport diner side by side and right next to the tarmac. The airport looked too good to be true so I booked in.

As I neared Fredericksburg the sky began to darken. The weather was not fantastic and it was deteriorating quickly. Air traffic control told me that a storm cell was sitting right on Fredericksburg airport. I didn't feel like it was an issue and grabbed a chart and looked for the closest airport with available fuel—Junction, Texas. I would land at Junction, grab some fuel for the plane and some for me and head on when the weather had passed.

I turned right, nosed the plane towards the ground and zoomed in over the airport. It appeared to be a very neat airstrip, a cluster of hangars and a lot of cars. Cool. I touched down and taxied to the fuel bowser, clambered out and had a look around. There were a lot of cars but not a person in sight. I could see one hangar door cracked open in the far distance.

I wandered in and said hello and shook hands with Sam, the apparent lone occupant of Junction's bustling airport, who was working on a plane. I asked him for the phone number to order a cab and he laughed at me. Junction didn't have cabs, he said, or food at the airport, but he offered to drop me off at a restaurant down the road. We hopped in his oversized ute and after driving past a freeway-side McDonalds and various other fast food outlets we stopped at a little

Texas shack. He passed on his details and said to call when I was ready for a lift back. There was no menu, just brisket sandwiches. There was nothing extra to add onto the sandwich, apparently that's where the brisket came in. It was a case of bread, brisket and bread. I looked around quietly hoping to undertake a little self education, but with no luck I asked what exactly was brisket. They laughed at me too. Turns out it was a cut of meat. I couldn't walk anywhere else, as this was the only option within walking distance. Instead I sat down under the Budweiser sign with my brisket roll and a Pepsi. It wasn't the Texan steak I had imagined.

Sam picked me up and I spent the trip back to the airport telling him just how much of a fan of brisket I was, and how hard it would be to leave that culinary delight behind. I climbed into the plane, ready and refuelled, and took off for the twenty-minute flight to Fredericksburg.

It was still a little showery but I had fun flying nice and low and looking at the Texas barns and farmhouses. With the airport in sight I overflew and joined the circuit to land, touched down in a gusting crosswind and taxied for the Hangar Hotel. This was something out of a movie, a war-themed hotel with a classic airport diner as its neighbour. It brought a whole new meaning to valet parking when I shut the Cirrus down twenty steps from the check-in desk.

I unpacked my bags then slipped the Cirrus away in a hangar. I had food, airplanes and a bed all within stumbling distance. I was in heaven.

One of the guys from the airport had come over for a chat just after I landed and mentioned that a local pilot would be interested in the flight and would come and say hello the next morning. He did just that and I shook hands with Bob Snowden, who lived with his wife Karen on the airport in what was a half hangar, half house. We walked over to his hangar and pulled up a chair between a yellow Piper Cub and a Ford Mustang. We chatted away for an hour and then Bob took me for a walk though a few other hangars and asked whether I would like to go for a fly. Of course I would.

I climbed aboard a bright yellow Beechcraft Staggerwing, a sleek and fast biplane. To many it's just another airplane but to a pilot it's one of the most amazing-looking aircraft in history, a vintage machine made of wood and covered in fabric. We started up the radial engine and drowned in a cloud of smoke, then taxied to the runway as the radial burbled away. We took the Staggerwing around Fredericksburg, a different type of flying than what I had been doing over the last month, and I was now in a completely different environment. That's another reason aviation is so amazing. A slight change in environment, a new aircraft and a new type of flying suddenly turned me into a student again, eagerly trying to learn whatever I could.

Bob and Karen were my hosts for a night out in Texas, an experience in Tex-Mex cuisine that more than made up for the brisket sandwich in Junction. And the Staggerwing flight was something I'll keep in my logbook forever.

It was bedtime, and in my room I bunked down next to a leather chair and an old telephone with a cord and a round dial on the front. Fredericksburg wasn't just an airport, it was an experience, almost like an amusement park except that the bar known as the "officer's mess" was off limits to anyone under twenty-one. I didn't want to leave, and told Bob and Karen I was good to go with the adoption process when they were.

Next morning I dragged the Cirrus out and topped up the wing tanks, thankful I didn't have to touch the ferry tank. I taxied to my valet position and loaded the bags, and after a goodbye to Bob, Karen and the crew at the airport I took to the skies, straight into a low-lying sheet of cloud and bound for Tennessee. The *Spirit of the Sapphire Coast* climbed through a solid layer of cloud above Fredericksburg in Texas and soon I was flying "on top." It was bright, sunny and still—perfect conditions to commit aviation.

I had a planned arrival time into Smyrna, Tennessee, a town just outside Nashville. Jeff Boyd, a very successful businessman and pilot whom I had met at the Frogs Hollow Aeroclub fundraiser dinner, had helped to organise the major service for the Cirrus there. Jeff had connections with Corporate Flight Management in Smyrna, which happened to be a Cirrus service center situated just about where I would require the 100 hour service. It was almost too good to be true. Jeff had been in the industry for a long while and had helped with planning, sponsorship, maintenance and so much more.

Corporate Flight Management were expecting my arrival midmorning; it was a fairly large service and they planned to get started straight away. On top of this, my mentor Ken, who was holidaying in the USA at the time, was in Smyrna waiting for my arrival, and I couldn't wait to catch up.

I levelled off and took in the scenery, still air and the broad accents of each controller. Given the ferry tank was packed away I planned to make a quick fuel stop in the small southern town of Greenville, Mississippi, before continuing. As I neared Greenville and started my descent, I couldn't keep my eyes away from the rather large grey storm sitting opposite the airport that was well and truly moving towards me.

I rolled to the left and right and as I crossed low over the Mississippi River I saw a steamboat sitting by the river's edge, exactly as it was supposed to. I conducted a quick orbit to slow down before joining finals and landing at Greenville. As I taxied from the runway I spotted the huge water tower with "Greenville" across the front. I wasn't even lost.

I climbed out and into the scorching heat. I had parked next to a business jet and in front of a small aviation business, another FBO (fixed base operator) who would organise the refuelling of the plane. I said a quick hello and went off in search of some cold water, to submit another flight plan and to check the ever-evolving weather. I called the 1800-WXBRIEF number and spoke with a really nice guy, telling him that I had come into Greenville towards some serious-looking storms. After a quick look over the forecasts his verdict was simple: I could track south immediately and hope to miss the storm about to pass over the airport, then once clear I could turn around and fly north-east towards Smyrna. It would take longer and use more fuel and there was no guarantee it would work. There was another option. I could book a motel, delay my arrival into Tennessee and not need to stress about anything except choosing what to have for dinner. It only required a little thought.

We began to pack up the Cirrus. By this stage lightning and thunder were creating a show that would play a starring role at the Greenville municipal airport any minute. The pilots of the business jet in front of the Cirrus quickly clambered in and proceeded to undertake a seriously spectacular takeoff. Just after becoming airborne into the now gusting winds they banked hard and left the storm behind them. I taxied the Cirrus to a worn-out, old but phenomenally huge hangar to park and unpack, sheltered from the heavy rain.

I was given a lift to the motel and thinking Greenville was an interesting-looking place, I asked the young guy driving if there was anything to see or do here. He told me that there was a restaurant a few meters from my motel and to "sleep there, eat over there and don't go anywhere else." I didn't ask any questions, I just did what he said. Somehow I had the feeling that Greenville, Mississippi might not appear in many tourist brochures. I was now late for maintenance in Smyrna but after a quick phone call I told them I would be there very early the next morning, so we would lose only half a day. I went to bed and woke up early yet again—at 3am—though with the knowledge that this time I wouldn't be facing a ten- or fifteen-hour leg but a casual flight of less than two hours.

A young guy from the FBO picked me up and we drove to the airport in his SUV. This guy was into car sound and audio systems and I had to hold my bags on my knees as everywhere else was covered in speakers and subwoofers, even the door handles had been removed. We pulled up next to the Cirrus in the large old hangar, our voices echoing in the cold early morning air. He then decided to show me just what his car could do: I will now go deaf ten years earlier than I otherwise would and the video of my distorted face will remain on the internet forever. It was amazing.

I said goodbye and dragged the Cirrus just clear of the hangar as I jumped on the phone and started to submit a flight plan. A lady answered and I began to provide the details she required: "Aircraft type, aircraft registration, endurance, persons on board, departure point, destination point." She stopped me mid sentence and asked, "Where are you from, where is your aircraft from, how did it get here? Don't try and tell me you flew it here! You're flying around the world? Why, how old are you?'

Her voice became more and more excited with every question. We spent twenty minutes just having a chat while I filled her in on what Teen World Flight was all about. By the end of our chat, although the flight plan hadn't been submitted yet, this lady was well enthused. "This has made my day, the most exciting call I have had in a long time!" she said. I laughed as we said goodbye; I was now late again. I started the Cirrus and the sound of 310 horsepower rumbled through the old hangar, a perfect noise to start the day. I took off above the lights and zipped though a layer of murky cloud. To my surprise, above the darkness was a magnificent sunrise.

The flight went quickly: two hours passed like ten minutes. I lined up with the runway at Smyrna, touched down and taxied under guidance from air traffic control to the hangar of Corporate Flight Management. A small group of people were waiting for me but no face stood out more than that of Ken Evers. I shut down and climbed out after a most enjoyable flight, and it was still only time for breakfast.

We all took photos and shook hands. I was introduced to a number of people including Dave Augustin, the co-founder of Corporate Flight Management. I unpacked the plane which was towed to the maintenance hangar, and Dave offered to take me to the motel where Ken and I could catch up for a couple of hours and then offered to take me out to lunch. Apart from not being able to check in at 7am, the morning was fantastic.

Ken and I sat in the motel lobby and caught up. We couldn't talk fast enough as we now had stories in common that so very few other people had. We spoke for so long that when Dave returned I was still in the flight suit and surrounded by my bags. I quickly changed before we all set off for lunch.

What followed was three days of the famous Southern hospitality. As the aircraft service was major it would take a few days so Dave had decided that the maintenance crew would work away and keep a log of what was completed, a log that I could review before I departed once again. This way there was no need for me to hang around the airport and instead could have a break and complete some other jobs that were well and truly due.

We had lunch with a very experienced 40,000-hour pilot based in Smyrna, the most time of any pilot in the Mitsubishi MU2 aircraft in the world. After an afternoon of jobs I was picked up once again and taken to the Grand Old Opry in Nashville, where Dave and I sat on the stage and watched one of the most famous live radio shows of all time. After the Opry we found ourselves at an Applebee's restaurant eating some kind of French dip, which may sound exotic but it was far from that, being a glorified roast beef roll that was apparently enhanced by dipping it in a French onion soup. As Dave dropped me off late that night he asked whether I would like to stay at his home with his family instead of yet another motel. It was a wonderfully hospitable gesture to which I agreed instantly and organised a time to meet up the next morning.

With my bags packed I moved from the motel and into a red brick house with an American flag flying on the front porch, it faced a grass airstrip and backed onto a river. It was everything I imagined a house and life in Tennessee to be.

Dave and his wife Danese, along with their kids Caleb and Chelsie, took me into their home and temporarily adopted me. There were still jobs to do such as updating the avionics, flight planning, phone calls and emails but fortunately I had time in between. I had dinner with the Augustins that evening, attended a family birthday lunch the next day along and set off for the Sonic Drive-In with Caleb, Chelsea and their friend Daniel. It was a takeaway where you could stay in the car while they brought the food to you and hung it from your open car window, something I had only seen on an episode of *The Flintstones*.

When the time came I was very sorry to leave. I had relaxed in Tennessee, as far as that was possible. The aircraft was now in great shape, everything had been looked over and I was ready to move on, though in the back of my mind I knew that things could become very difficult very quickly.

Dave stood by as I started the Cirrus, contacted air traffic control to ask for my clearance and instructions to taxi to the runway.

Without providing a clearance the controller confirmed I was an Australian and then out of the blue asked whether I followed Casey Stoner. Casey Stoner used to be the Australian motorbike rider in the MotoGP series. When I confirmed that "Yes, I follow Casey Stoner," the controller became excited and began to chat on a frequency and in an environment where chats are usually non-existent. I found out that Casey Stoner was testing the 2014 MotoGP bike even though he had retired. How about that? The things you learn.

I waved goodbye to Dave and taxied away from Corporate Flight Management. I lined up on the runway and took off, this time bound for the Outer Banks of North Carolina, the birthplace of flight.

With another few hundred miles behind me, a long list of different states and a change of scenery, I looked into the distance to see a familiar sight. Water, and a lot of it. The mainland of the United States, of which I'd seen an urban metropolis, desert, green bushland, desert, rivers, cities, desert, small towns, huge mountains and a little more desert had now come to an end. I had found the east coast of the USA, and in particular the Outer Banks of North Carolina. The Outer Banks were just that: waterways parallel to the coast, and scattered slightly inland of the ocean itself, a long thin landmass that followed the coastline.

I descended towards the Dare County regional airport, a quick fuel stop before landing at another airport a five-minute flight away, the one I really wanted to visit. I touched down, got out and refuelled. It was a busy little airport with aircraft flying skydivers up and banner towing aircraft displaying lengthy messages for all on the Outer Banks to see.

I had enough time to stretch the legs and have a look at a few aircraft scattered across the ramp before I set off for the day's final destination, Kill Devil Hills or Kitty Hawk, possibly the most famous airport in the world.

On 17 December 1903 two brothers from Ohio changed the way the world travelled. They conquered a dream of many who lived before them, many who strove for the same goal, and proved wrong the many who had not believed in their outrageous aspirations. Orville Wright successfully made the first sustained heavier-than-air powered flight. I was off to the First Flight Airfield, an airstrip only meters from the exact place where he made that very famous first flight.

I took off from Dare County, only just missing what looked like the entire bird population of North Carolina that had come by to say hello. I turned right and stayed nice and low, tracking for the airfield that I could almost see already. I crossed the coast and flew north alongside it, taking in welcome and familiar sight of beaches and bustling tourists taking in the sun. I turned over the airfield, which is done every now and then in the hope of spotting the windsock, but this time I wanted to look down and see the historic First Flight Airfield from above. I turned and began my descent, scooting down past the busy coastline and touching down meters from Wilbur and Orville's hangar. Unfortunately the Cirrus wouldn't fit in it, nor did it match its décor, so instead it sat outside and was tied down close by.

After securing the aircraft, I took a short taxi ride to a small motel. I quickly changed and had a drink of water before taking the taxi back to the airport. I spent a couple of hours just looking around, taking photos and trying to imagine what these hills had seen. I stood next to a long wooden rail, the actual rail that was used to stabilise the Wright Flyer on takeoff. I peeked through their workshop window and stood on a hill alongside the monument dedicated to the brothers and their phenomenal work and contributions. I was mesmerised, standing surrounded by aviation history.

I couldn't help thinking how aviation had evolved, what 110 years, war and commerce had changed. What would Wilbur and Orville Wright say if they knew a teenager could now fly solo around the world? Would they be surprised?

After a good night's sleep I was back in the aircraft which was full of fuel and ready to go. I backtracked the runway, taxiing slowly to the other end where I would turn and take off into the favourable winds. I stopped and started, trying to make as much noise as possible and scare away the lurking deer, because I know fast-moving airplanes and deer are not friends. After the last checks were completed I took off from the small airstrip and pointed west for the first time since leaving Australia, heading for Wisconsin.

Situated just west of Lake Michigan and north of Chicago, Oshkosh in Wisconsin is home to AirVenture, which calls itself the "World's Greatest Aviation Celebration." The Experimental Aircraft Association or EAA hold their annual fly-in during July and August each year, bringing in half a million people from all corners of the globe. This year one of those people would be me, along with the *Spirit of the Sapphire Coast*.

Since the beginning of the planning for Teen World Flight, the one event we aimed to attend was AirVenture, not only as an avenue to promote the flight and its associated goals, but as a way of meeting some of the international sponsors who had supported the flight from the beginning. I would fly to nearby Appleton before arriving at AirVenture, and afterwards head back to Appleton before continuing towards Canada and the North Atlantic Ocean.

A clear blue-sky day made life easy as I approached Parkersburg in West Virginia and flew an instrument approach through some fluffy white clouds that lay a few thousand feet above the ground. After thirty minutes to refuel I was airborne again, next stop Appleton.

I neared a watery mass known as Lake Michigan, one of the five Great Lakes of North America. The nose of the Cirrus pointed directly across the lake from east to west; to the left of the windshield and in the distance was Chicago while Oshkosh and Appleton lay to the right. As I reached the middle of the lake and aided by a little haze on the horizon, I lost all sight of land in any direction. It really was one of the Great Lakes. I passed over land and turned right, tracked right past the Oshkosh airport and continued onto Appleton. I was beyond excited. To think I was now here and overhead in my own aircraft was just fantastic, the dream of pilots all over the world. Every year 12,000 to 15,000 aircraft arrive at AirVenture, making Oshkosh's Whitman Field allegedly the busiest airport in the world for the week-long event. Fighter jets, airliners, home-built planes, private planes, ultra lights, blimps, helicopters: whatever flies will be at AirVenture. The challenge lies in accommodating the wide range of aircraft, having each pilot safely arrive at the air show in between a busy air display schedule. So how is it done?

Usually described in an eighty-page booklet, the arrival into Air-Venture can be simplified. Normally air traffic control and pilots communicate with each other, but when flying into the air show in Oshkosh the pilots are not allowed to say anything unless it is vital. Instead air traffic controllers will speak to an aircraft and identify it as "the red high wing" or the "blue biplane" before telling them where to fly or where to land. The pilots then confirm the message has been received and understood by "rocking the wings." The art of rocking your wings, a casual bank to the left and then to the right, has become an iconic part of the Oshkosh AirVenture air show and something that I had imagined doing since I first attended the show.

A very large number of aircraft take off and land on only a few run-ways, while each afternoon the airspace closes and air show performers zoom through the skies above. Large coloured dots are painted down the center of the runways, and after being directed to an assigned runway by air traffic controllers situated away from the airport, you fly towards the field until spotted by the controllers from the actual control tower. The now very well-known controllers will clear you to land on a specific coloured dot, while you may touch down on the "blue dot" there will be a number of other aircraft landing on the same runway at the same time, all onto a different colour spot. This is not recommended for colour-blind pilots. I would land on the Monday morning and the Cirrus was being put on display that day. Charles Woolley and the 60 Minutes crew were at Oshkosh to film part of the story. I too was there to work. I had an immense amount of flight planning to complete for the rest of the journey as well as a number of video conferences with schools back at home, organised by Telstra. At the same time, the aircraft had to be prepared for the journey onwards. I knew that the next month wasn't going to be the smooth experience of crossing the USA; I would revert to the kind of flying I had already done in crossing the Pacific. On the Monday morning I hopped into the aircraft at Appleton, while my family, 60 Minutes and a number of interested people were waiting at the show to see the arrival. 60 Minutes had flown to the USA to meet with me as I neared the halfway point, what better place to meet than at one of the biggest aviation spectacles in the world? A number of family and friends, many who had a lifelong dream to attend the Oshkosh air show at some point in their lives, had taken the opportunity to travel over and see the Cirrus and me arrive. With a few days to see through a number of obligations and complete further flight planning, it was an opportunity to also spend some time chatting with familiar faces. All I had to do was land at 11am. I took off from Appleton with the Cirrus accompanied by the clicking of cameras, nervous because I had read so many stories about landing at Oshkosh. I just wanted it to go well. I tracked low towards a certain waypoint; the idea was to find other aircraft all converging on the same point from different directions and form a single line, which sounded like a good idea. I arrived overhead and quickly spotted several aircraft, picked a black two-seat low-wing "RV" and slotted in behind with only half a mile spacing between aircraft. We all flew a certain height, speed and direction towards a point called FISK. On the ground at FISK were controllers with binoculars; their job was to identify you, ask you to rock your wings and then send you to one of two runways. They did just this, and when I heard, "White Cirrus, rock your wings," I couldn't help beaming. I was assigned a runway and continued tracking along railroad tracks and following the "RV" in front. Slowly but surely the Oshkosh Whitman Field appeared.

One by one the tower cleared each aircraft to land. I watched as the "RV" rocked his wings, turned right and descended for a landing.

'White Cirrus, turn now, cleared to land on the green dot." I turned right very low to the ground and flew along the runway, just staying airborne until the green dot appeared and the wheels of the Cirrus touched down.

'Good job on the green dot, turn left off the runway and onto the grass as soon as possible. Welcome to Oshkosh!" Woohoo!

I was on a high, excited and relieved that it been a success. I looked at my watch as I held up a sign signifying my parking position. Three minutes to eleven. Spot on.

I taxied into the main plaza of the airshow, the center and hub where all the action happened. I looked up to see family, friends and my manager Dave Lyall. They were nowhere near as excited to see me as I thought they'd be.

I hopped out and walked up to them where they were waiting behind a barrier. "What are you doing here?" my brother said.

'Ahhh, it's eleven o'clock, I am meant to be here at eleven.'

'No, it's ten o'clock.'

So some of my friends and some Aussies I didn't even know, as well as the crew from *60 Minutes*, had missed the landing and arrival. I had learned yet another lesson: North Carolina time is not Wisconsin time, and when you set off towards the west you need to change your watch back an hour. Damn.

16

OSHKOSH AND BEYOND

The *Spirit of the Sapphire Coast*, complete with its Australian registration, an Aussie flag in the window, a myriad of sponsor logos and the 500 Club names on the aircraft itself, sat quietly under the International Visitors Arch, taking pride of place on the air show line. Thousands of people came over to take a look, and every time we passed the Cirrus there were people peering into the windows, wondering where it had come from. It was all very cool.

There were interviews of all sorts and I was also able to shake hands with some phenomenal air show performers, including Mike Goulian, a pilot I have looked up to for many years. I also met Jack Pelton, the boss of the entire air show and the ex-CEO of the Cessna Aircraft Company, who had spoke with me shortly after my experiences in Wichita, Kansas. Being well into my trip now and chatting with Jack was great, he had only the kindest things to say about the flight and at the same time he was in the middle of running the air show! I also caught up with Bob and Laurie Carlton. Bob was the pilot who had flown the jet-powered sailplane at the Avalon air show back in Australia. To have such people take an interest in the trip was fantastic.

We spent a day with the *60 Minutes* crew, filming all sorts of snippets around the grounds. I was slowly learning just how much work went into a story on the *60 Minutes* program. Those guys work damn hard for what we see in a fifteen- or twenty-minute package.

I caught up with Jack Weigand, the twenty-one-year-old Californian who had broken the record for the youngest pilot to fly solo around the world, landing on the very day I took off. Only four pilots under the age of thirty-seven had flown solo around the world, and it was rare to have the two flights overlap. I spoke with Jack at length. He was a great guy, quiet and reserved yet encouraging in every way, regardless of who would hold the record in the end. Later in the week we caught up with Carol-Ann Garrett, a phenomenal woman who has taken on the world in a single-engine Mooney aircraft several times. Almost everything Jack and Carol-Ann said was reassuring, giving me some peace of mind about the next stage of the trip.

We spent hours speaking with schoolchildren back in Australia. Partnership with Telstra enabled me to connect via live streaming with a number of schools and colleges, including my own high school back in Bega. We were up well into the night thanks to the differing time zones but the response we received from the kids was fantastic and made it so worthwhile. I felt we were achieving our goal to inspire youth, not just in aviation but in other areas they might choose.

On a few mornings I stayed away from the airport to work on the flight planning from the USA onwards. Although most of the work had been completed, a few things had been left out. It was better to tackle these in Oshkosh having gained the experience of the flight so far; if I wanted to change the way I was going about anything, this was the time to do so.

AirVenture Oshkosh was a wonderful experience and I felt I had achieved so much: I had made new friends, promoted youth in aviation, spent time with sponsors, taken a trip to Milwaukee to do a live cross for the *Today Show* in Australia, had worked with *60 Minutes*, had rested and repacked. Above all, I had landed an aircraft in the world's biggest air show. Life was good.

The departure from Oshkosh for Appleton, where I would repack and prepare the ferry tanks and HF radio aerial, was a long process. I arrived in the morning ready to fly and with the attitude that I would take things as they came. Many planes were leaving Oshkosh that day and we had no idea how long that would take. I completed a pre-flight check on the plane, untied it from its tiedowns and had a large group of people help pull it to the flight line. I climbed in and started up, then I waited.

I had read all the instructions on how to depart Oshkosh safely: a heap of paperwork. A number of aircraft had all arrived at the end of the runway to wait their turn to take off, and I moved forward to join them. Two to three aircraft were being lined up on the runway at once in the hope of clearing the congestion on the taxiways. It was amazing, there were jets, warbirds, ultralights and home-builts all within 100 meters of the Cirrus. It was as diverse as you could imagine and for an aviation nut like me it was brilliant.

The controller became curious, "VH-OLS, Where exactly are you from? Oh my, you've come a long way!'

I lined up and when cleared, I took off. The controllers wished me well, not once but twice, even when I was well out of sight and on my way. They were great guys.

We were required to stay low and track in a certain direction before having the freedom to fly as we pleased, so I levelled off only a few hundred feet above the ground. The problem was that all the aircraft had different airspeeds. I banked to the right to overtake a Piper Cub, a slow little yellow airplane that became a yellow blur as I zipped past. After I had turned to track for Appleton, a Cessna 172 appeared in my right window. I had never been so close to another aircraft in my life. As fast as he was there, as fast as I reacted, he was gone.

I touched down in Appleton just as I had down earlier in the week, parked up and began to work away. The doona cover was removed, the ferry tank and wing tanks refuelled and the HF aerial reinstalled. After being packed the aircraft was back to how it was when we crossed the Pacific Ocean. Although I didn't need the tank to fly from Appleton to my next stop at Bangor in Maine, it was a great opportunity to test the tank over land. It hadn't been used in a while and the last thing we needed was to have something go wrong over the icy waters of the North Atlantic.

It had been an amazing week, with one more stop in Bangor before heading into Canada I was about to say goodbye to the USA. In the next week I hoped to successfully find myself on the other side of the pond, sitting in Europe.

I woke in Appleton early, made my way to the airfield and pulled the plane from the hangar. In no time I was programming the flight plan into the avionics, a leg that would take me into and then out of Canadian airspace before landing in the northeast corner of the USA.

I waved to my distraught Mum and proud Dad, the family who still remained after the air show. It would be a long while before I saw a familiar face again and as I removed the park brake and taxied towards the runway I felt just a little anxious. The flight went quickly and was reasonably relaxed, though I had a few jobs to do. These included testing the ferry tank. As soon as I was in the air I began to transfer fuel; it felt like forever since last time I had done that. The tank seemed to be working just fine as I zipped into Canadian air space, and in no time I was crossing Lake Ontario and skimming the border of Canada and the USA. A controller queried my registration and accent, simply wanting to know what was going on. I told him about the flight and how I was on my way around the world, all in the hope to arrive back in Australia in a month or so. He was blown away, and he asked whether I would like to track directly over Niagara Falls. That didn't take a lot of thought.

Guided by him, and trying to watch where I was going, I fumbled a bunch of cameras as I flew over Niagara Falls. I was at 5000 feet but had a fantastic view of the main circular falls that lead into a long narrow gorge under the large bridge linking Canada to the USA. To see the sheer volume of water and the way it moved was phenomenal, not to mention the "Maid of the Mist" boats that now looked like bath toys. It was moments like this that made me realise just how far I had come, but also just how far I still had to go.

The rest of the trip to Bangor was uneventful, tracking over the kind of rural scenery—trees and meadows as far as the eye could see—that I imagined was typical of this part of the world. Very little in the way of towns or villages. I touched down at the Bangor airport with nearly full wing tanks on the Cirrus. The ferry tank had been used for most of the flight and to my excited relief it had functioned perfectly. I parked up and caught a ride to the little terminal, had a quick chat about the Customs and other requirements on leaving the USA. This took some time: USA security was both complicated and tight. There was little to do to the airplane, I filled the wing tanks but left the ferry tank as it was. With a little fuel still in the ferry tank the next leg would allow me to completely empty it, which I needed to do to determine exactly how much fuel was on board for the flight across the freezing Atlantic to Reykjavik in Iceland, my next stop. A few airport employees whisked me off for lunch in Bangor and insisted that I try the lobster for which Maine is famous. We ordered a small plate of lobster and, being a little unsure about that, I also ordered a quesadilla for insurance. You can never go wrong with a quesadilla. (Yes, Mum, the lobster was okay.)

I was given a little gift bag that included a stuffed moose called Monty, who joined a growing zoo of stuffed toys that had been gathering in the Cirrus throughout the trip. That had started with a minion from the *Despicable Me* movies, named Mike by my Facebook followers. The gang was slowly growing.

I arrived back at the motel and met up with a reporter for *Channel 5 News*, a news station that reminded me of a movie set in a small town. After a quick chat it was off to bed.

With first light being 4:30am I woke worried, the last thing I needed was to miss my takeoff. I called Customs to double check the final requirements and it was lucky I did; a form was missing from the small tree of paperwork already submitted, without which I was going nowhere. I spent the next hour on the phone and laptop trying to sort the issue and eventually I was good to go. When something like this happens after all those months of planning, you begin to doubt yourself and wonder what else you might have forgotten. All you can do is continue and hope the guy at the other end of your flight is friendly.

I said goodbye and climbed on board. I sat Monty the Moose next to Mike the Minion, and after organising the paperwork around me I took off from the USA for the last time.

I crossed the border from the USA to Canada and it was a bittersweet moment. I didn't want to leave the USA, but the only way I was getting home was in the Cirrus, and if I wanted that to happen I needed to get a move on. I began to hear controllers and pilots speaking French on the radio, and though I had spent a few years learning to count in French class it was safe to say I had absolutely no idea what they were saying. The dense dark green trees began to be separated by little lakes and it was just as you would imagine Canada to be. The lack of civilisation was confirmed by a loss of radio coverage. I just couldn't talk to anyone but that seemed normal around this part of the world; the controllers had even told me it would probably happen. I requested descent after I found cloud at my cruising altitude, a quick look at the outside air temperature indicated that ice could form on the aircraft in these below zero conditions and therefore the warmer air down lower would be a better option.

I tracked visually for the airport and set up for a landing, just off to the right a floatplane took to the skies and turned away from my path. The runway was huge. Goose Bay in Newfoundland is a common stopover when crossing the North Atlantic. It sees some very large aircraft, although the Cirrus didn't really fit that description. I touched down and taxied towards the Woodward FBO. I remembered seeing a picture of the building online very early in the planning stage. It had stuck with me and now there it was, I was actually in Canada. I sat quietly in the plane and kept everything closed up as Customs drove up to the aircraft, they looked very official so I kept any emotion to a minimum. It turned out they were absolute champions, all they wanted to do was chat about the flight: "Why on earth would you want to fly around the world with one engine? Are you okay?'

I unpacked and dragged my bags inside, the Cirrus sat next to a broken United Airlines jet and an orange water bomber. I had watched a TV show called *Ice Pilots* about ferrying a water bomber across the North Atlantic and in typical reality TV fashion they made it look as if they were attempting the feat with a kite that faced a guaranteed fiery end. That said, I didn't want to make too many assumptions until I was sitting sipping tea in the UK.

There were a few young Canadians running the FBO and they asked all sorts of questions about the trip and took a few photos with the Cirrus. We organised Customs and refuelling, restocked my supply of oil and chatted away about life in Goose Bay. I mentioned how I spotted the endless lakes on the way into Goose Bay and we began talking about float planes, which led to them finding out I had never been in an aircraft on the water. They decided they needed to fix that. Within twenty minutes the owner of Air Labrador, a float plane operator based nearby, was on his way to pick me up. Instead of checking into a motel I was suddenly going flying. I like a little diversity in my day.

I hopped on board a twin-engine turbine Otter which underneath had two enormous floats that bumped back and forth against the dock. There were two pilots and one was the highest time Twin Otter pilot in the world with over 48,000 flying hours. They loaded timber, or "lumber," into the rear of the aircraft and I squeezed into a seat right at the rear behind the heavy load.

We idled from the dock and flew off. I sat back and looked out the window taking in the lakes and bushland as they passed by. We touched down on a lake in the middle of nowhere, taxied around a small headland and parked up against a dock. It was old and broken, the water looked cold and I didn't think I should walk on or anywhere near it. The dock led to a little island but the island was all on its own. The pilots set the timber in a pile centered on the small piece of land before a helicopter appeared over the hill. The pilot sat the helicopter down and proceeded to secure the load. He was slinging timber underneath the helicopter and taking it to an Australian construction site just over the hill. This was way too cool.

On the flight back to Goose Bay I hopped up the front in place of the co-pilot. I was now taking in the tree-covered Canada from the cockpit of a lumber-loaded floatplane. I might as well have been Canadian.

At three the next morning the alarm went off in my motel room. I had changed the tone because it had gone off in the early hours of the morning one too many times and I was starting to hear it in my sleep. Hoping to wake up fresher I had chosen an upbeat, positive jingle. It made no difference; 3am was 3am. I was planning on a 5:30am departure. Weather information was vital and I had asked the forecast to be faxed through to the FBO office at 4:45am. I needed to check and double check the conditions. There couldn't be too much cloud due to the low temperatures in the north, and below-zero temperatures and cloud meant the water droplets would freeze when they made contact with the aircraft, creating ice and quickly degrading the performance of the Cirrus. Scary.

I arrived at the FBO but the weather forecast hadn't. While I chased it up on the phone I began to prepare the plane for another departure. I checked the oil and then secured the oil cap. It's funny how a flight over water suddenly makes you paranoid. I must have checked that the cap was on properly at least five times. I packed the aircraft and headed back inside to find the weather forecast was sitting on the fax machine, I grabbed it and said my goodbyes.

I spent the next ten minutes next to the Cirrus, squeezing my legs and arms into a bright orange immersion suit. The Switlik Company had kindly sponsored the suit and a life vest, the immersion suit was a fitted full-body garment sealed at the hands and neck and including fully sealed boots. If I had to ditch in the North Atlantic I wouldn't survive for long. The immersion suit was designed to lengthen the survival time by keeping the body warm and dry for as long as possible. It was heavy and cumbersome, almost like wearing snow ski gear from the 1980s. The seal around my neck was tight. I knew for certain that not a drop of water could enter the suit, and with the life vest on top of all that I knew that this was not going to be a comfortable flight.

I squeezed into the left seat among the bags and equipment and put on my belts, started up and began to program the avionics, sort out the paperwork around me and check the HF radio. The HF wasn't working. I didn't know what had happened but I wasn't receiving any signal through my headset. I jumped on the phone and called Darren Gibson from Macleay Aircraft Maintenance in Kempsey back in Australia. He had installed the HF and I figured he would be the best one to speak to. Within minutes we had a solution and the welcome, yet unwanted, harsh squelch of the radio began beaming through the headset.

I called up air traffic control and requested 7000 feet for my flight, even though for a leg spent almost entirely over water the lowest safe altitude for flight within cloud was higher than 7000 feet over Greenland. Instead of tracking directly to Reykjavik in Iceland I had decided to fly over the tip of Greenland. If the weather was no good at Reykjavik or I had any issues on the way I could choose then to divert to an airport in Narsarsuaq just to the west of my flight path. I started the engine. I was off to Europe!

17

THE PHANTOM MENACE

I tracked over land on the climb to 9000 feet, noticing immediately just how cold the air was. The temperature gauge sat well below zero and I knew it would only get colder. I levelled off and ensured the first ferry transfer was out of the way. The tank had been bone dry just before refuelling in Goose Bay so I knew exactly how much fuel was on board, something that gave me significant peace of mind. I transferred from the standard VHF aircraft radios to the overwater HF radio even though I wouldn't need it for long. I could speak to the air traffic controllers from Canada, then switch to the controllers from Greenland before finally chatting to the guys in Reykjavik.

I flew all the legs of the flight early in the day because as the afternoon went on, typically the weather would deteriorate. I was fairly relaxed, the sky was clear yet the water looked cold.

This leg was renowned for aircraft icing and the experienced pilots had expressed the need for caution many times throughout the planning stage.

The cloud and water vapour in the air would form as ice on the aircraft if the air temperature were below zero degrees. When ice forms on the aircraft it blocks any view from inside the cockpit as the windshield becomes opaque, but more worryingly it builds on the wing and changes the shape of the one device carefully moulded to keep you in the air. The worse the ice on the wing becomes, the more lift the wing loses, up to the point where it will stop flying altogether. Ice grabs on to anything it can, even a propeller blade spinning 2600 times a minute. Basically, ice is dangerous. Very dangerous.

I began to zigzag back and forth to remain clear of cloud, which at this stage wasn't a big issue as it was still fairly clear. I continued to do this for hours but there came a moment where I could no longer stay visual and clear of the icy clouds. I had looked everywhere hoping to see an opening but had no luck. Everything happened so quickly, the next thing I knew I flew into the cloud. The Cirrus was designed to fly low and while it didn't have the ability to outclimb the weather, it could descend into what was hopefully warmer air. The problem was that this far north all the air was cold; you would have to end up very low before the temperature climbed back above zero and the ice on the aircraft began to dissipate.

As ice began to form on the windshield and the leading edges on the wing began to thicken and frost, I hoped against hope that the cloud was thin. When you don't have much flying experience it is hard to gauge just how bad a situation is. I knew that other pilots out there would think this was nothing. In fact it didn't look all that bad but as some pilots say, any ice is too much ice. All the same, I kept thinking of something I read once: "You begin life with an empty bag of experience and a full bag of luck. The goal is to fill the bag of experience before you empty the bag of luck."

And then the cloud suddenly thinned and finally disappeared and the sun shone down on the Cirrus's white wings. I looked down and saw a sight I will never forget. It was Greenland. It was a place of brown mountains that looked like shattered rock, with snow and ice in its crevices and cracks. Nothing green could be seen anywhere, of course: I remembered as much from my primary school days where I learned that Greenland was ice and Iceland was green. But in the waters surrounding the land were icebergs, real icebergs, small mountains of blue green ice sparkling in the sun. They were beautiful, but they were also a constant reminder of the water temperature and the conditions I was flying over.

I had little time to absorb all this before Greenland disappeared just as quickly as it had appeared. I passed the far eastern point of the island and turned right to align with Reykjavik. Next stop was Iceland.

The weather ahead looked okay. As the hours slipped by I decided to climb higher to 11,000 feet to avoid the cloud below. I knew at some point I would need to descend and hoped to do that ahead where the cloud had cleared. I had no wish to be sandwiched between cloud and the North Atlantic Ocean. The top fastening of the immersion suit was unbelievably tight; suffocating at this point was not especially appealing, and I held my hand between it and my neck. I contacted Iceland Radio on the standard aircraft VHF radio, and after a few attempts and some patience I was able to hear them. They gave me clearance into their air space and told me to keep tracking towards Reykjavik. There was still cloud, but it was not so thick above the airport and I could track for a landing visually.

I reached top of descent, calculated as the distance from the destination airport, and knew I needed to descend now to make sure I arrived over the airport at the correct altitude.

Cloud was still a problem. As I sat and delayed the descent I stared out the front window, watching conditions worsen to the point where even at this altitude I would enter cloud shortly. I had to descend through the cloud layer and I hoped it was thin: a frightening thought. I nosed down and slowed the aircraft as it entered cloud and watched the outside air temperature indicator drop even further.

It was cold, minus twenty degrees Celsius cold. The ice started to build and I watched very carefully. Ice makes the aircraft slow down due to the extra drag but the descent was causing the aircraft to increase speed; due to the simple laws of gravity, we were heading well and truly downhill. I was confident that with the current weather report I would break free into clear air very soon and therefore be free of the worst of the icing conditions. I needed to do that; after all, I couldn't go back up. The ice had formed on the wings and windshield and there was little doubt it had also formed around other parts of the aircraft including the propeller. At least it didn't seem to be getting worse.

But then I spotted the biggest problem of all. The long wire HF radio aerial was strung between the wingtip and the tail of the Cirrus. The air was warming and the ice was beginning to break off the aerial, creating an unbalanced piece of steel wire that began to swing like a skipping rope. I was worried that the wire would break, something I had been warned about if ice formed on it. If it broke from the wingtip it could swing back towards the tail, catching somewhere and potentially causing all manner of serious issues. With the ice nearly gone from the wings I began to slow down, hoping to stop the swinging wire. I was scared.

I wished I had more experience in dealing with icy conditions, but as I went through the checks in my mind I did feel I had made all the right decisions. If I couldn't reach Reykjavik, however, I had no option in the middle of the North Atlantic but to divert to another airport. But where? And how much fuel would I need? Could I refuel with avgas somewhere else? What about clearances? And weather?

The air temperature was climbing, the swinging aerial slowing down and eventually—to my massive relief—the nose of the Cirrus finally found clear blue sky. I was within minutes of Reykjavik airport and my knowledge of routine kicked in: I joined a final approach onto the runway. It sat on the edge of a town that looked interesting, all uniform, small, colourful houses like something from a postcard.

I touched down and breathed out for what felt like the first time in a while. I had made it and resolved never to fly a single engine airplane from Canada to Iceland without icing protection ever again.

I parked between a bunch of other aircraft, and climbed out as best I could in the immersion suit. My handler was nearby, and we said hello. He seemed really nice, but his English was not good. I waddled inside with my passport and bags to complete Customs and noticed that the cumbersome suit felt a little strange, sticking to me so that I looked like a cryovaced piece of steak. It took a few moments before I realised what had happened. At 11,000 feet I had pulled the tight neck seal away from my body but when everything became busy I had let go and flown the aircraft to the ground. On the ground the air pressure within the suit was still the same as at 11,000 feet above. With a swift movement I broke the neck seal and let the air rush into the suit. It sounded like a semitrailer letting off the air brakes.

I unpacked and spent twenty minutes fixing the HF radio aerial. The metal wire had well and truly been stretched after its impersonation of a skipping rope and it needed tightening. I slipped the Cirrus into a hangar and found a taxi to the center of Reykjavik, desperately needing food and sleep.

I placed my bags in the back of the taxi, hopped in the front passenger seat and said hello, but the driver's response was nothing but a smile. I had no idea how to speak Icelandic; I think I may have accidentally skipped over that option in high school. Instead I held up the address for the motel: Spítalastígur 1, Amtmannstígur 5, Reykjavik, Iceland. I could have attempted to pronounce it but it would have only complicated the situation. He hesitantly nodded and we set off. I assumed Iceland was only a small country and therefore we could only get so lost and having just confirmed the amount of water surrounding Iceland in the North Atlantic, I knew we weren't going far.

The conversation was hardly riveting. I sat and watched as the little colourful houses zipped by like illustrations in a geography textbook. Even the motel wasn't a typical one, more like a little unit for a family. I checked in and soon found myself sitting on the couch of a unit, still wearing the flight suit. Before long I threw the bags into a pile just inside the door and the lifeless body of the orange immersion suit lay across the floor. I was tired and it was already 9:30pm, but I was hungry and it was still broad daylight outside.

My body clock had already been diagnosed as clinically insane, it had been through so many changes and I think it was beginning to just take things as they came. I quickly changed and walked to the center of town to find something to eat before bed. The town was a hive of activity, the sort that could make me assume it was lunchtime, whatever else my watch was telling me. I walked along the strip of restaurants, stopping to read each menu, but there was no English in sight. Anything that had been translated into English still had Icelandic words hidden here and there. I'm a fussy eater and there was no way I was taking any chances on an Icelandic delicacy.

Just as I was about to give up at 10:30pm, I walked around a corner to find a familiar coloured sign—Subway. It might have been in Icelandic and the girl behind the counter might have only spoken a little English, but I had been to Subway a time or two and I had the pointing to what you want through the glass thing well and truly down. I pointed and she laughed at me while making my contraption of a meal, which thankfully looked like one prepared back at home, no surprises there. I paid with a credit card as I had no Icelandic kroners and headed back to the unit. This was the first time I had been in a country where the language spoken was not predominantly English.

Iceland lacked a little in this department but as a country it really interested me, partly because I had never really thought about it before. I had never imagined travelling to Reykjavik in the same way I had longed to visit to England or Italy. I figured that while I was there, with two full days before my next leg, I would make an effort to see as much as I possibly could.

I planned to tackle the aircraft on day one, it needed to be repacked, refuelled and readied for the flight to Scotland, the next step. Customs, the departure details, weather and specific times had to be organised with my handler, BIRK Flight Services. If I could squeeze all of this into one day then I could relax and have a look around before taking off again. It would be a challenge, but all I could do was try.

I set off for the airport and began working away. In most cases we used a fuel truck for refuelling but on this particular day the trucks were delayed, so I chose to taxi the aircraft to the fuel bowser. My handler was a young guy who I discovered did speak English; it was just his accent—and my Aussie one—that made communication a little more complicated than usual. Within an hour we had the ferry tank filled and we had thrown all the equipment that lay around the aircraft into a little car. Once back from the bowser I slipped the plane back into the hangar where it was slightly warmer, then took the time to carefully repack and give the plane a quick clean. I double-checked the little adjustment on the HF aerial, spoke to a few interested passers-by who knew enough English to chat away, then finally hopped into the car for a ride back to town. The *Spirit of the Sapphire Coast* was once again ready to go.

I was excited to have a few hours left in the day and impressed at just how quickly the plane had been prepared. BIRK Flight Services were used to private international flights and had everything worked out pretty well. I decided to spend the evening walking around Reykjavik township as the unit was fairly close to the center. Good booking, Mum!

I found a church sitting on the top of a hill and decided to wander in and have a look around. There was a lift that took you up to a viewing deck, so I handed over a few newly acquired Icelandic kroners and walked inside. I think the lift used to be a refrigerator and they had painted it silver and tied a rope to the roof, it was tiny. I was crammed inside with a French couple and in typically awkward fashion we stood silently watching the numbers increase as we made our way to the viewing deck. Suddenly the lift stopped and my now close acquaintances said something in French. We weren't at the top and whatever they said was a bit more alarming than *bonjour*. We picked up the emergency phone and spoke with the operator. It turned out that the French couple spoke English also, which was great as we were going to be spending the next little while cementing our friendship. Up to this point, along with flying and all the other jobs, I had shared experiences via social media using photos, videos and blogs. I was due to film a video blog on my phone soon anyway and with time to spare, why not now?

There's nothing like breaking the ice by asking, "I know we're stuck in a lift, but can you film me, please?" As the Frenchman held my camera phone I started to chat away, explaining my experience of the leg from Canada to Iceland, only to have the lights in the lift shut off in mid speech. Very quickly and swiftly the French lady pulled out her phone, switched on the flash to create some impromptu stage lighting, her husband kept filming and I kept talking. I had only just met these people but we were a gun team!

The lift finally moved and I took in Reykjavik from above before risking my wellbeing in the lift once again. That evening I booked a back-to-back tour for the next day. I decided to take a trip to the Blue Lagoons hot spring and the popular Golden Circle. I went to bed at about eleven, and was surprised to see how light the sky still was. It was never really dark; the sky always had a glow about it.

Next morning I woke early, unpacked my carefully structured backpack and filled it with a towel and spare clothes. My camera was charged and the blogs, emails and updates had been done the night before. I walked into town and hopped on a bus. First stop was the Blue Lagoons, a hot spa located in the Grindavik lava field in southwestern Iceland. There were a few tourists who had come there in order to swim in the warm silica- and sulphur-enriched waters. I joined in the fun and spent an hour swimming around the volcanic rocks. Nearly two years before I had seen a ferry pilot's blog describing his visit to the lagoon on the stopover in Iceland. Now here I was in the exact same situation, which was very cool.

Soon afterwards I was back on the bus and we arrived in the center of Reykjavik after a drive through the countryside. I hopped off, grabbed something visibly safe to eat and jumped on another bus. We set off this time with a tour guide to the Golden Circle, a tourist route that extends 300 kilometers from Reykjavik into central Iceland and back. We stopped at a phenomenal waterfall, the Gullfoss, before watching geysers erupt from the geothermal ground. As well as looking between two meeting tectonic plates and towards a far-off glacier, I sat back and took in the history of Iceland from a very local tour guide. Wow. Iceland was a phenomenal place.

I arrived back into Reykjavik late, but while it had been a huge day it was worth it in every way. While other people were being dropped at the door of their motels, I was let out at the front gate of the Reykjavik airport. Under my towel and camera was the handwritten flight plan for the following day, I had to drop into the FBO office and have the plan faxed through to an air traffic control center. With this out of the way and the plan approved, I made my way to the unit to pack and head for bed. Reykjavik is cold, even colder early in the morning. I was up early and busily packing the last of my clothes. The one-knee-on-my-bag manoeuvre hadn't become any easier since the first time I tried it back in Wollongong, and the poor zipper was holding on for dear life. I phoned a cab driver and asked to be picked up, holding the address of the unit in my hand and proceeded to tell him where I was.

'Spítalastígur Street, you know, Spit-a-lass-ss-ss-ss-tigger Street." Nothing. The cab driver had no idea at all. I also had no idea and we couldn't even piece together a normal conversation, let alone define a distinct position on planet Earth. I gave up. Even though it was very early in the morning I said thank you and decided to walk to a main road where I could hail a cab. Hopefully the ridiculous flight suit would then provide a hint as to where I needed to be.

I had a sleeping-bag-sized clothes bag, a flight bag, a backpack, the immersion suit and a bunch of other little things to carry. It took forty-five minutes to find a main road and besides my usual clothes and number of duffel bags, I had a bright orange suit draped over my back. I looked like the latest circus act to grace the shores of Iceland. Everything was heavy and for the first time in my life I wished I knew the local language. If I had, I could have been sitting patiently on the steps of my unit waiting for the cab to arrive.

I found a cab. The driver actually understood me, which was phenomenal, and in no time we were on our way to the airport. I hopped out, handed over the last of my kroners and headed to the aircraft. I had the weather forecast in hand, a folder full of all sorts of goodies and had spoken with the handler in detail as to the day's flight. Although he wasn't a pilot he had dealt with this type of flying a lot. He mentioned another light aircraft that would be departing for my next destination, Wick in Scotland, also. Not only would they be heading for the same destination but also be flying at a similar time. I recognised the registration. TAD was a little red aircraft on its way around the world. The two guys who were flying the plane had also been at the Oshkosh AirVenture show and though I hadn't spoken with them directly I had naturally taken a keen interest in the aircraft and what they were attempting to do.

After another painstaking pre-flight, I somehow squeezed into my favorite immersion suit and took to the clear blue sky. Although it was cold it was clear; the risk of icing at this point was nil. All I was required to do was take in the view, and what a spectacular view it proved to be. As I passed 5000 feet on my climb to 9000 feet, I tracked directly overhead a glacier, an unforgettable sight, a solid layer of ice extending in a circular shape and extending miles ahead of the aircraft. I remember asking myself the question we were taught to ask ourselves from the beginning of our flight training: "Where would I land the plane if I had an engine failure right now?" I had asked myself that question thousands of times before, but I had never had the answer of, "Oh, that glacier over there will do."

I overheard TAD speaking with air traffic control, quickly said hello and asked to speak with them on the frequency 123.45, a "common chatter" radio station where the strict structure of aviation radio was left behind. They had departed from Reykjavik just behind me and had also begun the flight to Scotland. We spoke about my journey in comparison to theirs and even exchanged contact details as we flew. I did have to have a chuckle to myself; networking above Iceland between two single-engine aircraft is not your usual social interaction. They sounded like great guys, I let them go as I began to transfer fuel, wished them well and thought that maybe we would see each other in Wick.

When I levelled off at 9000 feet the sky was clear and I was smiling. Yes I was over the North Atlantic in a light aircraft, a place where swimming was highly frowned upon, but it was completely different to the previous leg.

The tailwinds pushed me towards Scotland and I kept thinking about the land mass known as Europe. Once I was in Scotland I wouldn't have to look at this much water for quite some time, and that was a nice thought. A wisp of cloud appeared ahead but it was so thin it was nearly transparent. The Cirrus skipped through it but within a fraction of a second the leading edge of the wing had become extremely frosty. That was a little wake-up call, a reminder of where I was and the need to keep my wits about me.

I was handed over to the air traffic controllers in the UK and started my descent into what had become a warmer yet very cloudy sky, a scene typical of UK weather. I entered cloud and stayed there for quite some time, mostly speaking with a lady in the control tower at Wick airport located in far northeastern Scotland and up against the water's edge. I broke visual and descended quickly to avoid having to fly an approach using the instruments through the cloud. Just as I was clear I looked down to see patchwork-quilt-like fields with a small castle in the center. Yep, I had found Scotland.

After the five-hour flight I landed in very gusty conditions, taxied from the runway and around in circles for five minutes while trying to sort out where to park. Although I was tired I was actually more relieved than anything. I had crossed the North Atlantic Ocean and I never had to do it again.

I met my handler Andrew and for an hour we shuffled around paperwork in a very basic-looking building. It was a tiny airport and the Customs requirements for my entry into Europe were nowhere near as strict as I had imagined. The most strenuous question I was asked was whether I wanted a cup of tea. Considering this would be the only Customs engagement until leaving Greece, I had to say I was surprised at how casual it was, but I was cool with that.

We pushed the Cirrus into a humungous old hangar. It was so big you could have almost flown the plane inside it. It was old all right but they told me it was safe, after all it had to become old somehow. As I undressed, or rather awkwardly fell out of the immersion suit, an elderly couple wandered up to say hello, carrying a picture of me and one of their relatives from Australia. They had heard about the flight and wanted to pop by and say hello, not only from Scotland but from those back at home.

Jumping into a car that finally had the steering wheel located on the proper side, I was driven to a little motel where I would spend just a night before setting off flying once again, the only planned back-to-back flying on the trip. There was a little daylight left and I had taken in the narrow Scottish streets and old buildings on the drive from the airport, so once settled I decided to walk through the main area of town just to say I had seen a little of Wick. I wandered in and out of a few stores before finding a bakery that looked like something from back at home so I zipped inside to try and find something for dinner.

They had pies! The sign said "Meat pies." This was amazing. "So can you tell me what's in your meat pies?" I asked. "Just mince," she said.

'I'll take one with sauce, please.'

Although I was keen for an Aussie meat pie, a form of food that I had not seen anywhere else in the world, I can assure you that this was as far from an Aussie meat pie as you can get. In Scotland "mince" means absolutely anything presumed once living and now found concealed within an envelope of pastry. The pie had the consistency of Spam and a perfect geometrical shape, as if it had been shaped with a circular cookie cutter. I took one bite and made a beeline for the rubbish bin, then another beeline to the pub where I ordered a chicken schnitzel. Not even Scotland could ruin a chicken schnitzel.

I carefully folded the used, battered, note-covered flight plan and filed it away in a container along with the other legs already completed. I then removed a fresh white envelope with "Scotland to England" on the front. Each flight-plan envelope had been carefully put together well before I left Australia, so I needed only an hour or so of study to refresh my knowledge of the next flight. Half of my flight plan envelopes were now tattered and used, but the Telstra online tracker had made a turn and was now tracking "back down" from Iceland towards Australia. I had passed the halfway point. Progress.

Because the flying was so constant and the preparation had been non-stop I had little time to look in detail at all the different locations I would be flying over. So when a Facebook follower asked whether my journey included Newcastle in the UK because he wanted to photograph me as I flew over his home town, I had absolutely no idea. After a little research I let the guy know that I would be passing over Newcastle at around 5,000 feet.

I left Scotland after an uneventful morning preparing the aircraft, entered into cloud and intercepted my flight-planned track while climbing to 5,000 feet above the ocean. I watched the patchwork-quilt-like countryside pass underneath and although the thick cloud dissipated slightly it was still far from a clear blue-sky day. Having not refuelled the ferry tank in Wick, I used the leg to England to pump the last remaining drops into the wing and ensure the tank was again bone dry. It was only four or five hours from the northernmost point of the UK to its southernmost point: amazing when you think how far a four-hour flight will get you in Australia.

Flying in the UK seemed quite straightforward, although I had doubts about the way air traffic control handed me onto the next controller "down the line." No details of the aircraft or flight path were passed on, and I had to explain it all to the new controller from scratch. By the end of the day, I had a very clear idea about who I was.

I found it was possible to choose what "type" of surveillance or services I wanted: in other words, how much advice air traffic control would give about the whereabouts of other traffic and other airspace issues. I was stumped when they first asked; I had absolutely no idea what was on offer and had never heard of this approach before. When I queried my options the controller went on to explain, but he talked so fast I struggled to keep up. All I understood was that cost varied among the different options. I didn't know the finer details so I went with the most expensive one, figuring this was not the time to cut costs when dealing with something I didn't really understand, and in an unfamiliar country too. I decided I would rather skip dinner that night than breach London's airspace or see the whites of the eyes of another pilot. If I could have paid someone to bring me an inflight meal and a movie, I would have. The eastern coastline of the UK sat off my left wing while each town zipped under the aircraft. My plan was to fly south until I reached the coast, tracking straight for the White Cliffs of Dover, then once I had overflown the cliffs I would turn right and follow the coast to the day's final destination, Lydd. I had decided to stop at Lydd for a very good reason. Fred and Linda Rankin from the Frogs Hollow Aeroclub spent half the year living in England and the other half in Australia. They had UK backgrounds and broad English accents, but they also had the good idea of escaping the English winter and fleeing to the warm Sapphire Coast of New South Wales, one of the greatest places on earth.

Fred and Linda had heard about a potential stopover in England while I was planning the route, and I had decided to spend two nights at Lydd before moving on to France. Fred had wanted to plan a little gathering at a local English pub and although the chances of delays and diversions were high we decided to go ahead and take our chances.

Besides, Mum and Dad would be there too. They wanted to meet me wherever possible, but because the flight's budget was beyond tight, their options were limited. Besides they had contributed to the flight in any way possible already. That said, after being in the USA for Air Venture, it was only a short hop across the pond to England (that is in their highly advanced, temperature controlled, jet powered, food and alcohol equipped travelling machine… not a Cirrus). This meant that for one of the final times on my trip, there would be a bunch of familiar faces waiting to say hello when I touched down in England. I was looking forward very much to seeing Fred and Linda and Mum and Dad, and on the way there was one thing I had to do: take in the White Cliffs of Dover.

While I was speaking with the Lydd control tower I peered over the nose of the Cirrus. The English Channel was clearly visible, but I could see nothing that resembled the White Cliffs of Dover. I knew what to do, however. I had the cameras at the ready and as I crossed the coast I banked hard to the right. The green patchwork fields had ended abruptly, and there, underneath me, were enormous, perfectly pure white cliffs. I was blown away. and as I looked back towards the north I truly understood just what the White Cliffs of Dover were—a picturesque foreground to a history-filled landmass, one that we only wish could tell stories. I had spent hours watching, reading and learning about the young pilots who flew over these iconic cliffs during World War II. Though there are still a few of these heroes left, for someone my age the war remains part of history, something with which I have absolutely no direct connection, except for my imagination and what I have read or seen on TV or film. I stared at the White Cliffs in awe, and also took in the nearby harbour at Dover, something I had seen a thousand times in a textbook, on TV or during a movie. I couldn't believe I was really here.

I looked back over the wing at the disappearing white coastline before focusing on a landing. I joined a long final approach and descended towards the English countryside, touching down and coming to a stop just clear of the runway. The controller explained to me where to taxi and when I looked carefully I could see a marshal in front of a large crowd of people over by the terminal. I parked the Cirrus, shut down, clambered out and began to say hello.

I was excited. It had been a relaxing flight with a lot to see, a little to learn and not too much to stress about. I had just seen something indescribable and now was on the ground saying hello to Mum and Dad, the manager of the airport and a group of media who had been patiently waiting. After a few quick conversations I walked across to thirty or forty people standing behind the security fence. I was so glad they had taken an interest. I looked into the crowd, looked away and then looked back immediately, recognising some familiar faces from the Frogs Hollow Aeroclub, people I had never expected to see in England.

Debbie Keys and her daughter Georgie had been visiting the UK and had told me they would come by the airport to say hello. Just behind them stood, Col and Bev Hazel. No one had mentioned that they would be stopping by. It was great to see them all, a wonderful surprise.

I left the aircraft where it was and spent an hour talking with all sorts of people inside the terminal. There was even an elderly Sri Lankan man who gave me a handful of Sri Lankan currency—he wanted to shout me lunch when I finally arrived in Colombo. There was so much support for the flight and so much excitement to see the Cirrus arrive in Lydd, it was simply a great afternoon.

We packed away the plane and before long we were standing at the doors of the Queen's Head in Icklesham, East Sussex. We'd come from the thought of a "potential gathering" at the Frogs Hollow Aeroclub to a real English pub, and it was surreal to finally be there. We had managed to dodge several vehicles on the ridiculously narrow and winding lanes to get there: I was discovering that the narrower the roads, the faster English people seemed to drive. They must find that kind of thing fun. Luckily the drive ended at a pub.

We spent the evening chatting away and I was asked many questions about the flight so far and where I was headed after leaving England.

The room was buzzing—unlike me when I had my first pint of Guinness—but silence quickly fell when a story about my flight popped up on the nightly news. It's hard to describe what it feels like to be in an English pub with a group of people who have gathered because of a flight you have made, and then to see your own face on an English TV channel. It was strange but exciting to have an evening away from my racing mind that seemed to be stressing about something at every waking moment. When the night was over and I was more than ready for bed, we checked into the Ship Inn in nearby Rye and I went to sleep.

I woke next morning to the knowledge that once again I had one day to prepare the aircraft. I had to fill the ferry tank and it was time to wipe the oil from the underbelly of the Cirrus. I was also up against another issue. The plane was nearing a required fifty-hourly oil change, originally planned for France. I needed to buy and take fresh oil and an oil filter from England. It was all very heavy, not what I wanted to carry anywhere, but we had had trouble sourcing it in France. I spent an hour calling ahead to try and secure a hangar in Cannes because I needed somewhere clean and tidy to change the oil, but that turned out to be harder than I thought.

With little luck organising anything in France I decided to look at my options. Maybe it could be done in England instead? I crunched a few numbers. Each service had to be completed at a certain time: there was a little leeway but no exceptions. Apart from that, I needed to know whether a service in England would leave me with enough hours to fly back to Australia before the next one. If I didn't think this through I could end up in Indonesia with a grounded aircraft. I didn't think there would be too many Cirrus-certified engineers in Indonesia.

After a while I decided it was all possible, phoned a local engineering company and explained the situation: "Would there be any chance you could give a Cirrus a fifty-hourly service? When? Ahhh, would now be okay?" All of a sudden the Cirrus was towed from its hangar and a local company was hard at work on the plane. They cheerfully told me not to worry, just to take in the sights and let them do the hard work.

The service meant an extra day in England and one less in France. This didn't worry me too much as both were countries within Europe meaning no Customs rescheduling or issues with paperwork. All I really needed was liaison with Mike Gray from White Rose Aviation. A key component in the flight's success, he had been working with me to organise all the overflight and landing clearances for each country.

With a day now up my sleeve I made a last-minute decision to see London really quickly, and so Mum, Dad and I hopped on a fast train that took us to the center of the city. Once off the train we walked from the Underground and into the bustling streets, jumped on a red double-decker bus and took photos as famous buildings and locations zipped by. I ran from place to place, took a photo in front of Buckingham Palace, poked my head into the Tower of London, drove across London Bridge and gazed upwards at the London Eye before buying a new stuffed toy, a bear guardsman, to add to the ever-growing flight crew.

After only a few hours and with sore feet we took to the Underground and hopped back on the fast train. As we travelled to Rye I reflected that I had just seen London in record time. I had completed a round of the Monopoly board for real. When the morning sun began shining through the window of the Ship Inn I got up and quickly headed for the airfield. Just down the road, through complete coincidence, was the Eastbourne Airshow, a phenomenal display of flying by the beach. I had only been told about it the day before, although I had a big day ahead to finalise the maintenance and prepare the aircraft I had decided to sacrifice a sleep-in to see one thing in particular—the Red Arrows.

We stood on a typical rocky British beach among thousands of other spectators and watched a Spitfire and a Lancaster bomber, two of the most iconic British aircraft, take to the skies over their very own home. Soon after a fleet of red aircraft arrived as the star attraction of the show. The Red Arrows are the British Air Force Aerobatic Team, a world-famous group of red Hawk jet aircraft that trail thick blue, white and red smoke while they perform breathtaking aerobatics. As the Red Arrows disappeared over the horizon it was back into the car and off to the airport.

The Cirrus was pulled from the maintenance hangar complete with new oil and paperwork confirming that it had been inspected. We filled the ferry tank and double-checked all we could, I spent hours looking through paperwork, finishing up blogs and responding to emails. I had also withdrawn a large quantity of US dollars, having heard what the countries towards which I was now headed would and wouldn't accept as payment, and I knew plenty of US cash was vital.

Although the last few days had been far from planned, the jobs were nearly complete. I was almost ready to fly on to France and I had been rested and revived up to a point. To be able to spend time with familiar people in a comfortable environment was worth every moment. It was now up to me to fly through a further seven countries and back into Australia, only then, when the flight was over, would I be able to catch up with family and friends again.

As the busy few days in England came to an end I finished packing and casually read through the posts and conversations on social media. A photo caught my eye. It was an aircraft overflying Newcastle in the UK at approximately 5000 feet. A perfect shot of the aircraft's underbelly, an oily white Cirrus tracking from the north to the south.

I was now glad we had wiped most of the oil from the belly of the plane, but how on earth did he take that photo?

18

HIGHS AND LOWS

Like every flight so far, the routing Ken and I had chosen from Lydd to Cannes needed to be approved by air traffic control. I had been told that the Eurocontrol air traffic system could be a nuisance. If the routing was not approved a notice of rejection would be sent back with no information given about the reason. Working out why your route had not been approved was a guessing game. This time, however, I had struck it lucky. Andrew Bruce from Far North Aviation in Wick had already given me Eurocontrol-approved flight routes for all my European legs up until Greece. He had gone beyond the call of duty to help in seeing the flight become a success.

With the flight plan approved we pulled the plane from the hangar and completed the usual pre-flight inspection. The Cirrus was fresh out of Eagle Aero Engineering and thankfully there was very little to do before the four-hour flight over the English Channel, the French mainland and into Cannes in the French Riviera. For the first time in my flying career I had been given a "slot time," a definite departure time set so I could fit in with other air traffic in the area.

Next up, I said goodbye to Mum and Dad. To have them travel home from Oshkosh and the airshow in the USA via England had been fantastic but now they would be heading back to Merimbula and waiting there for me to arrive in early September. I wasn't really fazed by saying goodbye to their familiar faces; so much was going on that there was no time to think about anything not directly related to safely arriving at the next destination. Being preoccupied with that helped me a bit. Mum, on the other hand, not so much.

Once in the plane I started up and sat and waited for my allocated slot time before contacting the tower. A voice with a strong English accent gave me taxi directions towards the runway and with a wave through the window to Mum and Dad I was off. I lined up and with the checks completed I ascended towards the clouds, focusing on picking up my planned route and climbing as directed by the controllers. Within seconds I was told to turn over the English Channel and track outbound towards France. As I listened, replied and conformed to the orders I felt the engine give a slight shudder, a slight cough that within less than a second was back to normal. I was instantly as alert as if I had just downed four cans of Red Bull for breakfast.

This wasn't the first time the Cirrus had coughed early in a flight: it had done the same thing when I left Christmas Island in the middle of the Pacific. Then the aircraft had been extremely heavy and I would have had to circle overhead for hours to burn away the fuel and therefore the weight before landing. Instead I monitored the trends, and with the engine running smoothly I had made the decision to keep going. It was a very hot day and I believed the aircraft had experienced vapour lock, a small air bubble that enters the fuel lines on the engine and therefore momentarily starves the engine of fuel; after a slight cough it picks up again and runs as normal. Since then I had asked Rex Koerbin back at Merimbula Aircraft Maintenance some serious questions, and had also spoken with the Corporate Flight Management engineers back in Tennessee. Everyone agreed that although a little vapour lock would wake you up, it was quite normal and nothing to worry about.

All the same, the last thing a pilot wants to hear is the engine cough, especially when your plane is flying over a body of water such as the

English Channel. You have to be in a plane a few thousand feet in the air and over the sea to really understand what it feels like when a smooth-running engine misses a beat. However, with information gleaned from various aircraft engineers in the back of my mind I decided to keep tracking towards France.

As I climbed over the Channel I looked back over my left shoulder and took one long last look at the White Cliffs of Dover and the UK itself. I could already see land ahead of me and wished all water crossings were like this. Directly off the nose was France and to the left were Belgium and the Netherlands. I couldn't believe how many countries were within reach with the fuel I had on board.

Even though the Channel was hardly vast in comparison to the bodies of water I had seen from the Cirrus since leaving Australia, I sat there thinking about the people who had attempted to swim across it. As someone better equipped to float than swim, I was happy to be above the water rather than in it.

The French coastline zipped under the nose just before I climbed from 9000 feet to 12,000 feet—and for a very good reason. I had been told of a few hills known as the French Alps along my flight path, and I knew they were rather large. A high cover of cloud sat only a few thousand feet below me, yet off the left wing was a snow-capped peak poking through the cloud. I immediately thought of the cartoon where a pilot suddenly sees a mountain goat in his windshield even though he is flying quite high. This was true mountain goat in the windshield territory.

Ken and I had discussed the flight through the French Alps when we were sitting around the kitchen table at home. The Cirrus could fly only so high. As it climbed the amount of oxygen in the air reduced and oxygen, along with fuel, was what fed the hungry engine. As the oxygen reduced so did the performance of the plane. This would continue until the Cirrus could simply climb no more, it would more or less run out of breath. The French Alps in places exceeded the height to which the aircraft could climb. This situation would lead to a "mountain goat strike" and the end of Teen World Flight.

The solution was to choose a path through the French Alps, to fly along the valleys and the lowest-lying land. The map was covered in airways or roads in the sky. Each airway had a lowest safe altitude; if flying within cloud it was necessary to stay above this altitude at all times to ensure you remained clear of terrain. Ken and I had planned a route that carefully zigzagged through the Alps, staying at 12,000 feet for the entire flight.

Sitting comfortably at 12,000 feet and breathing with the aid of my oxygen cannula, I peered through the clouds at the largest mountains I had ever seen in my life. At one point the lowest safe altitude just nearby was a whopping 17,600 feet! After a while the mountainous terrain started to drop away as the coastline neared and looking back it was hard to comprehend just what I had been flying over.

Since crossing the coast I had been overrun with French, not just the accent but also the language itself. Nearly every pilot apart from me was speaking to the air traffic controllers in French, and vice versa. This felt odd. Normally I could listen out to other aircraft and gain a little knowledge about who was doing what and where. Not now.

I was given permission to descend into the French Riviera. The coast was in sight and it looked absolutely beautiful. I was doing okay with the French accent so far although I had to listen carefully as the controllers spoke so quickly. They cleared me for an approach that took me out over the water, where I would turn and track back towards the coast. I watched as my destination, Cannes, zipped under the left wing and back behind the aircraft. I was switched across to the control tower and told the controller that I was visual with the airport and requested to track visually for a landing. She had no idea what I meant.

I continued over water until I was fifteen nautical miles off the coast and wondering whether I should have just filled up the ferry tank a little more and kept on going. With a crackle of the radio I was told to turn back and so I pointed towards the airport, being told where to track and how to join the airspace just over the runway. This time I had no idea what the controller was saying. I couldn't understand her accent and I had to listen hard just to work out whether she was speaking French or English.

For the next ten minutes my favorite phrase became "Please say again." The French controller was getting quite irritated, yet every moment we struggled to communicate was another moment closer to arriving over the airport. We spoke back and forth, each time a little more slowly and with a slightly more "refined" rounding of the vowels. It didn't really help. For the first time during the flight I became quite irritated myself, though I made sure my finger was away from the radio transmit button before expressing exactly what I was thinking about the situation. No translator would have been needed and I thought I had better warn *60 Minutes* about that particular piece of footage. Finally we understood each other, and with our little conversation nearly over I began my descent and turned to line up with the runway.

For a moment I thought I had landed in paradise. I was directed by the control tower to a parking spot in front of the very official and fancy terminal and carefully navigated through the fleet of jets owned by the rich and famous. Wow. I really get to park here? I thought. But my joy was short-lived. I was told, "There is a newspaper here that would like to have a photo with you and the aircraft, and once you are done we will move you to the other side of the airport.'

After shutting down, stretching the legs and doing a quick newspaper interview complete with translator and confused though smiling French reporter, I taxied across to a grass parking spot, much more as I had expected. I closed up the aircraft and packed my bags into a van. We stopped by another aircraft and picked up a pilot and his wife. I said hello and attempted to start a conversation but received only blank looks and an awkward smiling nod. Oh right, I thought, no one spoke English. It had been an okay flight and the biggest issue had been the language barrier and difference in accents. There was a lot more of that to come. After a garbled conversation to organise refuelling for the following day I hopped in a cab, bound for the motel in Cannes.

With the flying behind me I watched out the window as Cannes zipped by. The place was amazing and everywhere I looked seemed to scream "money." We pulled up at the motel and I read the taxi meter. No. Impossible. I nearly had to sell the Cirrus to pay for the cab fare alone.

As I unpacked I grabbed the air conditioning remote but everything was written in French. I pressed a few buttons, a red light began to flash and the room started to become warmer. I told the front desk about my slight dilemma as I set off for a walk into town, they laughed at me and said something I didn't understand.

I carefully dodged the Vespa riders with their determination not to live, while drooling at the cars parked on the sidewalk. Bentleys, Lamborghinis, Ferraris, Rolls Royces and the rest, many with international number plates. I had no idea what these owners did for a living but I had a feeling they weren't pilots.

It was a typical French scene, with little cafes and restaurants by the water and thousands of people wandering the streets. I wandered around the marina where the yachts were parked, millions and millions of dollars worth of machines as far as the eye could see. I was just blown away at how the walkway onto the boat extended from the hull, let alone everything else that was going on.

I had walked for a couple of hours round Cannes, but after another long day I was ready for bed and I grabbed something to eat before walking back to the motel. I can't remember what I ate, but it wasn't that exciting. However, what little I had seen of France was amazing. I had seen a vast amount of different cultures and ways of life since leaving home, but Cannes seemed different. It had character.

I woke up to a motel room that simulated the conditions of the polar icecap; I had no idea which air conditioning button the man from the front desk has pressed, but it had no doubt worked. Due to my lack of skills in reading French I decided to leave it as it was. Better to be cold than hot.

I only had one full day in Cannes and needed to somehow find my way back to the airport to organise the refuelling for the Cirrus while I packed the plane for the next leg to Greece. Having only just resumed a normal breathing pattern after paying the first cab fare from the airport to my motel, I had to find another way to get around. I knew I was too young to drive a car and had no faith in my ability to drive on the wrong side of the road but there was one other option. I could join the locals, lose all will to live and hire a Vespa. So I did.

Before I knew it a black van had pulled up in front of the motel, a little French guy hopped out and introduced himself. On the phone only an hour before he had told me that no licence would be required to ride the 50cc Vespa. What was more, I could hire one for the day and still pay less than a oneway cab fare to the airport. Sweet. He wheeled a shiny red step-through Vespa, something I had only seen in a Jim Carrey movie, out of the back of the van. I hadn't ridden any form of motorised machine with only 50cc since I was seven. I asked the same question over and over again, "Will that Vespa carry my not-so-French and not-so-slim self up the steep hills around Cannes, and will it get me to the airport alive?" He laughed a little harder each time I asked, apparently confident I wouldn't have a worry in the world.

He organised a time to meet and pick up the hopefully intact scooter from a hopefully intact rider that afternoon and said goodbye. I now had my very own set of wheels, kind of, for the first time since leaving Norfolk Island. I packed a backpack with everything I needed for refuelling, threw my legs over the red Vespa and pulled on my white open-faced helmet. Wow. I was practically French.

I zipped out and onto the wrong side of the road. The Vespa had one gear and with the throttle wide open it sounded like a blender attempting to puree rocks. Even so, its noise was slightly drowned out by the hundreds of other scooters now huddled around me, so maybe that was a good thing.

With the GPS strapped to the handle bar and programmed direct to the airport, I set off and swerved through the little streets in the center of

Cannes with a smile from ear to ear. This was fun. Although I had not planned this, I soon found myself on a highway, keeping as close to the median strip and as far off the road as possible. Because I was an unlicensed rider the 50 kilometers per hour speed limit was set in stone, not something to experience on a highway when everyone else found 100 kilometers per hour so much more convenient.

Before long I pulled up outside the terminal and took off my white helmet. I wasn't quite the type to be seen on a little red scooter but the fact I was in France seemed to make it okay. I hid the helmet in the seat and set off with my backpack. That ride had been serious fun, but now it was time to concentrate on preparing the aircraft. At the desk I asked about a fuel truck to be told that I would need to taxi the aircraft across the airport and to the fuel bowser where I could refuel myself. After giving them a ten-minute crash course on how to refuel a ferry tank I had them convinced that holding up the bowser for over an hour would be a bad idea and miraculously the fuel truck was on its way.

I unpacked all the equipment from the Cirrus and laid everything on the ground. There was stuff everywhere. As I was about ready to refuel the truck pulled up with some fantastic news. "We can't drive the truck on the grass, just taxi the plane and put it on the sealed concrete over there," they said. I took a breath and repacked the plane, hopped in and started up. I had to request a clearance from the tower before moving anywhere, and as we were chatting away the refueller returned and began yelling through the door.

'Oh, actually, it's okay, just pull it forward ten meters and we can refuel there.'

I apologised to the tower and crept a couple of meters forward before shutting down. The guy pouring the fuel spoke no English at all and his mate stood by translating. They had a quick chat and told me that once refuelled the plane would need to be pushed back to the old position. Another crash course in refuelling a ferry tank let them know that it would be near impossible to move the newly refuelled plane onto the grass as it would be too heavy.

I hopped back in and started up, said a sheepish hello to the tower and requested taxi to the original concrete pad. After a little conversation they agreed to let me leave the aircraft there overnight as I was departing early the next morning. Maybe they just didn't want to hear from me again. We parked up and finally began to pump fuel into the wings while I emptied the plane once again and laid the ferry tank out flat before beginning to fill it with fuel.

We had wasted over an hour just moving the aircraft fifty meters from the grass to the concrete, but at least I was now really good at packing and unpacking the plane. I tried to relax and as I was bent over with my head crammed into the cabin the airport manager showed up. He was extremely apologetic about the confusion and offered any assistance he could, but with all jobs covered we ended up having a casual chat. It was hard to have a structured conversation when every second word was, "Sorry, say that again," or simply a blank look when I accidentally used some form of Aussie slang, but the Frenchman was not going to give up.

As I continued refuelling he popped his head into the cabin with his iPhone in hand and said, "Oh, listen, you will know this!" I recognised the song and the singer, but I had to take a second to make sure what I was hearing was correct. It was Slim Dusty belting out *Waltzing Matilda*. How on earth had this guy found this song? I had just ridden a Vespa, walked the streets of a French city, played my part in a Monty Python-type translation session and was now listening to Slim Dusty sing *Waltzing Matilda* crammed in the cabin of the Cirrus with a guy whose favorite word was "sorreee." I still laugh at the memory of the whole scene.

I repacked and locked up. It had taken a few hours but it was over and I was ready to ride on. I organised a departure time for the morning before mounting the red menace of a machine that screamed horsepower, hit the electric starter and unleashed each and every one of its 50ccs.

I rode straight back to the motel to take care of a bunch of emails I needed to sort out, along with writing a blog and studying up on the leg to Greece. The usual jobs took an hour or two before I needed to focus on a new issue, Egypt.

My route was to take me to Rhodes in Greece before a flight down to Aswan. However, Egypt was currently in a crisis bordering on civil war. With the situation worsening daily we really needed to look at our options.

We had people contacting us left, right and center asking for an update on what we planned to do; the situation in Egypt was extremely volatile. I had first started thinking about our other options in England. If we decided to divert we needed to do it soon in order to have the correct permits and clearances approved. A flight without those could mean being arrested, something which was not on my bucket list.

I was headed towards a part of the world that could certainly be described as interesting, a part of the world where ferry pilots had come to grief, a part of the world where bribery, or "excessive targeted tipping," was considered near normal, where people would take advantage of any situation if it meant making money. Anything that would make the transition through a complicated country as smooth as possible was certainly to be wished for. We juggled the options and with the help of Mike and White Rose in England we decided to change the routing. Instead of Aswan I would spend a night in Aqaba, Jordan, before continuing on to our originally planned stop in Muscat, Oman. With the decision made the approval process began.

I sent emails to update everyone on the route and I was constantly in contact with Dave Lyall as he let the appropriate media people and sponsors know about our change in plans. I looked at the issue of flight planning and luckily had the correct charts on hand as Aqaba sat not too far away from Aswan. I would still depart for Greece the following morning but would spend one extra day there to make sure everything had been lined up correctly, then I would head to Aqaba, just north of the Red Sea. Sounded okay in theory.

With the jobs completed and the next day's flight plan studied, I grabbed some board shorts and a towel and the keys to the Vespa and set off around the center of Cannes, the area I had walked through on the night I arrived. I had a near-death experience at an intersection that consisted of eight lanes proceeding in five different directions and decided the best way to stay alive was to follow someone. I cruised up and down the water's edge, trying hard to concentrate on the road each time a Rolls Royce or Ferrari drove past, as I took in the sights of the French Riviera. I spent a couple of hours just riding around, taking on an uphill winding road that gave amazing views of Cannes before heading in the opposite direction to find a slightly less cluttered beach on the way to Nice. I parked the Vespa on the sidewalk and dove in the Mediterranean Sea for a quick swim. It was amazing, picturesque and very European, but very different from the beaches in Australia, the best in the world.

When the day was over I parked the Vespa behind the black van where the little French guy wheeled it up the ramp and closed the doors. I handed back the helmet, GPS and keys and found myself feeling a little sad to see it go. That said, I wouldn't be seen dead riding a red Vespa wearing a white helmet around the beaches in Australia. Apart from the refuelling process, this had been the most relaxing day of the entire trip. I had been concentrating so hard on staying alive that I forgot about the issues of the flight, where I was going next or how far was left to go. It was great.

I grabbed a Subway before heading to bed. Boring I know, but the French guys behind the sandwich bar asked where I was from. They had asked every single customer the same question before attempting to sing them some kind of song relating to their home country, a song that finished with a Subway sandwich and a tip jar that was well and truly full held out for my contribution. After some kind of impromptu song about kangaroos and some serious laughter, I headed back to the motel.

19

AROUND THE MEDITERRANEAN

After I woke up in Cannes the next morning I packed and went downstairs. I clambered into a cab and we set off for the airport. My planned departure time was 9 am, which was later than I had hoped or expected, but due to various regulations at the Cannes airport it was the earliest time I could take off. I was given a ride throughout the airport grounds to the Cirrus which was still sitting on the concrete pad; within half an hour it had come to life and was warming up.

The list of waypoints was enormous; I sat and entered each and every one into the avionics and worked though the checklist. The flight was to take me over water to Italy, then over water again to the Greek mainland before a slight right turn towards the Greek islands. Although there was a lot of water, the fact that I would be able to spot land occasionally was calming.

I taxied to the holding point of the same runway I had touched down on after departing England only two days before, rolled along the centerline and the Cirrus became airborne, straight out over the waters of the Mediterranean. It was fantastic.

The coast disappeared and I settled in, being handed from one air traffic controller to another. The accents became a little less French and much more Italian, confirmed by the first time I heard, "Ciao!" The Mediterranean Sea came to a solid end as it lapped up against Italy. A high, mountainous spine running through Italy had meant crossing the long and thin country would have to be done at 11,000 feet. Even then I would need to track for the lowest valley between Italy and Sicily.

I peered down through the blue sky and could see iconic little red roofs clustered together on the Italian mountainside. It was hard to comprehend just where I was. Yes, the roofs were red but so were the ones in western Sydney. You had to look hard to take in the mountains, the villages and the water separating Italy and Sicily. It wasn't until I looked at the online tracker that evening that I really realised just where I had flown.

As the east coast of Italy met the Ionian Sea I watched land disappear and heard the accents change once more. I concentrated on doing the jobs I needed to do and soon the ocean abruptly ended, this time up against the Greek mainland. As quickly as land had appeared it disappeared as I turned right and pointed towards the Greek islands in the Aegean and Mediterranean Sea. Islands were continuously popping up off the left and right wings, they were everywhere. Rhodes, where I was due to land, was one of the easternmost Greek islands. I flew over dozens of tiny landmasses before I reached it.

The arrival was a non-event; the air traffic controller swiftly instructed me to descend towards the ocean and lined me up for an instrument approach. With the weather on my side I became visual with the airport and a Boeing 747 airliner on a final approach to the runway. The long sealed runway lay parallel to the coast. At one end sat the city of Rhodes, my new home for a few nights before I moved on to Aqaba. It looked like a bleak city from the air; there was a severe lack of white buildings clinging onto the cliff faces—nothing like the welcoming landscape I had expected.

I was told to stay clear of the airliner—good tip—and to fly an approach behind the jet for a landing. I touched down and kept the Cirrus moving quickly, hoping to get off the runway as fast as possible.

There seemed to be a lot of traffic for a small island and many large commercial airliners parked parallel to the runway.

It was all too easy. I had been so focused on the issue with Egypt that I had just wanted this leg over with, and now it was.

Or that's what I thought.

I taxied from the runway and gave the air traffic controller the name of the handling company that would be looking after me. Off to the right was a ground marshal and I headed in his direction before following his lead and bringing the aircraft to a stop. He waved and walked off, so I began to pack up inside the plane so I could just hop out and leave. As I cleaned up the mess, a little white car pulled up beside the *Spirit of the Sapphire Coast*.

This did not surprise me. In many of my stopovers so far someone had come to say hello and welcome, and even in some cases I was given a welcome gift.

But this was Greece, and things turned out to be very different.

I opened the door and said hello to the woman who had just climbed out of the car. There was no hello in return, instead a short and sharp, "Who are you and what are you doing here?'

I was slightly stunned. "Hi, I'm Ryan Campbell, I am on my way around the world solo and have been in contact several times in regards to my stopover here in Rhodes.'

'I am the airport manager. We know nothing about you. You should not be here. You have to leave.'

Oh crap. There's one less Christmas card I'll have to send out. Her English turned out to be not the best and many of the things I said just caused her to assume a blank and slightly confused expression. I told her I couldn't just leave and handed her the paperwork for all of my clearances. From the look on her face I could see this had the potential to be quite a big issue. I climbed out of the plane and into the car, fully aware that we were not going sightseeing. We were headed for her office.

For forty-five minutes we argued, or rather she did and I listened with the occasional nod. I apologised over and over again, my handler had not turned up and I had very little else to say. All the clearances had been obtained and I had entered Rhodes in a completely legal manner but apparently a twentyfour-hour notice of arrival had not been given. In the end that was not our issue. The handler, who I was paying, had not told us that Rhodes specified giving notice. Today was the first I had heard of it.

Her solution was quite a straightforward one—she wanted me to leave. ASAP. The problem was I had no fuel in the aircraft, I was in the middle of the Greek islands not knowing where else to go, and even with endless amounts of fuel I didn't yet have the permits approved for the flight to Jordan. Regardless of what she thought, regardless of what actions she decided to take, I was going nowhere. I decided I would rather argue with her than run out of fuel or be shot down by some foreign air force, another two items that never made my bucket list.

After a little while a Greek man walked into the office and introduced himself: my "better late than never" handler. He spoke with the woman in Greek while I awkwardly stood by. I knew they were talking about me and that the conversation did not concern the sights Ryan would most like to see while he was in Greece. They somehow came to an agreement. I awkwardly waved to the woman as my handler told me to leave and leave right away, and we wandered outside and just kept walking. "Sorry about that," he said. "She's not the easiest to get on with." Really? But she had seemed so nice, I thought.

'I told her you were leaving tomorrow and she finally agreed. She wasn't very happy about it. Don't worry about her, though. I'll make a phone call tonight and you can stay for your three days.'

I wasn't sure what to say. It had now been a couple of hours since I landed, the plane was locked up but uncovered and awkwardly parked. Luckily I had my bags and was off to the motel. We organised a time to refuel and repack the next day, I would pop by about 4:30pm and fill up the ferry tank. Other than the refuelling I would complete all my other jobs at the motel and stay away from the airport.

I thought long and hard about what had just happened while the cab driver set off for the center of town. It had rattled me a little and I now felt I was far from welcome in Greece, almost as if I shouldn't be here at all. That said, I had few options. I decided to update everyone about my exciting afternoon when I arrived at the motel then go and find dinner, to just forget about the flight until the following day, when I would finish the planning then go and refuel.

I was staying in the Old Town. Rhodes Old Town has been occupied since 4000 BC and is the oldest inhabited medieval town in Europe. I got out of the cab and walked across a moat and into Old Town, as you do. There are more than 200 streets without names in Rhodes and I see this as the reason I became lost. I was still in the flight suit, I was carrying a lot of bags and equipment normally left in the plane and I was lost up a steep cobblestoned street. It was exciting to be there but I could not wait to drop everything and get changed. I wanted to look around, but not like this.

I finally found and checked into the Nikolas Hotel. Mum had spoken with the owners and they were excited to have me stop by. I wandered in and shared my experiences of Greece so far and with a surprised look on their faces they showed me to my room. I threw everything on the floor and after a cold shower crashed out on the bed. I sent an email to let everyone know of the day's happenings, put together a quick update for the blog and social media and packed away the computer. It was time to forget about the flight.

I woke up with the Greek sun streaming through the window after what had been a good night's sleep. With only a few little jobs to do before heading back to the airport in the late afternoon I had the morning to look around, so I bundled my washing together and took it downstairs on my way to breakfast then headed out.

I needed to print off some paperwork and scan a few legal documents for future overflight and landing clearances, then I would email them through to Mike at White Rose so he could organise the finer details. Normally that wouldn't have been an issue, but the motel didn't have the equipment to scan or print, in fact it seemed that very few people in Rhodes did. Instead there was one so-called printing shop that took care of everything, even for the local university students studying on the island. I had a mud map and some comfortable shoes, so I packed my backpack and set off for a walk.

The day zipped by, I found the printing shop and organised the paperwork. I had walked the cobblestoned streets and managed to take in the architecture. It was hard to understand just where I was standing, if only the walls could have talked. I was frequently lost in a mix of tourists and locals as I walked past the shops that lined the ancient streets. Even small details such as doors and shopfronts were ancient and often beautiful. Although the shops were selling souvenirs, locals lived in the old buildings right alongside. Rhodes was the reverse of a commercial city.

I walked outside the walls of the Old Town and took a look around the marina to find a beach close by that I hoped to visit the next day if the plane was finished and ready to go. After a late lunch I attempted to find the motel hidden back among the unnamed cobblestone streets.

I jumped into a cab and took off for the airport, arriving right on 4:30pm and went inside to find my handler. We had organised to meet at Customs, where I would have to go through security to be allowed out on the tarmac where the Cirrus was parked. I spotted the only person I knew in Greece.

He gave me a wave but seemed to be in a hurry.

'We can't refuel at the moment, sorry. The woman is still here and we can't have her see you.'

He walked me up some stairs to a café where he found me a seat hidden behind a large wall.

'Stay here, I'll be back as soon as she has left." I sat behind the wall of the café for two and a half hours, quickly popping my head around the corner to grab something to eat, but otherwise just staying in my seat. I watched as the sun started to go down and became more frustrated the longer I waited. What if he had forgotten and gone home? I sure as hell wasn't going to walk around trying to find out.

He finally appeared but he didn't really say anything apart from "sorry." I began to realise that this wasn't the standard way they went about refuelling a customer. He let me know that my favorite person in the world had finally gone home as we zipped through security and tried to use the last of the daylight to refuel. As I unpacked the plane, he organised the fuel truck.

In a couple of hours the plane was refuelled and ready to go and after another thirty minutes trying to find a way to pay the refueller we slipped through security for the last time. I ordered a cab and bought a tub of chocolate ice-cream from the café. It was around 9pm and I had been there for five hours.

We pulled out of the airport and back to the motel. The cab driver seemed a little strange but he had some seriously catchy Greek music playing on the radio. While I sat and ate my ice-cream he turned around to tell me we would need to take a diversion, as there was a parade blocking the main road. I couldn't have cared less, all I wanted was to go back; at least until we turned off the main road while every other car continued towards the center of Rhodes. We were the only vehicle on a dingy and dark back road and I became a little worried. Maybe this guy was connected to the lady at the airport? Maybe this wasn't a taxi? Maybe this was the end and the *60 Minutes* story would be based on abduction and not a solo circumnavigation?

I though about it for a second but that was all it took. This guy was letting me eat chocolate ice-cream on the cream leather seats of his Mercedes. With that much trust in me he was obviously a genuine guy.

We eventually did get back to the motel. I zipped by a little café and ordered a gyros for a very late post-ice-cream dinner, a staple of the Greek diet with which I had fallen in love. It was similar to a mixed kebab that you could find back at home but tasted so much better.

I woke up early the next morning, took the freshly cleaned clothes, rolled them one by one, and with my knee pressed into the bag managed to strain the zipper closed.

The next few hours were spent finalising the flight plan to Aqaba in Jordan. I had the tracking details outlined and a flight plan form filled out and with the aircraft also ready all I had to do was submit the plan in the morning and take off. I was organised.

I decided to head to the beach that I had spotted the day before. Apparently it was one of the nicest beaches on the island. The sand consisted of coarse grey rock, there were white plastic chairs filled with people and tourists scattered throughout the ocean. I had a few hours so I walked around the perimeter to see what I could find.

There was a boat offering scuba diving, it was first come first served. I was surprised at how cheap it was, but it wasn't so cheap that oxygen became an add-on. I decided to have a go. I was in Greece, why not?

Kitted out and ready to go, I hopped into the shallow water with the instructor standing by. He told me to put my head under the water and have a go at breathing. I was surprised at the physical effort required to breathe out, something that was far from normal. I was a little hesitant but eventually stepped off the rock and into the deep water where I began to float. With one swift pull the instructor deflated my jacket, causing me to sink like a rock. I'd just been given all the encouragement I needed to learn how to breathe underwater, and quickly.

It was beautiful. There was not too much to look on the barren sea floor apart from a cave hidden in a rock wall. That did not matter: I had taken on a challenge completely different to the one I faced each and every day. I had to be careful to stay close to the surface because of the major pressure differences that affect the body when under water and then in the air. That said, scuba diving was still extremely exciting.

The day was coming to an end but instead of taking a taxi back to Old Town I caught a ride with the guys on the boat. I took in the coastline of Greece from the water at a level I hadn't been used to for quite a while. After getting changed I had dinner on the top of an old building, an opportunity to eat outside and watch the sun set over Greece.

It had been a great day and I had stored up some fantastic memories. Next stop Jordan.

But the Greek experience had shaken me a bit. I had been told that there would be unforeseen problems between Europe and home, and having spoken to a lot of ferry pilots I was aware of the sorts of things that might happen. The "targeted tipping" funds were stowed away in the aircraft; we had organised every handler to try and remove the issue of a dozen people trying to help at once and then charging for their trouble. Even knowing all that, and being focused on the issues caused by the Egypt diversion, I hadn't expected any problems in Greece. I had been taken by surprise and didn't like it. Unfortunately I feared there would be much more of this to come. For the first time during my flight I wanted to head home.

20

ON TO JORDAN

The next morning I said goodbye to the owners of the St. Nikolas Hotel. They had been fantastic and looked after me very well, even giving me a thirty-minute word-by-word translation of a local newspaper article about the flight.

I carried my bags outside the walls of the Old Town for the last time before finding the closest road and hailing a cab. I watched the last of the Greek countryside pass by before arriving at the airport. My handler was there and we both had the same idea: let's get the Cirrus and me out of here. Pronto.

I packed the bags into the plane and completed a pre-flight check. Just as I went to pay my handling charges I was told the only ATM machine was back inside the terminal and on the other side of security. I took a breath and off we went, I withdrew the money and fixed up the bill and just for fun we took on security one last time. I walked to the plane via the control tower, passed on my paper-written flight plan to be faxed away before being handed the printed weather forecast. Now I was good to go.

I clambered into the plane and carefully stashed away my Mars bar and bottle of Fanta. Some would say this is not the ideal breakfast, but there's not a lot you can do when you're faced with a vending machine.

I requested a start up and got immediate approval so with the engine warming I began the ritual of programming the avionics and working through the checks. After a few minutes tower let me know there was an issue with my flight plan, and told me to "just stand by and we will try and sort it out." I sat for ten minutes, just waiting, with the aircraft idling and with everything ready to go. Tower soon replied: they hadn't been able to resolve the problem and told me to come up to the tower. I shut down, locked the door on the Cirrus, grabbed just the iPad and my flight planning paperwork and walked briskly across the tarmac.

The flight plan had been faxed through but a notice of rejection had been faxed back. They had tried several times to change it, but without success. I had no idea what was wrong, although we figured they must have had some issue with the routing. However, as they gave no reason we had little to go on in trying to solve the problem. We sent several more plans with the prefix "re-routing accepted" in the hope they would provide a suitable alternative route, but once again they turned it down. When I sat down and looked over the chart again I could see a sliver of Israeli airspace that sat just to the west of Aqaba in Jordan. Maybe that was causing a problem. I re-routed the leg so I would not fly as close to the airspace but track further south and around it before heading north towards Aqaba for a landing. No luck.

We tried and tried: four hours later we decided to give up. I had been in contact with Mike about the overflight and landing clearances and we were still within the allocated time window, but we needed to move quickly. Mike contacted the ground crew in Aqaba and asked them to submit the plan from their end. We hoped that being so close to the Israeli airspace meant they knew exactly what was required and the correct tracking. I was now beyond frustrated.

After dozens of calls, emails and messages the flight plan was finally accepted. I received a copy and curiously scanned the details.

The difference between the original flight plan and the last and final accepted plan was one waypoint. Just one! But that change had taken six hours.

I said goodbye and scooted to the plane. It was now later in the day but the weather still looked stable. All flights had been planned for the morning to take advantage of what was hopefully the best weather, but luckily this afternoon seemed okay. This was no casual departure for me; I was late and I was on a mission. I started up and re-programmed the avionics as I taxied. I backtracked the runway and spun the Cirrus around, and with the throttle pushed forward: the *Spirit of the Sapphire Coast* built speed and became airborne. I turned left and picked up the flight plan track through to Jordan, taking a few last photos as I passed over the city of Rhodes. Although it had looked bleak on my arrival, I could now see and understand what I was looking at, and I was happy I had done that.

When I levelled off at around 9000 feet I was well over the ocean. I knew I was not destined to see land until I crossed the coast of Egypt and descended into Jordan. I fell back into the rhythm I had developed, overcoming the first awkward ferry fuel transfer, which meant shuffling from my seat and encouraging the fuel to flow through the air-filled lines. I then continued to transfer fuel, record engine trends and plan ahead for my arrival. Although just under five hours, the relatively short leg would take me from one world to another. I had never been anywhere that resembled the culture or lifestyle of Jordan. When I was thirsty I reached for my bottle of Fanta, only to find that six hours sitting in the cabin of the Cirrus had slightly warmed my one and only beverage. I was a little disappointed but with nothing to lose I jammed the bottle between two vents, carefully holding it still with my leg while allowing the cold air to hit the warm bottle. Half an hour later I cracked the lid on what was a freshly chilled drink. I couldn't believe it had worked and for the first time that day, I had a win. Bear Grylls would have been impressed.

The water soon came to an end and what looked like an endless sandy beach turned out to be Egypt. I crossed the coast before turning left and heading towards Jordan and although I was only over Egypt for a short while I was blown away by the landscape. Everything was just the one colour, a monotonous sandy grey and gold blur that stretched as far as the eye could see. If I looked extremely carefully I could see the outlines of seemingly camouflaged cities and towns. I even spotted a near invisible airport.

I was headed straight for Jordan on the northern tip of the Red Sea, but this also meant I was headed straight towards Israeli airspace. As I expected I was told to turn right and track down the Red Sea until requested to turn back. I followed orders and when I banked to the right I spotted Aqaba off the left wing. I would end up there at some point, I just didn't know when. I was told to remain at 13,000 feet and tracked for miles and miles until approved to turn back, when a 180-degree U-turn lined me up with the runway at Aqaba and I was told to descend.

The closer I came to the ground the more I realised just where I was. I was about to touch down in the middle of the desert. It was a scene straight out of the Bible; the only thing missing was a camel. In the distance a runway appeared, a long dark sealed strip that stood out like nothing else, mainly because everything within sight of it was a bright golden colour. The northern tip of the Red Sea disappeared underneath the nose just before I touched down. With a slight screech of the tires I had arrived in Jordan.

I taxied to what looked like the terminal where I saw a building with peculiar script I took to be Arabic on the front and beside it the word "Arrivals." That'll do me, I thought.

I leaped out into the driest and hottest weather yet. There was no welcoming committee, no one to greet me, so I unpacked the basics and wandered to the terminal doors. I needed to clear Customs before worrying about what to do with the plane and I was taken through to have my fingerprints and a quick photo taken. My passport was handed back before I was introduced to my handler, a nice guy with a true passion for aviation. I found that throughout the trip, regardless of the culture, the country, the cost of fuel or the sights, a shared passion for aviation meant that casual conversation was easy. With only one night in Jordan I needed to have the aircraft refuelled immediately. The next day was a long leg to Muscat in Oman which would see a good nine hours spent over Saudi Arabia. I was already late and we needed to get a move on, otherwise I would never get to bed. The handler showed me where to taxi. They had a fuel bowser near the local aeroclub hangar where we would refuel and then park the plane.

With the Cirrus pulled alongside the pump I began to empty the cabin. The equipment lay everywhere and the slight wind took hold of some foam sheeting and gave it an impromptu lesson on how to fly. I was working on unpacking so my handler went for a run in an attempt to restrain the foam. It kept him busy for a little while. We began to pump the fuel into the ferry tank after I had filled the wings and it took quite a while, but patience was something I had learned.

The diversion to Jordan had happened so quickly I wasn't really familiar with the local area. As I pumped away I asked the guy, "How much is the fuel here?" I took his: "Ah, I might tell you that when you are finished," as another way of saying "expensive." I was right, it was seven dollars per liter. After a pumping a good 700 liters into the Cirrus, I didn't need a calculator: someone to administer CPR would have been more useful.

I hopped in an old ute with my new mate and we set off for the motel after attempting to submit the next day's flight plan. The security was insane, they wouldn't let me back onto the tarmac even though I had just landed an aircraft in their airport. The security guy had a large gun so I kept my opinion to myself, but he and the handler traded words for a little while. Finally they let me zip in and out of the office, the plan was faxed away and the plane was good to go.

As we pulled out of the airport I had my eyes fixed on the palm trees, passing highway and general tidiness of the area. I suddenly looked up to see a bunch of camels crossing the road. All part of the experience.

The motel, which turned out to be nice, was in the center of the city of Aqaba. The buildings and shopfronts all had signs in that peculiar font with a little English to help alongside, although I didn't need that when working out what to have for a late dinner. Across the road stood a huge red sign attached to a red and white building. KFC.

This was the only thing I could relate to home or Western civilisation, everything else was very different. After dropping my bags in my room, I wandered inside and ordered something to eat and paid with the only cash I had, a US $100 bill. I have no idea what the conversion rate was, but a few of them gathered around the calculator to work through the issue. I was handed a heavy handful of Jordanian currency which I didn't even bother counting, as it would have been absolutely no use. I might have just paid for the most expensive KFC ever. Six hours delay in Greece had been frustrating but in the end it was worth it. I wandered back after dinner, on the way buying a small stuffed camel to add to the collection of crew in the Cirrus, and had a chat with the guys on the front desk. I told them I would be checking out early, they mentioned I would miss breakfast but a "breakfast box" could be organised for me if I wished.

Sure, why not, I thought. What could go wrong?

21

THE MYSTERIOUS EAST

I had gone to bed late and got up early; my bags still sat packed on the floor because I had taken out only what I needed for a few hours sleep before moving on. The diversion to Jordan had meant an extra day in Greece while we waited for the overflight and landing approvals, but now I needed to climb out of bed and find my way to Muscat in Oman. This would not only enable me to make up for lost time, but would at least put me back on the planned route for the flight.

I woke up and crammed the few essentials into the end of the bulging bag, pulled on the flight suit and headed downstairs. It was very early, about 5am. I was up against a 1,300-nautical mile flight that would take about ten hours. Most of that would be over the barren landscape of Saudi Arabia. I checked out of my room and was passed my preorganised breakfast box, a plastic bag with a container inside. I had food, my ride was here and I was on time. Today was off to a good start.

We arrived at the airport and was I dropped at the terminal doors with my bags; my handler intended to wait for me on the tarmac while I cleared Customs. Once that was sorted and I was let out the front doors, it would just be a matter of pre-flighting the Cirrus and taking off.

I wandered inside and found the check-in desk and then the queue for Customs. I was surrounded by foreign tourists and Jordanians, all preparing to take a commercial flight. Just like an airport at home, really, except that I was in a very different culture and environment. Everyone looked at me wondering why on earth I was wearing what I was, why I hadn't checked in my bags and what I was carrying in that plastic bag.

I handed over my passport and the General Declaration form, I just needed a stamp and I would be on my way. But the guy behind the glass apparently had other ideas. He spoke little English and didn't seem comfortable with what I was trying to do. I waited patiently, though with a knot in my stomach, as he spoke with his supervisor, then another guy and then a few other strangers. After I had been in the queue for almost an hour my handler, my only Jordanian connection who was sick of waiting for me on the tarmac, turned up. I have no idea what he told them but my passport and Gen Dec form were stamped very quickly.

The amount of cash I had to hand over was enough to look as if I was buying a share in the airport, not paying for avgas. I signed a few forms and gladly accepted parting gifts from my handler consisting of hats, bottles, pens and other merchandise from the Aeroclub of Jordan, said goodbye and boarded my plane.

While I waited for my clearance I watched a Jordanian Airlines jet pass by my wingtip and very soon was I following him to the end of the runway and readying for departure. Aqaba is situated in a valley so the avionics and paper charts showed a long, thin, low-lying section sheltered by monstrous mountains along either side. They were so large that the runway pointed directly into the valley to keep arriving and departing traffic clear of the hills.

I was cleared for takeoff and told to climb on the runway heading until I reached 9000 feet, a very long climb with the aircraft as heavy as it was. It was hot and the Cirrus didn't like it at all. With the nose held low I climbed at a much higher airspeed to try and keep the important bit up the front nice and cool. After the "forever" climb I finally reached 9000 feet, was cleared to turn right and pick up my track to Oman. It was then I looked back over towards Aqaba and realised just how far I had flown up the valley.

After levelling off I began to set up for a long flight. I twisted around and messed about organising the first ferry transfer and then settled back in my seat facing the right way. As I entered the western side of Saudi Arabia I started to take down notes and chat with the various air traffic controllers.

I was hungry but I always seemed to be hungry, and just as I thought about eating I realised I had the breakfast box full of goodies. Best day ever. I hadn't looked but maybe it was a muffin? Maybe a packet of chips? Maybe a fruit box?

I grabbed the plastic bag and sat it on my lap, cautiously but excitedly untying the knot, only to be swiftly smacked in the face by a very strange smell. I am far from a skinny kid and therefore know my muffins very well, and I can assure you the smell did not come from a muffin.

I peeked inside the Styrofoam container. Oh no. It was a full cooked breakfast, with eggs, bacon, beans and something green. The sausages had now escaped the situation and lay in the juices in the bottom of the plastic bag.

I could have cried. No way in the world did I think they would pack me a hot breakfast. I had cherished this potentially food-filled package through an hour of Customs and now four hours of flying. Worse than that, the smell was far from healthy and I was trapped inside the cockpit for the next six hours. What on earth could I do?

I unbuckled the belts and climbed into the back. I went through everything I had and found several plastic bags that I pushed together in an evil attempt at pass the parcel. I then lobbed it over the ferry tank into the back of the plane. I was of course still hungry.

I took a few photos of the sandy landscape, a mix of rich red and light golden sand that extended as far as the eye could see. After a few hours of flying I took a few more photos of sand, this time a mix of rich red and light golden sand extending as far as the eye could see. I fixed up a few jobs and checked that everything was still running smoothly and then became phenomenally excited when I spotted the one sealed road that disappeared on the horizon and took its photograph. Around it was a mix of rich red and light golden sand extending as far as the eye could see.

I soon worked out there wasn't much else to Saudi Arabia. The thought of having an engine failure and ending up stranded in the middle of the desert made me shudder; I hadn't watched enough episodes of Bear Grylls to handle that. Okay, I did have an Official Bear Grylls Survival Kit, but even that wouldn't be enough.

I spotted green crop-circle-like objects at one point mid flight and quickly took photos with eager interest. In the middle of nine hours of picturesque sand sat these green circles, obviously regularly watered. What on earth were they?

The flat endless sand began to turn into mountains, Saudi Arabia whittled away and soon became Oman. I was getting closer to the day's destination.

I was within range of Dubai and the Middle East, the mountains of Oman had risen from the flat desert ground and clouds had started to appear. I was really looking forward to flying past Dubai as two friends, Brennan and Lisa Single, had moved there from Australia not too long before. I was so close to familiar faces but still so far.

Air traffic control was fairly quiet and one controller took the opportunity to query me on the details of my flight plan. I had written my "endurance," or time I could spend in the air as 1300, or thirteen hours. The controller wanted to know what on earth I was flying and I can assure you that "a Cirrus" was not the answer he was expecting. He then asked what was I doing and after I mentioned I was flying around the world solo in a Cirrus and he had confirmed my age, the radio came alive as a handful of pilots launched a bunch of questions.

The general unprofessional chatter gradually quietened down, I was now over water and nearing the top of descent. With the required clearance I pushed the nose towards the desert floor, next stop Muscat.

I was cleared to fly a "localiser" approach that would put me on a long final approach to the airport. I could follow a distinct path to the ground. Each distance from the airport had an associated height and if I flew these heights I would arrive at the end of the runway, right where I needed to be.

I joined the approach and let air traffic control know. They asked me to keep the speed up as I was one of a few aircraft inbound to Muscat. What they should have said was: "You have half a dozen jet airliners chasing you, fly significantly faster or you will become a small smear on their windshields." I continued flying as I listened to air traffic control slow each jet down: "Slow to 160 knots please due to preceding traffic." I was scooting along as fast as I could, but I knew the pilots of the airliners were cursing the little kid in the whippersnipper-powered plastic toy that was currently ahead of them in a fierce battle with the laws of physics.

I found the runway of what turned out to be a huge airport that again appeared against a sandy backdrop. The runway was so large that when I touched down I still had to apply power in order to find the first taxiway so I could make my way to parking. I turned to the right, headed towards a far-off marshaller and parked the plane among a few Saudi Air Force C130 Hercules aircraft. They were painted in camouflage, a rich red and light golden sandy colour.

My handler was a young girl who was extremely helpful and polite. Not once was I called Ryan, nor Mr Campbell or Sir, it was always "Captain." I laughed a little inwardly at this, especially as everybody else—Customs, the refuellers and every single person at the hotel—called me "Captain" too. I couldn't have felt further from being one:

to me a captain was someone with neatly combed grey hair who flew an airliner and had been flying planes for longer than I had been alive.

We took an air-conditioned mini bus to the terminal and walked to Customs, where my handler proceeded to escort me straight past a phenomenally long line of people and to the front of the queue. This Captain thing was kinda cool, I thought. Maybe I needed to dye my hair grey and find a comb. After Customs I was driven to the motel, they sat me down, gave me a warm, wet face washer and took my bags, telling me, "You have a phone call, Captain." People called me? People knew where I was? I had moved up in the world that far?

Wow. The caller could have been a telemarketer for all I cared. It turned out to be the handler back at Muscat airport to confirm fuelling and departure requirements.

After my phone call I went to my room. The humidity on the short walk from the air-conditioned lobby out into the open air stopped me in my tracks and I had to remove my glasses as they fogged up immediately. I found my room and saw my bags had beaten me there. At least that was cool. I ordered dinner and sent updates as I ate, answered emails and worked through the social media chatter. It was always a good feeling to read people's comments regarding the flight and I missed very few during the entire journey. Before long I was in bed.

I had one full day in Muscat, the one day I would normally spend in refuelling and preparing the plane. My handler had told me that if I returned to the airport that day I would need to be in full uniform, obtain a full security clearance and proceed through normal security just to gain access to the plane. I thought about the options and worked out that even if we tried, it wasn't 100 per cent confirmed that I would receive the clearance I needed. And so I made the decision to take the day off. I had my flight plans with me at the motel where I could study up on the next day's flying and I would refuel the following morning nice and early before my departure.

This level of security, the language barrier and excessive use of the word "Captain" was something I had been told to expect in some places, and evidently Muscat was one of them. This was why I dressed in a flight suit covered in Australian flags, bearing the words "Pilot" and with the renowned four golden bars on my shoulders, something normally reserved for the guy with the neat grey hair. Wearing the uniform, I had been told, was an absolute must for the countries between Greece and Australia: I needed to show authority and rank. I remember telling Ken I would fly in a white shirt and black pants, I could even put the sponsors" logos on my back! His answer was an uncooperative and stern, "No." He had then unrolled his flight suit to show me what I needed to wear. Along with showing who was in charge of the aircraft, the uniform was fireproof and had more pockets than I had gadgets. This included an inside pocket to hide my passport and cash.

Less than a year after my journey ended I saw on the news pictures of a pilot sitting in his light aircraft on the ground in a foreign country, surrounded by camouflaged soldiers with automatic rifles. Each and every soldier had the barrel pointed at him. He had been intercepted by a fighter jet and told to land. He was in serious trouble. This type of "international relations" as outlined in the movie *Top Gun* required a subtle approach in order to have a happy ending, and a few bars on the shoulders and a suit to show your rank and position were only going to help. Unfortunately for this pilot, he looked as if he was dressed to go to the beach. Nice sandals, though.

I took on the day, working hard to finish up the paperwork, emails and phone calls to square away fuel and clearances for the remaining legs to Australia, then I donned my boardies and hit the pool.

I ordered lunch, they dropped it by and I ate under the sun and by the water. I was sick of trying to convert currencies and I needed to eat. Why stress over exchange rates? I had a burger and chips, which was about the cheapest item on the menu. It was one of those cute burgers that fits in the palm of your hand, accompanied by a quarter of a potato surgically divided into small sections. I wasn't fussed that the meal wasn't too large and just hoped that "25" in their currency somehow resembled "25" in ours. It didn't. I had just eaten the world's most expensive hamburger. It made the fuel supplier in Jordan look like a charity.

After lunch and another swim I had one more job to do. The significant amount of US dollars carefully placed in the Cirrus had been whittled away by my experiences in Jordan and now I needed more. I called the front desk but after having no luck at the hotel itself I ordered a cab, figuring I would zip down to the servo to find the closest ATM.

I pulled on some casual clothes and grabbed my passport wallet, which held credit cards and a pen and paper. My passport itself was always in the flight suit and this wallet was the next most important item.

I hadn't really been outside in Oman all that much and I took the short drive as an opportunity to video the surrounding city. I signalled to the cab driver to wait when we pulled up at the service station, zipped inside and started to withdraw the cash.

I needed $2,500 US to cover upcoming costs, including fuel, but this ATM produced only local currency and without a bank nearby it was my only option. I began but each transaction was limited to a certain amount, each card also had a daily limit and somehow I needed to keep note of how much had been withdrawn from where. With my pen and paper in hand I got stuck in. I soon found out that one $100 US bill somehow transferred into a thick wad of local cash around two centimeters thick. I placed it in the passport wallet and kept withdrawing cash, the wallet becoming thicker and thicker.

I walked out of the service station with the equivalent of a little over $2,500 in US dollars. In Oman that translates into a small briefcase of cash and I looked as if I had just robbed the place. A few people were shocked but none more than the cab driver as I climbed in with cash falling from the straining passport wallet. I had absolutely no excuse not to give this guy a tip.

The taxi driver dropped me at the motel, my handler was picking me up the following morning so I had nothing to organise except something to eat for dinner. I wandered downstairs to a restaurant, sat down and looked through the menu. After I had ordered, I suddenly realised I was past ready to go home.

I ordered the Australian sirloin steak with pepper sauce. As to how much it cost—don't ask.

22

ACROSS THE INDIAN OCEAN

By now I had been away for just over two months. I calculated that I had been flying for about 150 hours. Only another forty or fifty to go before I was home.

I woke up in Oman early, not only because the day's leg to Sri Lanka would be strenuous and long but also because the intense security and the inability to get to the aircraft on my day off in Muscat meant refuelling was best left for the morning of my departure.

I packed my bags and made my way to the lobby. Even in the early hours of the morning the humidity hit me like a thick wall of water. My handler picked me up from the motel, we got into a silver Hyundai and set off into the darkness. We chatted as we drove, and I told her I needed to find some form of food to take with me. This turned out to be quite a challenge at such an early hour. In the end we stopped at a service station, I wandered inside and bought a bunch of items that were far from the "ideal" culinary choices as suggested in the food pyramid.

At the airport, security was as tight as I had expected. There was no doubt about that. We manoeuvered through the international terminal, again lugging the bags and equipment. My passport was examined and the paperwork and General Declaration forms signed: the most emotionless people seem to work in airport security, I have found. Then we headed onto the tarmac in the darkness, boarded a little bus and set off towards the Cirrus.

I spoke with the handler about refuelling. I had a long flight over water and through a part of the world where the weather could build significantly as the day wore on, and I really needed to be on time. I would unpack the plane while the handler organised the fuel truck and while the refueller filled the wings I could sort out payment, using the ridiculously large pile of cash I was still lugging around, before hopping up on the wing and filling the ferry tank myself. All I needed then was to strap everything in, pack my bags on and around the tank and set off. It sounded easy.

But no matter how well thought out your plan of action might be, if the fuel truck doesn't turn up you might as well have stayed in bed. The Cirrus had been emptied, all the equipment was spread across the tarmac and we just stood by waiting. The departure time was nearing and I was frustrated but my handler was so apologetic that I could hardly feel bad, nor look annoyed.

The day's flight was to take me through India's airspace, not some-where listed on the "places to fly before you die" list I had compiled with information from a range of ferry pilots. I had heard many stories about issues transiting through India and descriptions of interesting moments from pilots who had decided to stop over on the mainland. Originally my flight route had included a potential landing at Cal-cutta and Bangalore. However, discussion among experienced pilots resulted in a plan that was probably more achievable and would—we hoped—produce fewer problems. One of the first steps was to substi-tute any Indian stopovers with two nights in Colombo, Sri Lanka.

As I sat inside a small office keeping a keen eye on the Cirrus and everything I owned scattered on the ground around it, I was becoming really anxious. A little over an hour later the fuel truck finally arrived. I double-checked it was an avgas truck: discovering that it contained jet fuel would have just topped off my morning.

Finally able to get things going, I looked at my watch and realised I had a little over forty minutes before my planned departure. I had become quite good at this ferry tank business and with the wings completely full I took over and filled the auxiliary tank. I was in a hurry and it was hot, I looked as if I had just ran a marathon but I had the tank full of fuel in record time. I asked for various items like a dentist yelling for a drill, and worked to secure the tank while people handed me bags and equipment. I had the tank covered, the bags on top and tarmac around the Cirrus clear. I was only half an hour late.

I threw copious amounts of cash towards the refuellers. They did not apologise for their delay and were less than grateful for the money, which was in the currency of Oman, not US dollars. Well, you can't please everybody. I hopped into the plane and said goodbye, started up and pointed the air vents towards me before contacting air traffic control. I heard: "Victor Hotel Oscar Lima Sierra, please note the airport is closed from time 00 to time 30. Clearance and your departure will be available

after time 30." It was two minutes past the hour, meaning the airport had just closed. Two minutes!

After a little more time spent in the picturesque office with an apologetic handler, I finally made it into the air and I couldn't have been happier to leave. The early morning sun lit up the desert, which very quickly became the coastline and then the endless Arabian Sea.

I climbed through a layer of cloud towards 9000 feet and watched the day unfold as I worked through the first ferry fuel transfer. I had become quite comfortable with flying the Cirrus in the overwater ferry configuration—I had completed a takeoff at maximum weight out of Hawaii, I had successfully completed a number of ferry fuel transfers, and as for the HF radio, well, that could be worked out on the way. I would never completely understand or like using the HF radio but I had little choice. Always looking for a way to do things better, I had time to think as I cruised over the Indian Ocean.

Many months before, as Ken and I sat around the kitchen table planning the flight, we had spoken about this leg from Oman to Sri Lanka. This had been at a time where I was being drowned in new information, trying to find a way to remember it all, to place it in my mind and understand where and how it would apply to my flight. At the time we had discussed the implications of ditching the aircraft into the ocean.

Landing the plane on water was never a desirable situation, of course. However, the method of landing differed, depending on where the emergency took place.

The best "worse case" would be to ditch into a smooth, warm lake in the USA and to be taken in by a loving family for a good feed and a hot shower. After that not so likely option, a ditching near the shore of a well equipped country such as the USA, Australia or anywhere in Europe would be the next best: somewhere allowing a state-of-the-art rescue to take place quickly. From there the options grew worse: a ditching near a less than well equipped country or island, in an area where radio coverage was limited to the HF, in the middle of an ocean where rescue crews would require extensive travel. The unpleasant possibilities were endless. One of the worst, however, was a ditching during the leg from Oman to Sri Lanka, the leg I was currently flying.

The reason for this could be stated in one word. Pirates. I had watched the *Pirates of the Caribbean* movies. The pirates had seemed like a good bunch of guys with a sense of humour and a drinking problem. However, I was soon told that those who cruised the Indian Ocean were far from being the good guys. They didn't have impressive beards or hooks instead of hands or large sailing ships or copious amounts of rum. Instead, if you were forced to ditch the aircraft, they could target an activated distress beacon—the kind installed in the Cirrus. They would then carry out their own "rescue." Although we could never know exactly what would happen, the meeting would be anything but hospitable.

As with all the potential issues our risk mitigation plan took into account the threats throughout the Indian Ocean. We worked out an alternative method of alerting emergency services that did not include the use of the emergency locater beacons, a plan that would use the support team back at home to our full advantage. You should have seen Mum's face when Ken started the pirate conversation.

Meanwhile, here I was at 9000 feet and air traffic control had transferred me from the Middle East-based controllers to those in India. The HF was still a challenge to use; although set up within the Cirrus as well as it could be, the reception was average at best. And on top of that was the Indian accent.

I had one goal, to see the coast of India pass under the nose of the *Spirit of the Sapphire Coast.* The greater part of the water I had needed to cross would be behind me and Sri Lanka would be not too far away. My casual thoughts of Jack Sparrow and his pirate gang would be replaced by the thought of dry land, a bed and something to eat. After more than eight hours in the air daylight was fading. I should have already been on the ground but thanks to the refuelling operation in Muscat I would now be arriving at night.

There were dozens of boats floating well off the west coast of India and what I had thought were the lights of civilisation on the mainland turned out to be fisherman bobbing up and down in the ocean. However, before long the lights of a city became unmistakable. I was so close.

I was now back using the standard aircraft radios, chatting to a controller I could understand quite well and it was all fairly straightforward. I had arrived over the southern tip of India before turning right and aiming for Sri Lanka. I stared down at the lights, the dimly lit streets and the buildings crammed tightly together. Regardless of what I told myself, there was no way I could really comprehend that what I was looking at, below me, was India. Once over the water again I didn't look back at the land at all. Instead I focused on the ocean in front of me and hoped to spot the lights of Colombo.

Finally I was told to descend, but into a cloudy, murky mess. The closer I came to land the darker the sky became; however, a few thousand feet above the ocean I broke free of cloud. The sky was pitch-black but I spotted a dark sliver of land littered with lights.

With little time for the relief I felt on seeing that fantastic sight and knowing I was across that patch of ocean, I was given a clearance to land and with an unexpected change of plans I turned over the coast to line up only a few miles from the runway. It was a monstrous piece of bitumen and I think I could have taken off and landed the Cirrus several times before running out of the sealed, smooth tarmac. I slowed down, quickly ran through my checks and moments later the tires screeched onto the runway. To the right of the runway centerline lay the all-too-familiar ocean but to the left was endless tarmac, a car park for aircraft. As the Cirrus slowed down I spotted a large airliner with "Sri Lanka" written up the side. Unless he was also lost, I was fairly certain I had found Sri Lanka.

The control tower gave me taxi directions, a long-winded list of alphanumerical designators relating to different taxiways which I jotted down before looking at the chart for Colombo's main airport and working out where I had to go. I soon found my handler, a small group of guys waved me in and waited as I shut down. As soon as the propeller stopped moving they began looking all over the aircraft before trying to peer into the cockpit. I hopped out and said hello. They were just as excited to be there as I was.

I was expecting to see a few familiar faces in Colombo. The *60 Minutes* crew including Charles Woolley had flown across to film a few segments for the story that would air when I returned home. It turned out that the joys of airport security and obtaining clearances for filming, among a few other challenges, had made it too complicated for them to be on the tarmac when I arrived.

My handler, along with his very excited co-workers, took a few photos before they all grabbed one of my bags and helped me onto a bus. It was not just any bus, but a full-sized one used to shuttle an airliner load of passengers to the terminal. Tonight it held a kid who had hopped out of his toy plane along with his handler and a few bags.

We swished through security, which was a non-event where I just stood by and smiled, except when being compared to my passport photo, and did everything I was asked to by my handler. I could tell he had done this a time or two before and he was a serious kind of guy—finding someone like that was sometimes a good thing. We laid out a plan of action for the next day and decided on a time to refuel.

I said goodbye as I hopped into the car and sped off towards the motel. So far so good. However, I soon learned that I had left something out of our risk mitigation document: travelling by road in Sri Lanka. Road rules were non-existent, each car seemed to have the option of full throttle or full brakes, nothing in between. The first lesson appeared to be "how to just miss everything." Then there was the mystifying use of the horn. At the strangest times the driver would stand on the horn and appear to lose his mind in a fit of road rage, but when a car almost T-boned our taxi he didn't move an inch, no horn, nothing. I didn't think you could be approved for a scooter or motorbike licence if you had any reason to want to continue living.

I stepped out of the cab still shaking and paid the driver, giving him a tip for delivering me to the motel in a semi-conscious and relatively sane state. I checked in and dropped my bags inside the door of my room. Despite the near-lethal cab ride I was still hungry. I had called Lincoln Howes, the producer for the *60 Minutes* story, just after touching down, and even though he was a fair distance away he had decided to make his way to my motel for a catch-up. I was looking forward to seeing him: I would get to chat with another familiar face and with only one day in Sri Lanka we could organise the filming in between refuelling and the other jobs.

When he arrived I shouted him a beer, which I figured he would need as much as I did. We had a few more before he had to drive back to his motel. We chatted away about the flight so far; even though emails had been exchanged I had not seen the *60 Minutes* crew since the AirVenture airshow in Oshkosh, USA, around a month before. It was great.

I said goodbye and organised to meet the following morning at the crew's motel closer to the city. I made my way to my room, jumped into bed and just lay there thinking.

Being in Colombo felt odd. I had always wanted to travel to the USA and had done so before my trip. Europe was always appealing and countries such as Iceland and the Pacific Islands had been exciting. But I had never wanted to go to Sri Lanka, I had never really thought about it much. We had chosen Colombo because it seemed a logical stopping place, and from then on it had become a name, one of many included destinations. But to actually be in Sri Lanka was strange, to be in a culture that was so different and in an environment far from anything I had experienced before was truly eye-opening, as I was shortly to discover.

As a tourist, you usually hop off the plane with all your belongings in hand. You trek around the sites with a camera and a backpack. The greatest source of stress is watching what you eat and keeping track of your passport, but little else causes too much worry. I had been a tourist many times before and loved that feeling, but travelling in the Cirrus was very, very different.

I felt more directly involved in what I was doing every day.

I was constantly thinking and working towards the next goal, challenge or job. I didn't feel like a tourist, there was more to the situation than just me. I had an aircraft in my possession and I worried about that constantly. Was it where I put it? Was it being watched? What did I need to do to keep on top of anything that could happen at any time? Had I forgotten something? Beyond the day-to-day duties was also the constant worry that something might go wrong, I knew all too well what that would mean in the media and who that would affect. It was my job to prevent that from happening.

All these were feelings and worries that had begun the morning I departed the Australian coastline. Although they dwindled here and there when I was having fun, such as when I was riding that Vespa in France, they were always on my mind. I knew they would stay there until the day the Cirrus was parked back at home. At this point in the trip, I couldn't wait for that moment. More than anything else I wanted to be home.

Whether I was flying that day or not, the alarm always rang early to remind me of how much I had to do. On this day I was being picked up in a van that the *60 Minutes* crew had sent from their motel with the hope it would provide a more sedate ride than a local taxi.

It didn't. We cheated death time after time, and my tendency to believe in a higher power strengthened a little more for each kilometer we survived. I decided it was best to take my focus away from the road and look at what Sri Lanka had to offer instead, or at least whatever I could see of it through the blur of the windshield.

Travelling in a car, taxi or a van to and from the motel or airport was one of the rare times I was able to take a look around each destination. During this particular ride into Colombo, which lasted an hour, I could see the Sri Lankan streets lined with shacks and each small business operating out of nothing more than a tin shed. There was traffic everywhere, it was chaotic and nothing defined the moment where the road ended and the sidewalk began. The levels of poverty were shocking, the way of life and standard of living were far from anything I had seen before. Yet little did I know I had not even reached the slums.

I will never forget crossing a little bridge that spanned a murky, thin river filled with opaque brown water. On either side were makeshift shacks that actually touched the stream. People had set up their homes on the riverbanks, homes that could barely be classed as adequate shelter. It was something I had seen only in school geography lessons: my teacher, Mr Daniels was an absolute champion. He had grown up in India and shared so much about his home country and the surrounding areas such as Sri Lanka. I had seen these images on a Friday afternoon documentary in the classroom, but not in real life until now.

The slums disappeared behind the van as we vibrated violently along the road. The shaking could have been caused by the potholes, or most likely the buffeting around the Toyota Hiace as we approached the speed of sound. I just wanted to get out. This driver was nuts.

We finally arrived at a fancy motel and I walked inside to find Charles Woolley and the crew sitting in the lobby. I sat down and began to fill them all in on the happenings of the last few weeks. There were countless stories to be told. We also decided that I would set off to find an ATM and withdraw cash to pay for the fuel before filming a scene at the local markets. We would then take a ride in a tuktuk, a semi-stable three-wheeled form of popular transport consisting of a small motorbike modified with the addition of a "cabin." The rider sat in the front with passengers in the back, and the open sides meant holding on tightly was something of a must. After the tuktuk ride I would make my way to the airport to refuel and would fill the plane on my own before attempting to make it back to the crew for a quick segment at sunset overlooking the ocean. It all sounded simple.

After piling the camera equipment into the back, we all hopped into the van so the same driver who had picked me up earlier in the day could take us to the markets. It was a fifteen minute drive combining laughter, disbelief and fear, and it all seemed great fun largely because I wasn't on my own. We were dropped off at what I was told were the true local markets, a place hidden away from tourists in the back lots of Colombo. It didn't take long to see what they meant. We were the only white people in sight, sandwiched among the locals out shopping for their groceries.

We stood by the van as the locals watched and the sound guy, who had a habit of sticking his hand up everyone's shirt, fiddled around to secure a small microphone out of sight. We had a quick chat about the plan before setting off for a walk through the markets. I soon noticed every eye was on us. I strolled along casually with Charlie as one of the crew lugged the huge camera and the sound guy held a microphone on a boom over our head. Our goal was to catch a snippet of the culture of Sri Lanka; one experience of many during a journey through fifteen different countries.

We stopped by a Sri Lankan man and a crowd gathered around as we admired his selection of chillies. They were green and towered in cane baskets placed on the ground. He also sat on the ground behind his produce patiently waiting for a customer but I don't think we were quite what he expected. Charles asked for "a chilli," a single chilli, and handed over a Sri Lankan bill. The man smiled and immediately set to work, he grabbed a plastic bag and began filling it with hundreds of green chillies. Regardless of what we tried to say, he wouldn't stop, not until his scales had reached one kilogram.

We wanted one chilli, we now had one kilogram of chillies. I was all for value for money, but this was insane. All we could do was laugh. The growing crowd watched as Charles removed a single green chilli from the bag and broke it in half and in unison we took a bite and began to chew. The locals, who spoke very little English, began to laugh hysterically. They could see our faces and knew I thought I was going to die. Again. Not only that, but I was picturing the confined cockpit of the Cirrus and imagining the long flight to Indonesia scheduled for the following morning. I had a feeling this chilli was travelling on a return ticket.

Only moments after handing the full bag of chillies back to the salesman, complete with a "no refund required," another Sri Lankan man popped up in front of me with something that resembled an elderly tomato. He didn't speak a lot of English but "this chilli hottest ever" wasn't the best sales pitch he could have gone with. We smiled at the locals and said goodbye to the chilli salesman. I think he stills holds the record for the highest profit earned from a single transaction.

We continued on through aisles of food stalls and the smells, the sights and the atmosphere were amazing. As we chatted away Charles was picking up strange food, including dried fish that lay in the sun, but the locals knew we weren't there to purchase anything, they just wanted to be involved, jumping in front of the camera at every chance they got.

We waved goodbye and began the logistical nightmare of organising two tuktuks to ride alongside each other and yet somehow end up back where we started. Charlie and I clambered in one while the camera and sound guy hopped in another. We scooted in and out of traffic, one hand gripping the handle and the other pointing in awe at the sights of Sri Lanka.

In the rush of trying to capture all the shots they were looking for, along with making it to the airport to refuel, it was easy to overlook what was actually going on at that very moment. I was in a tuktuk with Charles Woolley, being chased by a camera crew through the streets of Sri Lanka, all for a program to be run on national television based around the story of my wildest, most out-there dream. All of this just for an ordinary kid from the Sapphire Coast. A prime example of what can be achieved with courage and commitment.

Our jobs for the morning were complete, we dropped the crew and the camera gear at the motel and the driver and I continued towards the airport. Three of us spoke with the driver, giving him directions and trying to tell him to wait at the airport until I was finished. It was a hopeless effort and although we thought he had the plan correct we would only know when I wandered back from refuelling to find a ride back to the motel or an empty car space.

The day fled by as I met my handler, we worked our way through security and began to empty the Cirrus. Just as in Muscat the fuel truck was delayed, but this time when it arrived it had three forty-four-gallon drums of avgas sitting on a trailer. Fortunately the fuel had been organised well before my arrival; the three drums put aside for the Cirrus was all the avgas available in Sri Lanka. Without that fuel I would be stuck in Colombo.

A couple of hours passed as we carefully filled the tank. I was constantly thinking of the next leg, eleven hours to Padang in Indonesia the following morning, and therefore added each and every drop from the three drums. We refuelled, strapped and secured the tank and repacked. The Cirrus was good to go. I walked outside the terminal and began to look for my driver. It had been three hours since he had dropped me off but he suddenly popped up in front of me, enthusiastic as ever, and asked whether I was ready to leave. I had no idea whether he understood anything I had said that day, but he sure had been patient.

We missed the sunset after the delayed refuelling process but managed to find a restaurant and have dinner before bed. It was strange to be sitting around a table discussing the next major event: the moment I would land back in Wollongong.

I said goodbye to the 60 Minutes crew who were due to catch an early flight out of Colombo the next morning and beat me home by a couple of weeks. I survived the final commute from the center of Colombo to my motel and sifted through the flight plan and paperwork before bed. I had sent an email earlier that day to confirm one final time, after several emails over several months, that avgas was still available in Padang. This was the last time I would need to do this, as after Padang I would be "direct to" Broome on the west coast of Australia.

Then I got an email in reply:

'Mr Campbell, No, sorry, no avgas in Padang. Thank you." Oh. Great. As I had done so often before, I called Mike Gray from White Rose Aviation in the UK. Mike had organised every overflight and landing clearance and their limited validity meant that any changes in plan would require a little teamwork and understanding of when we could legally fly. Besides this, it was part of Mike's everyday job to safely navigate a range of pilots and aircraft across the globe, so he had a phenomenal understanding about where avgas was available around the world.

It was now late as Mike and I ran through the options. I kept telling myself that when stressed it is really easy to make a simple situation more complicated than it needs to be, so I had to step back and look at the big picture. This was simple: There was no fuel in Padang in Indonesia and if I flew to Padang I would be stuck. The only avgas in Indonesia was in Jakarta and a quick flight plan showed that if the aircraft was full of fuel it had the range to make it there. The problem was that Sri Lanka's complete supply of avgas was already in the Cirrus, and that wasn't enough to make it to Jakarta. Clearly I was not going to be departing for Indonesia the following morning. Mike suggested adding a stopover in Malaysia but at this hour we both agreed any decision to re-plan to a new destination and still depart the following morning would have been ridiculous and dangerous. I called the lobby to cancel my taxi, emailed home to update them on the changes and turned off my alarm. I would go to bed and work towards a solution with Mike the following day. It meant another full day in Sri Lanka and would put us a day behind, but the options were few and far between.

23

TO MALAYSIA

There was no doubt that I had found myself in a challenging part of the world: a place where simple things could become complicated, where the language barrier could cause problems and vital yet straight-forward requirements such as keeping track of available fuel could take a turn for the unexpected at the very last minute.

During the planning, after speaking with dozens of ferry pilots, I learned that the main logistical challenges would most likely occur between Egypt and home. This had already come true. Greece had pro-vided a surprising challenge because of the strange woman. We had diverted to Jordan because of the crisis in Egypt but not until after six hours and two dozen flight plans had been rejected because of restrictions around Israeli airspace. Muscat turned out to be a fort, the security changed our refuelling plans and coupled with a late fuel truck the departure was pushed back, causing the arrival into Sri Lanka to take place at night. Now our fuel plans in Indonesia, which had been in place for months, had fallen away from us. The question at the moment was: what had happened to the fuel we had been told was safely in Padang, Indonesia? We had confirmed the availability of avgas via email only days before. A full day of phone calls and emails with "Uncle Mike" from White Rose ended in a solution. I would now fly from Colombo to Kuala Lumpur in Malaysia. We had organised a handler to meet upon my arrival and refuel immediately. Because I was adding a leg to the journey and was already a day behind schedule, I would take off early the next morning and fly to Jakarta. There I would refuel and depart the following morning for Broome. It was constant flying, but it was best to move quickly through these countries and make it back to Australia, something I was looking forward to beyond anything I could explain.

I woke early the following morning with a freshly assembled flight plan; more importantly, I had to set my mind on a new destination. It was pretty depressing. All I could think about was returning to stand on Australian soil but it seemed to be getting further away. I had been counting down the legs until that happened and using it as my source of inspiration to take another flight over water, but now we had added another stopover.

When I arrived at the Colombo airport my handler led me to the weather briefing room, and after fifteen minutes of currency exchange enabling me to pay my bill I went through security. My large supply of US cash had disappeared with great speed, and finding a place to withdraw money throughout the last few destinations had been a bigger challenge than I had imagined. With the cash finally sorted we made our way outside and onto the tarmac, where I boarded a bus and set off towards the Cirrus to prepare it for a departure.

I kept glancing at my watch as I removed the covers and completed a pre-flight inspection by torchlight. The flight plan submitted before every leg of the trip not only outlined details of the aircraft, the pilot and the route, but gave a designated time for departure, allowing air traffic control to sequence you in with other aircraft leaving around the same time. For once I was early and though I had a few more little jobs I still had forty-five minutes before my scheduled takeoff.

My handler, who had been on the phone while I worked on the aircraft, ran towards me with a worried look on his face. The prime minister of Sri Lanka was due to touch down in fifteen minutes. If I was not airborne by then I would be grounded, they couldn't tell me for how long, just for a "significant delay."

No one should have to move that quickly at that time of the morning. I clambered into my seat and had the aircraft running while I was still trying to put my seat belts on. As soon as the engine was warm I was on the move and programming the avionics as I went, a tip passed on to me in Oshkosh by Jack Weigand, the then world record holder as the youngest pilot to circumnavigate the globe. Jack's advice about programming the avionics meant that putting in a flight plan wasn't such a mind-numbing job. It wasn't the only piece of advice he gave me; in an hour of casual conversation he passed on many little tips and tricks concerning the flight. Jack congratulated me on the flight so far and expressed his belief and trust that I would finish it successfully. My "what was it like to..." questions had all been answered, and I had left Oshkosh with the most important tool of all, a little more self-confidence thanks to his encouragement. With a clearance in hand I sat ready at the end of the runway. After a Sri Lankan Airlines jet touched down only meters from the Cirrus I lined up on the centerline and waited for it to taxi clear. Soon I was airborne. It was dark and within minutes I was hidden within a thick layer of cloud. I tracked for my flight path and climbed towards 9000 feet as the land disappeared and the ocean began. It was a fairly standard departure for me.

The darkness began to lighten up and within seconds I had reached the top layer of the thick cloud, only to pop out into thin air to one of the most amazingly beautiful and colourful sunrises I had ever seen. I juggled the art of analysing the foreign-sounding air traffic control transmissions while taking photos of the sunrise and flying the overweight aircraft. I was well on my way to Malaysia.

I continued with my usual jobs. It was strange to think that flying a single-engine aircraft with just under 1000 liters of avgas on board, including 600 in the cabin, continuously over water for ten hours, could be regarded as anything near normal. But by then it was. I was far from comfortable, but after well over 20,000 nautical miles I was as comfortable with the situation as I would ever be.

The forecast for Malaysia was for isolated thunderstorms. Although I had managed to depart early, the fact of a ten-hour leg meant that a late afternoon arrival couldn't be avoided. As I flew I transferred fuel, radioed through position reports using the HF, recorded engine trends and briefed my arrival. And I watched the sky morph into a dark cluster of ever-growing and towering clouds. They looked menacing: no way I could be complacent about them, yet again.

Approximately seven hours after leaving Sri Lanka, with three hours to go until I reached Malaysia, I spotted my favorite sight of all time. A sliver of dry land appeared on the horizon: Indonesia, partially hidden by the developing thunderstorms. As I was now nearing a solid and dry surface, I gladly packed away the HF radio and continued chatting with air traffic control on the VHF or standard aircraft radios. I began to hear dozens of aircraft requesting "traffic" to fly left and right of their original route in order to stay clear of the thunderstorms. Flying high over the Indonesian mainland, I was sandwiched between several massive ones. I joined the other aircraft and requested approval to fly left and right of my track. As we were all being overseen by air traffic control, any diversion of our planned route would have to be approved before we set about flying around the weather.

The day was becoming darker and the blanket of solid land soon turned into water again for the relatively short stretch of ocean that separated Indonesia from Malaysia. I was told to expect an ILS approach into Kuala Lumpur, a very precise instrument flying procedure that would bring me extremely close to the ground and hopefully all the way down through the bad weather. The instrument approach procedure was outlined on a piece of paper, or "plate." As well as having an electronic copy on the iPad I had with me hundreds of hard copy plates all sponsored by Jeppesen, an American aviation company specialising in aircraft navigational information as well as other aspects of aviation. I briefed the plate, a casual conversation with myself to outline exactly what I would do and when, because local terrain and airport position made every approach different in some way. With that job out of the way I continued dodging the storms before being given a clearance to descend. I left my cruising altitude and within only a couple of thousand feet I had entered solid cloud. It was a thick layer extending from 8000 feet towards the ground. I was vectored left and right, given distinct headings to fly by air traffic control that would ensure I was sequenced correctly for my approach. I kept descending before intercepting "the extended centerline" of the runway, meaning I was lined up for a landing and could continue my descent through the cloud.

It was a little exciting and unnerving but I had been in cloud for a long time, zigzagging through the sky as I listened to aircraft of all sizes requesting diversions around the storms. I had managed to stay clear of most of the turbulence and only been shaken around a little, now I was number one in the sequence for a landing into Malaysia. I kept going, approaching my "decision altitude," an altitude where if I was not visual with the runway I would be required to "go around," meaning I would need to climb away from the airport and follow distinct instructions to allow me to either try the approach again or divert to another airport.

Only a few hundred feet from my decision altitude, the solid cloud began to flicker and I glimpsed a phenomenally long and well-lit runway. Malaysia!

I touched down and made my way off the runway to allow for the dozens of other aircraft waiting for their turn at the approach. I taxied for my recently organised handler and almost immediately spotted him waving an orange-lit baton around the sky. I also spotted another familiar face, Malaysian James Tan, the youngest pilot to fly solo around the world at twenty-one. Prior to my departure James had been one of only four young pilots in their twenties to have taken on a solo circumnavigation. Like me, James had watched American Barrington Irving fly solo around the world in 2008 at just twenty-three, slashing fourteen years off the world record, and had been inspired. With Barrington's extraordinary achievement fresh in our minds several young aviators—Swiss pilot Carlos Schmidt, James, Jack Weigand and I—had found a new goal. Not only had James successfully broken the previous record, he was now there to welcome me to his home.

As always at the end of a long flight I was eager to hop out and stretch my legs before catching my breath and looking around. Another leg was over, another water crossing behind me, another step closer to home. I shook hands with James and was introduced to my handler, Jeff. He was a big guy with an even bigger smile and they were all so happy to be there.

I unpacked as James looked through the Cirrus, the fuel truck arrived and we topped up with fuel that was extremely cheap in comparison to the price in Muscat and Jordan. The next day's flight was not too long and I still had fuel left in the ferry tank, so I worked through a few calculations to confirm that we would only fill the wings, leaving the ferry tank as it was. This was a decision that would save time and stress.

After making sure it was neat, tidy and ready to depart the next morning, we secured the plane then walked under the wing of several corporate business jets and into the terminal. Jeff led me through Customs and Immigration before setting me free. We had a simple plan. James was determined to take me for something to eat before quickly showing me the Petronas Towers in Kuala Lumpur. He promised it would be a quick trip and he would have me to my motel in no time, I would head to bed as early as possible and grab a taxi early the next morning in order to meet Jeff at Starbucks for a wake-up beverage.

After a bite to eat in the terminal I threw my bags into James' car and we set off for the city center. There are few ways to explain what happened next. I had flown the majority of the way around the world and James had done so completely. He also happened to live in Kuala Lumpur and yet somehow we ended up lost. Really lost. We were looking at the city skyline in the distance, both mobile phones were flat and we had no way of looking up anything such as Google maps or using the GPS so instead, we just drove and took several slightly less than educated guesses.

A full four and a half hours later, nearing the middle of the night, I checked into my motel. I had a photo of myself standing in front of the Petronas Towers, which was no doubt kind of cool, but I also had the experience of actually finding the towers. It had been quite funny and a little frustrating, but it was a great story and nothing a good night's sleep couldn't fix. I collapsed into bed and quickly ran through the emails and paperwork for the next leg. Fortunately I had only recently planned the flight to Indonesia while in Sri Lanka so it was still all fairly fresh in my mind.

Just as I was about to pack up and get some sleep another email made its way to my computer: PLEASE HOLD AIRCRAFT AT WMSA UNTIL WE HAVE INDONESIA LANDING PERMIT (PERMIT STILL UNDER PROCESSED) AND PLEASE DON'T MAKING OVERFLYING OR LANDING INDONSEIA WITHUT PERMJIT ON HAND, HOPE PERMIT CAN APPROVED ON AUGIST 29, 2013 BTN 1200—1300 UTC AND IF I HAVE EARLY WILL INFORM YOU A.S.A.P DUE TO PERMITS NO. 4887, 5567 AND 6075 ARE NOT VALID ANYMORE

I re-read the email several times. Through the capital letters and imaginative spelling the message was clear: I had to hold the aircraft in Malaysia, a pre-planned permit was now invalid and a flight through Indonesia's airspace without a permit could end in a little involuntary formation flying with a fighter jet. As a requirement I had the "interception from a military aircraft" paperwork printed off and in the Cirrus. A list of signals, such as the fighter aircraft banking away or flying across the flight path, were outlined with their associated meaning. If you were intercepted by a jet they most likely wanted you on the ground. I had no wish to have to pull out that piece of paper to interpret what the angry guy with missiles strapped to his wings wanted. It sounds funny but it is very serious stuff.

I called Mike, who was on call in the UK twenty-four/seven. It was always a surprise to see where exactly he was in his day. Was he having breakfast or had I just woken him up in the middle of the night? Mike had been sent the same email and explained what I had feared—we were in a similar situation as in Sri Lanka where we were unable to fly the next day. It was disappointing and frustrating but it was a non-negotiable fact. I emailed everyone about the change of plans. We were all awake but it was important to all be on the same page. I didn't want Jeff to turn up at Starbucks at some ridiculous hour to find out I was still in bed or have Mum and Dad watching the live tracker wondering why it wasn't moving. Sixteen emails later we were all sorted. I called reception, booked in for another night and went to sleep. Completely alarm-free.

I was staying in a small and well equipped unit and after a sleep-in and a cold shower I set to work again, spreading paperwork and charts out across the table before sitting down to compile a job list. I had one full day in Malaysia, and there was nothing I could do about the Indonesian overflight permit: others were sorting the problem and all I could do was wait. I had no wish to venture outside my motel room, not because I didn't want to see Malaysia but because I had so much to do. There were many little jobs that hadn't been a priority but would become so very soon if not seen to. Over the last few weeks I had been trying to juggle endless emails, some of which had fallen through the cracks and some had been only partially seen to. I needed to sit down and clean everything up, to regroup before setting off on the final stretch towards home. After a day of constant emails, efforts to update blogs and organise the finer details of the homecoming, I sat back with a more relaxed attitude. The job list that had been compiled that morning was now a list of obliterated items, all enthusiastically scribbled out with a ballpoint pen.

I consumed some form of mildly heated room service meal before packing my bags. The overflight permit had been sent through midafternoon and our plans for the following day mirrored those that should have gone ahead on the previous day. I set my alarm and went to sleep.

The taxi driver I had organised the day before must have slept in; I waited in the lobby as they phoned another, who came. Fortunately it was a short trip through the dark Malaysian countryside to the airport, we pulled up and I began to unpack my bags again with the help of my handler Jeff. We grabbed a quick bite to eat before setting off through Customs and Immigration, then walked across the tarmac to find the Cirrus waiting, ready and willing to take on yet another leg.

It was a dark and wet morning, the aircraft was covered in dew and the cloud sat so low that it partially covered the lights that shone down on the apron from the tall light poles. While Jeff stood by and chatted I worked away to pre-flight the aircraft and to ensure everything was in order. Soon afterwards I clambered in and kicked the aircraft into life. Regardless of how long I had spent in it, I would never get sick of the loud rumble of the Cirrus as it ruined the early morning silence.

I waved goodbye to Jeff and taxied from the apron before taking a number of turns to find myself at the end of the runway. I took to the air and flew through the now ever-lifting cloud layer and into a sky that was growing lighter as the night became day. I set course towards the south and settled in for what would be a short flight in comparison to the others, a hopefully leisurely four and a half hours down to Indonesia where I would find the much-anticipated and much-required avgas.

I settled in for the cruise, focusing on emptying every drop of avgas from the ferry tank to make sure I would know exactly how much had been added in Indonesia and therefore exactly how much was in the tank for the eleven-hour flight to Australia. Just after I had finished transferring around ten gallons into the right wing, I saw the "estimated time to run" sitting at three hours and thirty minutes: I was nearly there! It was interesting that this time now qualified as a short flight. I took notes and looked out the window at an endless picture of rolling green hills, extremely high by the standards of those back home, but nothing in comparison to the French Alps.

It was all very simple. I tracked for the next waypoint on the list and kept in contact with air traffic control as I went. Each moment saw me edge a little closer to Indonesia. As I tracked south Jakarta was just off to the right-hand side of the nose, but I was asked by air traffic control to turn left and fly out over water because of the other traffic in the area. I would be put into a sequence of aircraft waiting to fly an instrument approach and when it was my turn I would descend through the cloud layer for a landing on Indonesian soil.

Before long it all started to become a little less simple. The controllers were very hard to understand, I would reply to their transmission and in many cases I just hoped it was correct. If not, they were sure to come back to me and repeat themselves, each time a little slower than the last. I turned towards Jakarta and continued inbound, descended as requested and was told to intercept a localiser, an imaginary extended runway centerline that would see me perfectly lined up with the runway. I was then transferred to a different frequency.

All the frequencies around the world had names depending on who you were speaking to, "approach," "clearance delivery," "tower," "ground" and so on. But the frequency I had been told to contact was completely new, one that I had never heard of, not even after flying through fourteen different countries. I transferred across and spoke with the controller, who was hard to understand. I was now tracking towards the instrument approach procedure where I would soon need to descend. He quickly transferred me to another frequency and along with his instructions provided the frequency itself. I had no idea why I had even been told to speak with this guy!

'Victor Hotel Oscar Lima Sierra, Contact tower on 123.4." I set up the frequency, whatever it might have been at the time, and quickly contacted the tower. At this point I was only miles away from the airport and had not been cleared onto the approach I had been told to expect. I called the tower but heard no response. I tried again and again. I flicked back to the previous frequency to let my contact know that there had been no response, he confirmed the frequency and I tried once more. As I flicked back to the tower frequency I heard a call for "Victor Hotel Oscar Lima Sierra." There was traffic information, a "traffic alert" for an aircraft in my two o'clock position. As I peered over the nose a large white Boeing 737, a private business jet, zipped by the right wing of the Cirrus. It was phenomenally close and phenomenally large, it was on climb out of the airport in the opposite direction to the localiser I had been told to track inbound on. I had never seen an aircraft pass so close and in the opposite direction. My heart-rate sky-rocketed. My hands began to shake. The picture was all wrong. I gave the Cirrus full power and climbed away from my altitude. I'm a person who rarely gets angry but this time I was absolutely fuming. I called the tower to inform them of just how close the "traffic" had come, also the fact I was not going to remain flying along a localiser that was obviously opposing the active runway. I climbed away and asked them firmly just what they would like me to do. They could tell I was far from happy.

Due to my position I was given another approach to fly, from over-head I set up to fly an approach where I would track away from the airport on descent, turn back inbound and continue down through the cloud. The controllers did not seemed fazed at all, even though the crew of the Boeing 737 also called the tower to inform them just how close they had come to another aircraft. Their response was simple: "That was another aircraft transferring between frequencies, he is on an approach and nothing to worry about."

I could not believe it. I was trying to fly an approach but my hands were still shaking, I really knew something far from normal had just taken place and began to wonder what might come of it. The whole episode had well and truly frightened me. Would there be someone on the ground waiting to have a "chat"? Would I have to recount what had happened?

I broke through the last of the cloud and spotted a runway, banked slightly and lined up on the centerline. I was so fixated on landing and getting out of the aircraft that I looked at nothing except the painted touchdown markers on the runway. I could not have described what Jakarta looked like from the air if it had been the last thing I had to do.

I taxied from the runway and towards the marshal. There were a few people standing around waiting for my arrival but nothing seemed out of the ordinary. I parked up and shut down before opening the door to say hello. "Welcome to Indonesia, sir," he said. That could have gone worse.

Although I believed what happened had been the fault of air traffic control, there was nothing said about a near miss with traffic outbound from Jakarta and I was happy the issue had not escalated into anything significant. I was, however, a little surprised someone hadn't at least mentioned it. Was this a regular occurrence? Did they consider it okay? I had already decided I would never fly a light aircraft in Indonesia again, except to leave the place of course, so someone else would have to find that out.

I stood by the aircraft and took a breath, I said hello to my handler and discussed what the afternoon would bring. I needed to clear Customs and Immigration and if we were departing the next morning we would also have to refuel. I grabbed my passport, a large black folder that had held every important document for the last two months, and the bundle of US dollars, and set off for the terminal.

After the awkward joy of Customs, a lesson in international translation, we wandered up a set of stairs to the airport refueller's office. I ordered three drums of avgas but was told I would have to pay for them in cash before the locals would wheel them across to the Cirrus. I counted out the US bills and handed them to the lady, who took each note and carefully examined them before saying something to my handler in a foreign language.

There was a small problem. She would not accept three $100 bills of US cash as each note had an imperfection. One had a small stamp in the corner and the other two had been folded in half at some point in their life and therefore were now apparently worth less. I didn't have an ironing board and iron in the Cirrus to rectify that so I took the notes back, held my breath and handed her three new bills. We had a deal.

I left the flawless bills in the office and made my way back to the Cirrus in a small van to find three drums of avgas already sitting on the tarmac on a small cart. We parked close by and began unpacking the plane. A small army of locals had gathered around and as I handed items down from the wing they carefully stacked them around the aircraft. Within minutes of having everything unpacked the heavens opened up and the sideways rain I had experienced in Pago Pago had now found its way to Indonesia. Everyone grabbed something, anything, and threw it into the back of the van before clambering in soon after. Within minutes all the equipment and each person was in the van and keeping dry, all except one guy who thought standing outside with an umbrella would be sufficient. It wasn't, but it sure was amusing to see.

The refuelling process had begun. We had three forty-four gallon drums of avgas, one hand pump and eleven people. Yes, eleven people—nine "helpers," two firemen and myself. The already complicated task was now made harder due to the rain. Avgas and water don't mix and if water was to make its way into the fuel tanks it could have disastrous results. I made it known that we would only be refuelling when the pouring rain had ceased, and even then we would have to dry the drums, pump and area around the fuel cap on the aircraft's wing before beginning. With this in mind, we waited.

When the heavens finally stopped emptying themselves, my small army clambered from the vehicles surrounding the Cirrus and started work. With everything dry, the locals set about pumping the fuel. The pump was a manual one, meaning the handle had to be rotated by hand for the fuel to make its way into the aircraft. I was in charge of the fuel filler and the wings were not too much of an issue, but the ferry tank was a different story. I was definitely the only person going to be pointing the fuel hose into the cabin of an aircraft I didn't own.

It was a slow process. We watched as the showers neared and rain began to fall, we would seal the drums, put the cap back on the tank and hop back in the van. Once it had stopped we got out and started again, only to partially fill a tank before the rain returned. It was a "rinse and repeat" task.

From the first drop pumped into the wing tanks to the last strap being secured on the internal ferry tank it took a full five hours, longer than the flight from Malaysia to Indonesia, and longer than any refuelling venture to date.

I was exhausted and never wanted to refuel an aircraft ever again, not in Indonesia anyway. The only incentive to keep moving was the thought of touching down on home soil in only twenty-four hours' time. I packed up the Cirrus, wandered through the terminal, met the little van once again and climbed in for the ride to the motel.

I sat back and admired the local culture as we crawled through a late afternoon traffic jam that barely moved, something that gave the locals a fantastic opportunity to sell anything they could through the passenger windows. I watched as the scooters zipped in and out of the traffic, some carrying more people than we would normally see in a car, plus the family pet. I took in the sights and smells of the local streets, businesses and way of life. It was now going on two months since I had departed the east coast of Australia and I was tired, not just from the sport of endurance refuelling but also from the trip as a whole. That said, it was a humbling experience to take in the sights and sounds of Indonesia and compare them to the phenomenal opportunity I had been able to pursue, the sights I had seen and the people I had met.

I checked into the motel, but not before going through security. This was something new: at the motel entrance was effectively airport security. I put my bags through the X-ray machine and wandered through the metal detector, my bags were taken and I was directed to the front desk.

It was bedtime, but not before food and the usual update of emails, blogs and a quick read through the consistently encouraging social media posts. A late night but an early start. Next stop Australia.

24

BACK HOME

I was very keen to reach Australian shores, not only because Australia is the greatest country in the world, but more importantly because it would be the last Customs and Immigration stopover. The ferry tank could be covered up, the HF radio would not be required again. And best of all, there would be no more water crossings.

I knew Australia was a large country and I would still need to fly from the west coast to the east coast before I was safe and sound back at home. It would all be new, since I had never flown west of the eastern states. This was another reason why I looked on the flight to Western Australia as just another leg, not one that would see me arrive back home.

I woke up in the darkness, packed up and loaded my bags into the waiting handler's van and we set off for the airport. It was strange to drive through a country that I had only been in for a matter of hours. I looked at the road signs, trying to convince myself that I was in Indonesia, knowing that even before I absorbed their messages the Cirrus and I would be airborne once again and bound for another country.

I asked the handler whether it would be possible to purchase some food along the way. It didn't have to be much, just something to keep me going for the eleven-hour flight. "No worries, sir," he said, "We can stop at Dunkin" Donuts." That sounded sufficient and nutritious.

As we pulled up in front of the terminal we glanced across towards Dunkin' Donuts but it was shut. Who would have thought at 4am? We scouted around and I quickly found a small convenience store. I soon emerged with a bottle of water and a pack of Oreos, the only edible products on offer.

We cleared Customs and Immigration before meeting the van on the tarmac. I quickly asked where the bathroom was: visiting one was sensible if the next eleven hours were to be spent in the aircraft. The bathroom turned out to be the most worrying sight I had seen in quite a while. I am fairly certain I was the first person in there for the last ten years. It was so bad that I walked back through security and into the terminal just to find somewhere a little more convenient, which to my relief I did. With security now cleared for the second time I took the weather information and my Customs paperwork, and after a pre-flight inspection climbed into the Cirrus. All I could hope was that the departure would be a little less eventful than the arrival.

With the aircraft warm, a clearance in hand and the checks completed, I taxied for the runway at the Jakarta Halim International airport. I lined up and gave the Cirrus full power, listened to the familiar groan of the engine and the churning propeller blades biting away at the thick humid air. Within moments the heavy Cirrus became airborne and climbed away slowly but surely, making only a slight left turn before picking up the track towards Australia and continuing the climb to 9000 feet.

I was transferred to a range of Indonesian controllers. One requested that I contact them as I passed the coast and again when crossing another waypoint well out over the water and therefore at the outer edge of their airspace. I agreed and continued. I began to overfly some significant mountains; even at 9000 feet the high terrain only just zipped underneath the aircraft. I focused on my flying while the mountains sat below, wondering where and how I would land the heavy aircraft if there was an engine failure.

As the land below gave way to ocean for the final time, I radioed air traffic control. There was no response no matter how often I tried, and it didn't take long to realise that this was because of the mountains that were now behind me. Instead I began to request a relay through another aircraft in the hope they would pass on my message to the controllers; although I tried several times I had no luck here either. I could either turn back and climb up above the terrain to find a position where I could contact air traffic control myself or keep going and wait until I was in contact with Australian air traffic control. It wasn't a difficult decision. There was no way I was heading back towards Indonesia, I was only heading in one direction and that was towards the beaches of Australia. If that meant the Indonesian ATC worried a little about my whereabouts so be it, but I'm sure they didn't.

I settled into the cruise and enjoyed the radio silence while I could. I began to unpack and tune the HF radio for the final time but no matter what I tried I couldn't seem to bring it to life. There was no rush, I was casually plodding along towards the boundary where the Indonesian airspace would become Australian and only then would I be required to speak with the Aussies for the first time. With the HF radio having retired for some reason I decided to take a different approach, I scanned through my paperwork and found the phone number for Melbourne Center, the Aussie air traffic control sector I would be speaking to very soon. I leaned forward and peered around the right seat to find the satellite phone Telstra had supplied me with, dialled the number and pressed the little green button.

The dial tone registered through my headset and the phone began to ring and then an Aussie voice answered from far away. It was hard to hear but I introduced myself, passing on a position report giving a set time, latitude and longitude and an expected arrival time at the boundary of Australian airspace. I cannot explain just how great it felt to hear an Aussie accent, especially from a controller. I could actually understand what the guy was saying. With my position report confirmed we decided to talk again when I crossed over the boundary. I said goodbye and hung up, wondering why on earth I hadn't used the phone more often.

I flew on and worked through the different tasks that were now very familiar. I transferred fuel after initially removing the air that seemed determined to block the fuel lines, recorded engine trends and monitored the systems. I continually calculated fuel figures, all the while ensuring I was pointing in the right direction as I watched the Australian boundary come ever closer.

I zoomed in on the avionics, dialled Melbourne Center again and counted down the nautical miles. I had a smile from ear to ear as the nose of the aircraft broke into Australian airspace, much the same smile that had appeared when first entering New Zealand's airspace after departure on that very first leg.

I was just happy to tick another box, and to know that after one more round of Customs it was all going to be familiar air space for the ride home. I dialled the number and spoke to my new friend in Melbourne. He could tell I was excited and the congratulations began as I passed on an estimate for the next waypoint.

Before saying goodbye he quickly asked, "You must be well and truly bored up there?" I wasn't bored, believing that boredom is generally a sign of having forgotten something important, but I was comfortable enough to wonder about the fact that yet again I was hanging over a very large ocean. Flying over water seemed to be getting to me more than it ever had before.

'How about I find you someone to talk to? There are a few guys out there," suggested the Melbourne controller. Almost immediately I had a call from an airline pilot. No land-based radio would have been able to reach me at my current position, so I knew the call came from an aircraft in the air space around me. It was from a jet bound for Bali. I chatted away with the crew, partly about my flight. They told me they thought I was insane but the flight itself was amazing. We talked for quite a while before saying goodbye. "We might even catch you on the way back," they said.

I kept going, calling once an hour to report my position and to give an estimate for the next waypoint while I completed the other jobs. There was a moment of excitement when I realised I had the pack of Oreos on board. They had dropped to the bottom of a bag while I went through Customs that morning, but now sudden hunger made them a very high priority.

I munched away on the only food source I would receive for over fifteen hours. I now realise that was probably not a good thing but at the time so many other issues seemed more important, such as safely leaving Indonesia or finding a bathroom that was not a risk to health, wellbeing or sanity. At least all the pre-flight immunisations were being tried and tested.

I watched as the time en route to Broome counted down, and when it fell below two hours my excitement grew. It was time to clean up around the cabin. For the final time I sprayed the top of descent insecticide throughout the aircraft. Before much longer I pointed the nose of the Cirrus towards the ocean and made my way towards 6000 feet.

As I neared the tail end of the flight, a familiar voice came across the radio: one of the airliner crew bound for Bali earlier in the day. They had landed there, the passengers had disembarked and they had reloaded the new passengers and refuelled before heading back towards Perth. Now they were overtaking me and would touch down in Perth before I arrived in Broome. I obviously needed a faster airplane, preferably one with flight attendants and room to walk around.

As picturesque as eleven hours of ocean was, the change in scenery provided a very welcome sight—the Australian coastline. The sliver of land slowly grew as I neared Broome and I was switched from the frequent satellite telephone calls to actual contact with Broome tower on the standard aircraft radios. I started to set up the cameras and sit straight up in my seat, with my eyes nearly as wide as my smile.

I tracked inland listening to the other traffic and could now pick out the beach itself, golden sand I had not seen since leaving home. The Broome controllers were great. They knew all about the flight and were excited for my arrival, but not before a particular plane brought reality back into the occasion. A jet was inbound to Broome and flying on a medevac status, giving it right of way to all other traffic. It was the Royal Flying Doctor Service and I am sure they were picking up a patient from Broome. I was asked to orbit in my current position off the coast. Now at 3000 feet I went round and round in circles, so close to land but apparently so far. The ocean meanwhile seemed so very close.

When, after ten minutes I was cleared back inbound, I watched the beach grow larger in the windshield. Ten minutes is a long time to orbit over water when the Australian coastline is in sight! I could see the airport just inland of the beach and the runway that awaited me. The controllers asked a few questions about my feelings and they also mentioned that a few people had sent "welcome home" messages. I was very cheered to learn that the message had come from the Frogs Hollow Aeroclub. I was cleared to join the circuit area for a landing and watched the beach zip under the nose. I was overwhelmed and so relieved: from the very beginning one of my great and everpresent fears had been engine failure over water, but now that fear was gone. The ocean was behind me and there was no reason for me to cross it in a Cirrus ever again. I completed my checks, turned towards the runway and moments later came to a halt on Australian soil. I backtracked the runway and the fire trucks at the airport sat just off the runway, waiting to shoot an arch of water to welcome me home. Later I was told that this was only the second time this had been done in twenty years. I taxied under the arch, peering through the water-covered windshield and hoping not to hit anything.

I was given a final welcome home from air traffic control, parked up and shut the aircraft down. It had been a long day and it was so close to being over. I kept the door securely shut as the Customs and

Immigration officers made their way to the plane. They asked whether I had remembered to spray the insecticide and I told them I had, holding up the half empty can as proof, but they seemed to think I should spray a little more just to be safe. As a small crowd stood around the Cirrus I took the can and filled the cabin with the insecticide again; they asked me to just sit, or incubate as I called it, for five minutes before hopping out. I had been in the aircraft for way too long and now every living object in that aircraft was now dead, and that nearly included me.

I opened the door and stood up and out onto the wing, I stretched and smiled before stepping down onto the ground. I was actually standing in Australia again. It was both exciting and an enormous relief. I signed a few final Customs and Immigration forms and thanked the firefighters for their welcome. Soon afterwards I was able to chat to the locals who had turned up to say hello. A woman came over and introduced herself and her husband, saying they had followed the flight from the beginning and had stopped by to welcome me back to Australia. She handed me a brown paper bag containing something I had craved for months. It was a simple meat pie and sauce, a real Aussie meat pie that in no way resembled the concoction I had purchased in Scotland. It tasted amazing. The couple were asking questions but although I was truly grateful for their gesture, my answers had to be delayed. No way was I going to let this pie be wasted, not after fifteen hours in the air on a packet of Oreos.

There were lots of people hanging around to say g'day. I answered questions while I unpacked the plane, then met some local business owners from Leopold Air, a scenic and charter operator located on the airport itself. After the Cirrus was tied down I was given a lift into town. The trip was extraordinary: I was in awe of the red dust, something I had never seen before. They dropped me off at the local rental car center. There were two rental car operators in Broome. One had declined my business due to my age but the other had agreed to set me loose in a real car. This was the best day ever. I slapped the P plates on the yellow Jeep, threw my bags in the back and set off down the road, still in my flight suit. I stopped by the Broome air traffic control tower to say a hello; the controller Bron and her family were great. They were thrilled just to have me drop by and say "hi" while I was excited to look around a state-of-the-art control tower. It was confusing, and I think I'll stick to flying. On the way to the unit I pulled up at the bottle shop to buy a drink before continuing on to the motel.

I parked the car, threw my bags on the floor of my room and let my phone ring as I was inundated with messages of congratulations and emails. My personal mobile had picked up Australian reception for the first time in well over two months and proceeded to have a heart attack in the corner. I switched on the TV and was immediately hit with the Aussie accent and the familiar Channel 10 logo. I then plugged my phone charger into the wall, straight into the wall, without the need for the forty-seven adaptors I had carried with me around the world. With all of this going on, I suddenly realised something. I was home. I had just landed an aircraft back in Australia, an aircraft that had seen over thirty destinations, fifteen countries and over 22,000 nautical miles. I had been so fixated on so may things that I hadn't understood the significance of landing back in Australia. I had my eyes set on the final landing in Wollongong and not on Broome, and although the flight was far from over I could see that so much of the risk was behind me. I sipped my drink, sat back and took in the moment, imagining it was a tiny glimpse of what the feeling would be like when the wheels touched down in Wollongong in less than a week's time. It was exactly the right note on which to go to bed.

When I woke up I lay in bed for a moment, confused. I had seen quite a number of motel rooms over the previous two months and didn't want to get ahead of myself, but I was pretty certain I was in Australia. As clarity dawned I confirmed I was not dreaming, I had actually landed in Broome. There was no better way to start the day.

I had two days there while I waited for the final oil change and inspection of the Cirrus. Although most of the work would be out of my hands, there were still a few things to be done before the engineers could get started. I headed off to the airport, and with the engine running I watched as the oil temperature rose, something that would make dropping away the old oil a little easier. I parked up against the maintenance hangar and shut down and while the engine covers were being removed and the old oil began to drain away, I emptied the cabin and started sorting through the clutter.

I removed the HF aerial, unplugged and packed away the HF radio from inside the cabin, switched off the various valves on the ferry tank fuel lines and covered the tank with the same doona cover I had used throughout the USA. After a few hours I was finished and the Cirrus looked willing and ready to head towards the east coast. All that was left was for the mechanics to finish up the service.

I wandered around for the rest of the day. I said hello again to the locals at the airport and went for a drive. I didn't miss having to study up on the next international leg through foreign airspace, calling ahead and confirming the requirement of avgas: I really didn't need to stress about anything. After an afternoon of emails, a blog, a catch-up on social media and the general tidying up of different jobs, I went to bed.

Next morning I hopped out of bed nice and early. I had been offered a seat on a flight around the West Australian coastline and I didn't take much convincing to accept. Here I was, spending my free day in an airplane. Funny that.

I spent the morning peering out the window of the Cessna with nothing else to worry about except taking photos. The other passengers were great company, and we stopped at a small dirt strip near a swimming hole before making our way back to Broome along the coast. Having flown most of my hours on the east coast of Australia, I was caught off guard a few times along the west coast, as someone had put the ocean on the wrong side. When anyone is flying north the water should be on the right, not the left!

After checking the now finished Cirrus I caught up with a couple of young pilots from around the area, packed my bags and found a pub that had chicken parmigiana on the menu. As I sat and ate I put together a flight plan for the next morning. I was off to Alice Springs and had been advised to stop by Halls Creek for avgas. It sat about halfway along my flight path, about five hours of total flying time. Not a long flight but one I was looking forward to.

The next morning was relaxed. I woke up and checked out of the motel before heading to the airport and unpacked the Jeep, hiding the keys and leaving it in the car park. After having had to watch so much for the last few months, the freedom and ability to move around as I pleased were amazing. I preflighted the *Spirit of the Sapphire Coast* and hopped in, taxied for the runway in Broome and took to the sky over the top of Cable Beach, the iconic stretch of sand separating Broome from the sea. With a goodbye from the guys in the control tower I set course for Halls Creek.

The barren landscape zipped past beneath me, endless plains of red dirt that stretched as far as the eye could see. I saw the odd road but nothing significant until Halls Creek appeared in the distance. I touched down in a hot, dry little airport and parked next to the fuel bowser. An attendant appeared from a small office and helped out with a fuel card for payment and I pumped fuel into the wings of the Cirrus. I wasn't in a rush but there was nothing to do in Halls Creek, so it wasn't long before I set off skyward once again.

The view outside the window was unchanging, although perhaps the red dirt was becoming a little redder. It was almost like flying over Saudi Arabia yet again. I continued to record engine trends just as I had done over water, a good habit that would be hard to break, but few other jobs needed to be done. As I neared Alice Springs I peered out the right window towards Uluru. I had always wanted to fly past the iconic Australian landmark but the limited hours I had before the aircraft was due for more maintenance meant that tracking direct to Alice Springs was a much smarter idea.

I contacted the Alice control tower and was directed to line up on an extended runway centerline. Among the red cliff faces and barren dirt I spotted a dark line that somewhat resembled a runway. It gradually grew into one as I slowed down and completed my checks. While I descended through the final stage of the landing, I looked across at the tarmac to a small line of light aircraft and on the end was a very familiar aircraft, a red and grey Falco F8L. This was a low-wing, two-seater wooden aircraft owned by Ian Newman, a pilot and friend from the Frogs Hollow Aeroclub.

I touched down and taxied clear before parking in front of the Alice Springs Aeroclub. As I expected, two familiar faces appeared behind the Cirrus for a surprise visit; Ian and Neil Bourke had flown out to Alice Springs to say hello and buy me a drink. They had played a huge role in my flying as well as the planning of the Teen World flight.

To see a few familiar faces, especially people I respected so much, was fantastic. I clambered out and said hello, my flying done for the day after crossing half of Australia in a little over five hours. I caught up with family friend Tony Norris, a very experienced pilot now based in Alice Springs, and after a quick chat we took the Cirrus and slotted it in a spare space in the corner of Tony's hangar.

That night we took the time to have dinner and a catch-up, and there were many stories to tell before bed. The following morning we made our way to the airport where we went about washing the Cirrus. This had normally been a job I did on my own and it was fantastic to have a helping hand. The oil was wiped clean from the underside of the aircraft, the windows were cleaned and the interior was repacked, all ready for my arrival in Wollongong.

Early the next day I flew off. While I was alone in the Cirrus, the familiar Falco flew alongside with Ian and Neil smiling away. That day's final destination was Broken Hill. We had put together a flight plan that included a fuel stop in a place called William Creek, and then onto Broken Hill, just passing alongside Lake Eyre. It was great to fly along casually with company and we could chat on a discreet frequency while we listened out for other traffic, allowing any notes to be compared on what we could see out of the windows. For so long I had been on my own, seeing some of the most phenomenal sights in the world but only able to share them by means of a few photos or a description in the blog that evening. Being able to chat and compare with others what I was seeing in real time was just great.

As we approached William Creek I called up on the radio, announcing our position and intentions. A young lady who was currently flying over Lake Eyre asked whether we would be needing any fuel. After we thanked her and said we could always use some, she told us to park at the airport and walk down the sealed road to the pub. The publican or the guy behind the bar would be able to organise some avgas for us. What? Fuel for the plane from the pub? Definitely a first.

I touched down just after the boys in the Falco and parked up— being the only two aircraft on the field, we certainly had the pick of the parking spaces. We wandered to the pub, taking a photo along the way with the "William Creek, Population 2" sign in the background. We ordered cold drinks and avgas and after adding our names to the writing-covered communal wall of the pub, we checked over the aircraft and set off again.

We tracked towards Broken Hill, taking in the scenery including Lake Eyre before casually watching the now familiar red, barren landscape begin to incorporate a little more shrubbery. It was a relatively short flight of only a couple of hours, made even shorter by the continued chatter on the radio and before long we were inbound to Broken Hill. The airport was alive with activity as aircraft of all shapes and sizes refuelled before taking the flight to Birdsville for the annual and very famous Birdsville horse races. We zigged and zagged between traffic before touching down: as I taxied from the runway two fire trucks sprayed another arch of water as a welcome to their town, another very kind and rare gesture.

While I unpacked the Cirrus, Ian and Neil refuelled the Falco and taxied by soon after. With a wave goodbye they set off for the east coast, where they would wait for my arrival. Broken Hill was very interested in the flight and the Cirrus in particular, with many faces, including the local newspaper reporter, popping out to say hello before I made my way to the motel. I checked in to my accommodation for the last time on the trip, unpacked my bags and grabbed a bite to eat before sitting back and absorbing the activity on social media. I tried to take in what was going on, as well as what was about to happen in less than two days' time. It was not easy, so I just went to sleep instead.

25

BACK TO DESTINATION A

My one free day in Broken Hill had been a relaxed one. A late awakening was soon followed by a trip back out to the airport to refuel; one of the members of the Aeroclub helped top up the tanks of the Cirrus before tying it back down for one last night. I sat down that afternoon, wrote a final blog and filmed a short video. I then stared blankly at the online tracker that stretched across the Teen World Flight webpage.

There was a blue line that left Wollongong just south of Sydney and squiggled its way east. It passed over the Pacific Ocean separating Australia from the United States mainland, it linked the west and east coasts of the USA before tracking for Canada via Wisconsin, was camouflaged in the blue of the North Atlantic Ocean, briefly touching Greenland before reaching almost the top of the world. The line turned a corner and rocketed towards Europe and through to Jordan before finding Sri Lanka via Oman, met Malaysia and Indonesia and came to rest in a large country known as Australia. The last part of the line stretched almost completely across the largest continent in the world. Now there was just one tiny gap, one that a few hours' flying would fill.

I had taken off from destination A well over two months before. I had seen fifteen countries, been to thirty-four destinations on four continents and covered nearly 24,000 nautical miles. The next day was the moment that everything had led to, one last flight that would end at destination A.

The following morning I woke very early and rose before the sun. This was not just another day, I knew—but I could not have guessed that over the next twenty-four hours I would learn several things I could never have expected.

The Royal Australian Air Force had shown their support from the very beginning. After many meetings and emails, the RAAF Roulettes Aerobatic Team had been approved to fly a display overhead to welcome my homecoming just before my arrival in Wollongong. While flying through Asia I constantly received emails regarding my homecoming day, mostly about what would happen and when, how the morning would go ahead and what I had to do. The plan was for the Cirrus to arrive at Wollongong just before 11am. The Roulettes would finish their routine and let me know when I was okay to descend over the escarpment and approach the airfield. *60 Minutes*, further media, microphones, airport access, public fencing and so much more had been organised. All I had to do was be on time.

I pre-flighted the Cirrus by torchlight, cleaned the windshield and hopped in as the sun began to appear over the horizon. I looked at my flight time to Wollongong and worked out exactly when I should leave Broken Hill. Then I sat back and waited. It was maddening. Maybe I could just leave and fly slower? This sitting business was giving me way too much time to think. Not thinking too much and just doing seemed to be the best approach; something that had actually applied to a great deal of the flight. As the carefully defined departure time neared I started up and taxied for the end of the runway. One last push of the throttle later and I was airborne, racing the sun as it lit up the morning sky.

As I set course for Wollongong I peered down at the avionics where both my groundspeed and tailwind or headwind component were displayed. These were the figures I had been staring at anxiously all through the fifteen-hour leg from Hawaii to California, yet this time they read very differently. It so happened that the strongest tailwinds of the entire trip were forty knots on the flight to Wollongong—the one leg that was meticulously timed so that my arrival took place at a very particular moment. I was now rocketing for home at well over 200 knots ground speed. Not ideal for the welcome, but I couldn't help smiling at the thought.

During the three hours I was in the air I watched as the barren red landscape became a more familiar, greener environment, as towns with very recognisable names began to zip under the wings. I had a lot of time to think. I knew where I was going to be landing but not what to expect. It was almost like a rollercoaster ride where you knew you were going to go upside down but just had to bide your time to see how it would really feel.

My overthinking and slowly melting brain were soon given a rest as another aircraft called me up for a chat over the radio. It was brilliant Australian aviation writer and Qantas pilot Owen Zupp. I had read a lot of Owen's writing, we had spoken at various times and among other things had discussed what it was like to pilot a jet airliner. Now Owen was flying a Boeing 737 on a Pathfinders charity flight to the Qantas Founders Museum in Longreach. As he couldn't make it to Wollongong, he wanted to check up on how the last leg was going and to wish me well. Regardless of what I was flying or where I had been, my love for aviation meant I was still extremely excited to be chatting to an airline pilot as he cruised past in his jet.

I neared the escarpment that sat high above Wollongong and the surrounding areas, a solid cliff face overlooking the low-lying coastal city. Although previous experience had shown that it could be a hassle in average weather conditions, there was no doubt that it was a spectacular sight to anyone flying above. I was way too early thanks to the tailwinds yet I managed to take a peek across the escarpment to Wollongong airport. I could hear the Roulettes on the radio as they prepared to take to the sky, yet could see a thick blanket of cloud that seemed to only cover the airport. Everywhere else in the atmosphere that day was perfectly clear. I steered away from the airport although I knew no one could have possibly spotted me. My watch told me that I had a significant amount of time to spare before meeting with the Channel 9 news helicopter off the high side of the escarpment. I decided to make a quick stopover at a little airport I had visited once or twice before, tracked for Wedderburn airfield only a few miles north of my position and joined the circuit area for a landing. I touched down and backtracked for the bowser. My safest bet was to top up the tanks and then take off in time to meet the chopper, and the problem was that there were very few people at the airfield. I was told they had all travelled to Wollongong where they were waiting for some kid in a toy plane. Luckily a few members of the aeroclub were on hand and very kindly donated some avgas to see me home. The other members were quite surprised to discover that I had dropped into their home field unexpectedly. That trip hadn't been planned and less than a handful of people knew I actually stopped there. In the excitement of the flight ending, we never even got around to updating the stop on my website.

I departed Wedderburn with full fuel and headed south towards a small lake, called up the news chopper and switched across to a frequency where we could chat without the stress of aviation radio calls. Once I had the helicopter in sight we met up and flew alongside each other; while the Cirrus was far from a rocket ship, the helicopter sure made it look fast. I had met the boys in the chopper for a little filming before my departure a few months before, and summing up the trip with a few more shots was exciting. I positioned the Cirrus carefully so the underbelly camera on the helicopter could film away, giving the odd casual wave when requested, and step by step we worked together to film a number of scenes. It was actually a lot of fun. Helicopters have always interested me, and to be flying around with one just having fun was so cool that I forgot all about what was supposed to happen next.

The chopper pilot casually reminded me that now was the time to head to Wollongong. We had been flying around for twenty minutes and the concentration required to not make contact with the strange, unfamiliar and large rotating wings on top of the helicopter had taken over my world, but now it was over. I flew slowly, allowing the chopper to keep up as I pointed the nose towards Wollongong, and when the escarpment slipped under the Cirrus it provided another 2000 feet of vacant air. I pushed the nose down and headed towards the airport, and in that moment I realised what was actually happening.

Years before this moment I had begun thinking about a dream, a ridiculous dream yet one that constantly occupied my mind. When I envisaged an around-the-world flight I had not imagined the paperwork, the logistics, the enormous amount of money required and attained through sponsorship, the planning, the preparation, the fatigue, the stress or any other negative or challenging parts of the operation. I had only thought about taking off from destination A and flying east through unimaginable terrain, cultures and experiences, to return to destination A. And now here I was only minutes from realising my dream.

I made a radio call to announce my intentions and shortly thereafter said goodbye to the chopper pilot, who hovered close by the runway abeam where I would touch down. I banked to the left and took a quick look at the crowd below where a number of bright red PC9 Roulette aircraft sat carefully aligned creating a large V on the tarmac, revealing my final parking space.

I turned downwind and flew parallel to the runway. I stopped looking at the crowd and focused solely on flying the airplane. A pilot's life, regardless of what anyone tells you, is dedicated to making smooth landings in front of others, especially if those watching are fellow pilots. I now had countless people in the crowd, the Roulette pilots and crew and family and friends of which so many were aviators, all waiting to watch my landing. Please, oh higher power somewhere out there, let this be a smooth landing.

I turned the airplane towards the runway and lowered some flap. The Cirrus is a relatively slippery and fast machine but by this point I had completed a few landings and figured I should have it worked out by now. I slowed the plane down and turned one final time to line up with runway 35, the same runway I had used to take off in the heavy Cirrus months before. I looked ahead and focused solely on flying the plane, concentrating on not bouncing the landing. I decreased the power as the painted runway zipped below. The *Spirit of the Sapphire Coast* slowed down as I held the wheels only inches from the ground and shortly afterwards heard a rumble from the landing gear. I let the nose wheel fall close to the tarmac before holding it in the air, knowing that if I could let it touch the runway softly I would have brought the flight to a successful end, most importantly with a landing to be proud of. Moments later the Cirrus met sedately with the earth, just as I had planned.

I took a deep breath and let the airplane slow down before exiting the runway. I made one last radio call before taxiing towards the crowd. I checked and double-checked that everything was set as it should be, as the last thing I wanted was to be caught up in the hype and excitement and leave the flaps down, an error you learn not to make in initial flight training. I turned towards the crowd and lined up with one of the Roulettes crew as he marshalled me in and brought me to a stop at the very tip of the now complete V I had seen from above. I flicked the final switches and pulled the little red handle, ceasing all fuel flow to the engine and bringing silence to the tarmac.

I was home. I was the youngest pilot and first teenager in history to fly solo around the world.

Part of me just wanted to sit in the plane and think about what had just happened. Instead, I secured the safety pin into the parachute handle that sat above my head, removed the keys and set them on the dash before opening the door and stepping up and out onto the wing.

I looked around and waved but there was so much to look at that I couldn't really take anything in. I stepped down off the rear of the wing and started to walk away before realising I had forgotten something. I quickly turned back and gave the Cirrus a kiss and a pat on its well travelled fuselage.

I had always laughed when people told me, "You will become attached to that airplane." All I can say is that you certainly learn to appreciate the only object between yourself and thousands of miles of ocean, especially the bits with icebergs in them. There were only two common denominators between each destination, each country, each scary moment, each memory and each achievement: the Cirrus and me.

I walked around the wingtip and met a group of family and friends on the tarmac and it was hugs all around. I was wide-eyed and dumb-founded, trying to take everything in but not really sure what I should have been feeling or thinking. Mum, on the other hand, was highly emotional and I could tell that there was no way I would be allowed to do this again. Dad was proud, stumped for words, yet knowing that little needed to be said. My brothers Chris and Adam and my sister-in-law Claire were ecstatic. I caught my breath before walking over to the fence to say hello to Nan and Pa. It was a wonderfully emotional moment that I will never forget. No doubt relief was what we all felt, but beyond the risk and stress was a feeling of achievement, not just for me but for so many people. After all, this had been a team effort.

I shook hands and received a hug from Charles Woolley as the *60 Minutes* cameras lingered around us. I couldn't help contrasting this with the situation so many months before when I'd sat nervously down the road waiting to meet "Mr Woolley" for the first time. Now I could see more than ever that "Uncle Charles" was genuinely excited to be there, part of the team and a friend.

While I continued to try and take everything in, I stood back at the lectern set up for the festivities where we listened to a number of people speak. The mayor of Wollongong gave an address before my mentor Ken Evers stood up and shared a few stories. Then as a surprise Gary Clark, the inventor of our mascot Ding the Duck, said a few words.

Gaby Kennard, the first Australian woman to fly solo around the world, had also flown down. To have Gaby take such interest and pass on her congratulations was phenomenal. She was one of only a few people who truly understood what the trip had been like. And there were so many other messages, memories and stories that could form a book in themselves.

With the more structured proceedings over, I was finally able to say hello to family and friends. I walked along the barrier and met hundreds upon hundreds of people who wanted to chat or to have a photo or my name scribbled on some form of clothing or picture.

It slowly began to hit me just what this Teen World Flight had been about. Not the world record, but its effect on so many people individually. I had been so fixated during every waking moment on working towards a successful end that I had not seen past it. I had read the social media posts but had not imagined the flight from the perspective of those who were following the whole story. My own passion had been to inspire young kids to become involved in aviation; now there were hundreds, proving that I had been successful. There they were, all crammed up against a fence just waiting to have a chat. Far too soon I was dragged away by my manager Dave Lyall to fulfill media commitments. Dave didn't want to end the fun either but there were television and radio interviews, and phone calls from journalists. We also had to finish up the filming with *60 Minutes*.

From there I parked the Cirrus with the help of a few friends and tied it down just as it was. I had one other job to do and I was running out of time. This was the day of the federal election. It had taken a lot of manoeuvring and hard work to move my arrival date back one week because of this, originally announced for 14 September by PM Julia Gillard. Annoyingly, once my date had been changed, the new PM had decided to do the same. Thanks for that, Mr. Rudd. With my brother I went to the nearest polling booth, where for the first time in my life I was actually old enough to vote.

From the polling booths we made our way to a local club. The day had grown old and a very patient group of Teen World Flight fans, including many young kids from the local Air League Squadron, were waiting to say hello. The next few hours passed quickly in telling stories and catching up with family, friends and very important people, such as Ken Evers. After that I headed towards the motel. I had an early interview with the *Today Show* the next morning and planned to leave Wollongong after refuelling. I was flying to Merimbula where another party was planned, and where I would meet many more people who had played such a key role in the flight. I was also looking forward to flying over the Sapphire Coast once again.

I sat back with a few friends and had dinner and a drink. Most of my family and friends had begun the drive to Merimbula where they would wait for the next day's celebrations. All this was a little too much to take in, but there was no doubt that I would now have plenty of time to think about it.

The *Today Show* interview was quite an experience. We had moved the Cirrus to the correct spot in the early morning light. The sound guy proceeded to wire some sort of microphone into the flight suit while I stood very still trying not to make the task harder than it needed to be. I had an earpiece, obviously stolen from the set of a Bond movie, in my ear. They counted me in and before I knew it I was being spoken to. I looked into the camera just as I had been told, constantly pretending that I was actually looking at somebody and not into the dark black lens. The conversation had turned. I was no longer the kid with a dream, I was no longer hovering on the edge of success or failure. Now I was successful. I had broken the world record, I had succeeded in the first phase of promoting youth in aviation and I had met our fundraising goal with our partner charity, World Youth International.

Once the crew had packed up and gone home it was almost time for me to do the same, to take off and fly south to Merimbula. I pre-flighted the Cirrus and left it sitting out the front of the Southern Biplane Adventures hangar in Wollongong. The owner Chris and the crew, led by their marketing whiz Andrew Musgrove, had been a great help by looking after me and the airplane each time we needed to meet up with media. Even better, Chris had cooked an early morning BBQ to mark the moment. Just before we began to eat I mentioned how dirty the Cirrus had become; the underside of the fuselage was covered in oil and flying with the helicopter at a lower level had brought along its fair share of bugs. After we had finished eating I said goodbye and walked outside to the Cirrus to find two young lads, Riley and Dylan, rolling around underneath it with a handful of now oily rags. I could see they were fixated with flying; the aviation bug had bitten them now too. They were working hard and helping out where they could at Southern Biplanes, including giving the Cirrus a clean for me. I was blown away and excited to see young guys with such a passion.

With the help of the boys we pulled the aircraft away from the hangar and I clambered in, started up and taxied for a departure to the south. I stayed low as I left Wollongong. I had been looking forward to flying stress-free down this coastline for a long time, and that's exactly what I did.

We had another planned "welcome home" event in Merimbula, and after saying hello to the familiar sights of the Sapphire Coast once more, I met up with two other aircraft. Along with Ian, who had visited me in Alice Springs in the Falco, was Drew Done, who also had a Falco. Drew was a member of the Aeroclub and one of the hard-working supporters who had put so much work into Teen World Flight. Both Ian and Drew turned their planes around and we flew the remaining distance to Merimbula together. As we neared I heard over the radio the voice of Ian Baker, a supporter and manager of the Merimbula airport. We chatted away to keep the waiting crowd amused and descended a little further before making an inbound radio call. I flew the Cirrus over Merimbula and along the airstrip, a quick glance at the ground showing a large gathering of people waiting on the tarmac.

After another round of the airport, I slowed down for the very last time and made a turn over what I will always believe is the greatest little town in the nation. I touched down on runway 21 at Merimbula airport, a runway that for me holds too many aviation-related memories to mention here, and taxied towards the final welcoming arch of water. The final marshal just happened to be Dad. I carefully followed his directions, as I always have, being such a wonderful son, and brought the Cirrus to its final stop. Although I had no wish to fly any further it was an almost sad moment to pull the mixture and cut the engine.

I repeated the movements of the previous day, securing the inside of the plane before stepping onto the wing as the aircraft was connected to a tug and towed through the cheering crowd. I hopped down and walked to the stage, a small box trailer with a portable PA system.

It is strange what effect little things can have. For someone who thinks maybe a little too much, the trailer was a prime example of what Teen World Flight had become. An achievement based on mateship, the result of the efforts of hundreds if not thousands of people, individuals, not taken over by a corporation, yet achieving all its goals. It wasn't the size of the trailer that mattered. It was the stories, the memories and the lessons I had learned from all the people standing on that makeshift stage.

I stepped down from the multipurpose entertainment and mulch-carrying platform and about five meters later was swamped by people who wanted to say hello. I soon learned that the flight had become a subject of serious interest within the local area. The *Merimbula News* was the source of news about the adventures of the Cirrus and me. I spent the next couple of hours just talking yet again and was blown away by the number of kids who just wanted to touch the plane.

As the time approached for the lunchtime airline flight the public were whisked from the airfield. It had been so good to see people wandering about looking at the aircraft of various shapes and sizes, something that I think should happen at Australian airports far more often.

I had a quick break before setting off for the Frogs Hollow airport; after all, it was Sunday afternoon and in my opinion a Sunday afternoon should be spent nowhere else. It was a very special few hours, a great way to end the flight. The caravan rolled on and we left Frogs Hollow and made our way to the local RSL club, the same club where I had spent many nights washing dishes while I was still at school.

As every pilot knows, it takes airspeed and money to fly. The Merimbula RSL had been my source of money and had given me the opportunity to find the airspeed. We had dinner before gathering around a large TV to watch the *60 Minutes* program. I sat among family and friends and watched the culmination of many hours of filming, emails and hard work by the entire *60 Minutes* crew. Although every scene was new to those who watched it that night, I would never be able to see the story from their point of view; for me it ignited a million memories at once.

We left the RSL and came back to our place. I unpacked my bags and sat them on the kitchen table. I had a shower in familiar surroundings and went to bed in an all-too-familiar room.

At last, finally, I was home.

EPILOGUE

On 8 September 2013 I woke up at home in my own bed. No early alarm, no foreign motel room, no ocean to cross, no aircraft to fly. It felt very odd.

Whether I liked it or not, a significant chapter of my life was over.

I didn't realise it then but I was playing a mind game, a "choose your own adventure" where the paved four-lane highway that has had one direction suddenly and unexpectedly branches off into a hundred different back roads, some leading to a dead end but others right back onto that highway, destined for even greater adventures. It was up to me to use the lessons I had learned to choose the right road. Part of that was writing this book.

I developed a headache from writing so many words, but those that have made it onto paper are simply the culmination of the thoughts whizzing around in my mind, the adventures and the moments that made me think, "I am going to tell someone about this one day." They have all come together to tell a story, one that I hope will be beneficial. This is the story of a normal kid. I hope your imagination will bring something to it and I hope you can truly take something away.

I spent hours wondering how I would finish this book, how I could bring the story to an end with the finesse of a storyteller, yet manage to pass on the lessons I wanted to. I wondered whether the best option was just to spill my thoughts into a final chapter, to share what was running through my mind, to have a one-on-one chat with you, the reader, to summarise. So here goes.

I often wonder whether I think too much. In fact I am sure I do, but anyone who is mad enough to want to fly around the world alone probably does anyway. I want to pass on every little bit of advice, every lesson and every experience of the last few years to each and every person on the face of the planet. You shouldn't have to fly around the world to learn these lessons and change your life in the way I have.

I started off as a very quiet kid. I couldn't speak in front of an audience, I was a nervous pilot under pressure and I had very little real world experience. I was a dreamer, often fixating my mind on one thing—the urge to fly, or simply to acquire a cool new toy—and not letting go for quite some time.

I looked up to people, whether family members or the aerobatic pilot who just scribbled his name on my new favorite poster; I would see the positive qualities in a person and strive to imitate them. I was easily bored. School holidays could not involve simply playing Play-Station, I needed something to do, something to learn or something to build. I was a hands-on kind of kid. Regardless what other kids were up to, I needed something to set my mind on at all times and although time with mates is beyond important, regular weekend parties didn't quite tick the box. I would soon find something that did.

Mum had always requested our beds be made before school, not smoothed over neatly but made into something that met and exceeded the expectations of the armed forces on inspection day. I am sure this was a good thing, but I was never motivated when it came time to actually make the bed, which was always a challenge. This goes for a lot of things. I was always sick on cross-country day and I considered school gymnastics the worst form of punishment still legal in the modern world. A double lesson of mathematics nearly brought on tears and physics always ended in a headache. They all had one thing in common—I didn't have an interest in them.

My active mind, the one that I am sure thinks way too much, suddenly found something it could focus on. My interest in aviation that had begun at six morphed into a pure burning passion at fourteen. All it took was a flight in an airplane. Nothing managed to get in my way, goal setting came naturally and my life changed for the better. I had never been able to focus on anything as I did on aviation. (If only I had had that enthusiasm for making my bed, or school for that matter, but I just didn't.) I began to learn some very important life lessons from my experiences in aviation. The responsibility normally first given to a young kid in a car was now handed to me in the form of an airplane at a much younger age. I might have been young on paper, but it was super important that I act like an old man on the inside, even if I had to sternly tell Mum not to touch that red button. I was given opportunities and responsibilities beyond my imagination, but that was what was exciting. As I passed each test and gained a little more experience, that active mind that thought way too much was still thinking, this time about a new adventure. Flying around the world.

I was a pilot, but so were many other young kids. I wanted to fly around the world but I was sure it was a stupid idea. If I didn't have the stamina to make my bed on a daily basis or to study a subject I didn't care about, what made me think I could achieve something unique?

Well. There is only one answer. It was my passion.

Your mind is very powerful. For the first time in my life, the burning desire to achieve something overcame negative thoughts. Months of the one idea churning over and over in my mind resulted in an email to the most successful Australian entrepreneurs and aviators of all time. Why did I think I could email Dick Smith and Ken Evers? The passion and burning desire again outdid the negative thoughts, it was my most likely option for success at the time, so off the email went.

With the initial support of Dick Smith and Ken Evers, I soon realised that my dream was becoming a potential reality. I started to learn a number of things very quickly; every day offered a new lesson of some sort, although rarely aviation related. As much as a practical plan this was a mind game, the challenge being to accept what was happening and create a mindset where it was possible to work through the difficulties and problems day by day. It's an attitude that can be applied to any type of personal challenge, certainly one beyond aviation. Although we planned the actual flight meticulously, the issues in even being ready to set off were bigger than I had ever imagined. Issues such as sourcing an aircraft, raising sufficient funds (something we did achieve, but barely), overcoming fear of the media, finding enough time in the day to work, eat, sleep and fly were ever present. This constant workload made life hard, but along with the burning passion to achieve the goal there was another factor. The flight had become public. It was now beyond just a thought in the mind of a kid who thought too much. It was the common interest of an ever-growing number of people.

I often say that if no one else knew about the flight apart from me, I would have given up a thousand times; because it was a public affair the urge to see it through was always there. This showed me personally—the kid who struggled with menial household chores—just what I was capable of with the right amount of courage and commitment.

The planning continued, the support grew and the stories of endless contributions, commitment and encouragement took over our lives. The planning stage soon became the flight itself and as well as being a full-on time for me it was definitely something of a challenge for so many others. I kept moving every day, the team kept the wheels well oiled and after many months of flying and many years of planning, we successfully carried out what I believe was one of the safest and most carefully planned around-the-world flights in history. The dream had become a successful operation. We had broken a record, inspired youth and benefited youth beyond aviation through the funds raised for our partner charity. It seemed we had inspired many other people too.

My life had changed from what was considered normal to the roller-coaster ride known as Teen World Flight, a ride that did not cease until 8 September 2013. Although the actual flight had been a big change, coming back home was a much bigger one, the transition from the everyday addictive adrenaline rush to a normal life. So much focus had been on my safe arrival back home that the end of the adventure was a complete shock. I knew I probably should do something but had no idea just what that should be.

On 8 September I woke up, got out of bed, went to the kitchen and opened the fridge door. After a few moments of indecisiveness, my inability to cook led me to skip breakfast before taking on the day. Instead I went to the airport. Of all the places in the world I could go, I ended up back with the Cirrus in order to begin taking out the ferry tank and carrying out maintenance before an air show I was hoping to fly to. I could have stayed home and shared stories with the family, but I didn't. Regardless where I was in the world, I still needed an adrenaline rush. If that was not available, at least I needed to be playing with the airplane.

The first week at home was spent undertaking maintenance and the following weekend I flew Mum and Dad in the Cirrus to the Narromine AusFly air show. This was the same event I had attended a year before to officially announce the plans of my trip to the public. Now I had returned to share the journey with hundreds of interested listeners. I remember standing up on the stage and before I had even said a word an entire hangar full of people were standing on their feet, all clapping, eager to hear a story I had yet to tell.

Media responsibilities continued. I spoke about my experiences on many radio interviews and made various personal appearances. Dave Lyall remained my right-hand man, organising many events including speaking engagements, which allowed the story to be told in much more detail. I accepted awards and attended various events I had never imagined being part of: whether being named the Australian Geographic Society's 2013 Young Adventurer of the Year or catching up with Dick Smith regularly. Every occasion seemed surreal, odd, in a way nothing to do with me.

As 2013 moved on, I was able to be introduced into the world of twin engine flying. Whether this was a sound decision or not, this opportunity saw me move out of home to Newcastle about 200 kilometers north of Sydney. I took on a new job flying twin engine Piper Chieftains moving patients all around the skies of eastern Australia, all while juggling different events and engagements. It was all part of the learning process, the process of bringing Teen World Flight into a new and slightly more normal life.

Although the flight will always be a part of my life, it was now a story to be told and no longer an experience to be lived. I was trundling down one of the many crossroads hoping that I had made the right decision, aided by the lessons I had learned. There have been many, but three have stood out above the rest. Goal setting is vital. Without the ability to organise my life into short-term and long-term goals, whether getting out of bed in time for work or finishing this story, I would have fallen in a heap. Set your own goals and work towards them. It is easier to write many chapters, one at a time, than to write an entire book.

Courage and commitment are extremely important. If you are at all a partially realistic person, no matter what your dream and no matter how unachievable it may seem, these are what you need. If you move ahead with these two qualities alone, all the other aspects will more easily fall into place.

The third thing is this: make decisions simple. As we all know, life is complicated. Whether you're faced with the daily grind of a job you don't like, the stress of bills or debt, the race to have the latest and greatest of everything or the myriad other issues faced on a daily basis, life always has a way of making things hard. When you are facing a significant decision don't let the little issues have an effect on your big answer, take a step back and look at the big picture, answer with a simple "Yes" or "No," stick with the answer and work out all the other smaller issues around that.

I believe the most important lesson to take away from Teen World Flight is this: ordinary people can achieve. How you gauge your ability to succeed in life is dependent on your attitude. Although I have learned a great deal from the last two years, I am the first to say my adventure has only just begun. Who knows where the next adventure will lead? I hope that my experiences lived and lessons learned can help in pointing other adventurers in the right direction.

In April 2014 I stood in Government House in our nation's capital as an official guest at the Governor-General's reception for the Duke and Duchess of Cambridge. I stood and shook hands with Prince William and we casually discussed flying before he confirmed that next time I set off around the world it must be in a helicopter with the Duke himself. To be given the opportunity to meet members of the Royal Family was an honour and another experience to add to the collection, another story to tell mates at the bar.

As I am sure many people question their own positions in life, I often wonder whether I took the right road at the end of Teen World Flight. The rollercoaster of emotions and experiences I have undergone since the end of my circumnavigation, such as meeting the Duke and Duchess of Cambridge, buying a new car, moving out of home, pushing myself as a pilot in a new job and always looking for new opportunities, have made me realise that I have.

The right road is one that has adventure and excitement, one that allows you to set goals and makes every day new, adventurous and exciting. One that makes you want to get up every morning and make your bed.

ACKNOWLEDGEMENTS

This is my attempt to express my gratitude and thanks to many people in far too few words. I could easily spend another six months naming individuals, sharing stories and personally passing on thanks to each and every person who played a part, big or small, in Teen World Flight, but that would take up more space than I have here. This is why I would like to explain what the word "we" means to me.

Whenever I described anything about the flight—the planning, my experiences during the flight, its beginning or end—I have always used that word. We took off. We were relieved to have reached the coastline. We broke a world record.

I was often asked, "But it was just you in the plane, wasn't it?" Of course that is true in one sense, but though this was a solo journey it was in no way a flight taken alone.

My wildest dream, at first hidden by doubt and insecurity, was carried forward by people who gave me unending support, belief and encouragement. Without them my dream would have remained just that. Teen World Flight was a success not just for me, the solo pilot, but for thousands of others. Without the support of each and every person, from our sponsors to strangers who wished me luck while walking down the street, the flight would not have taken place and the objectives of Teen World Flight would never have been met. And so every single person, whether a member of the main team or a well-wishing member of the public, is part of that word "we."

To Mum and Dad: I think we can all say that the journey of Teen World Flight was more complicated, stressful and worrisome than we ever imagined. There were challenges beyond our imagination but they were all successfully overcome. Thank you for your support, not only in my flying from the very beginning and Teen World Flight, but throughout my life. I promise the next challenge will be much more low key.

To Chris, Adam, Claire, my pilot mates, friends and family: as faces seen regularly, as influential peers of similar age, as pilots and most importantly as family and friends, you have all been phenomenally supportive of someone you know so well taking on something you might not have expected. I appreciate everything you have done so very much, and look forward to returning the favour in the future.

To Ken: well, what can I say? You took a young kid's crazy idea and played one of the most vital roles in making it a reality. You were always there, the voice that gave support and reinforced belief when I decided it was all becoming too hard. It is near impossible to explain my thanks for what you have done for me. I am looking forward to any flying adventures we share in the future. (Just not solo or in a piston-engine aircraft over water, okay?)

To Dick Smith: beyond sponsorship, beyond advice and beyond kind words delivered both face to face and in public, you passed on something even greater. Your reply to my original email was an electronic form of inspiration and encouragement, reinforced when I first shook your hand and during each encounter afterwards. Thank you for your belief in my dreams and for your contagious, unhindered sense of adventure.

To Dave Lyall: Mr. Right-Hand Man. Thank you for your initial interest in the flight, your generosity and flexible approach to my plans, your professional input and patience. Your team is fantastic, professional and easy to work with; thanks, Lloyd! Most of all, thanks for the good times and memorable laughs.

Taco Bell tastes better at midnight.

To the team at Harlequin, especially Jo, Adam, Camille, Romina, Sue and Lauren, to my editor Jacqueline and first editor Dave: if you had told me when I swapped Advanced English for Standard English class during my Higher School Certificate that I would write a book, I would have laughed. Thank you all for your patience, encouragement and dedication towards improving my storytelling and correcting my spelling mistakes. Thanks to you all, I have written a real book.

To Selwa Anthony: I must thank both you and Linda for taking a chance on me. Your experience and encouragement have given me the spur I needed to take on the challenge of writing this book. Don't be surprised if I drop around for another cup of tea and cake.

To members of the Frogs Hollow Aeroclub: your support for Teen World Flight was beyond anything I had ever imagined, but in previous years your support went far beyond measurable. What I learned in flying different types of aircraft, the experience I have stolen and the good laughs I have had helped put me in a position to take on the flight. Thank you again, I look forward to plenty more Sunday afternoons at Frogs.

To David and Leanne Green, Andrew and Caroline Dance and the Lamattina family: the most vital piece of the puzzle was of course the aircraft; not just finding a machine that upheld safety standards, but getting one in a way that was feasible and fair. Then we were equipped with the *Spirit of the Sapphire Coast*, an advanced and safe aircraft that met every expectation we had and achieved the goal with relative ease. Without your support and generosity the puzzle pieces would not have fallen together at the very end. Thank you!

To Mike Gray and White Rose Aviation: dear "Uncle Mike," on 7 September 2013 I arrived home. Not once did I see the inside of a jail cell, not once was I arrested and I am pretty sure I will be welcome back in every one of the fifteen countries I visited. Thank you for helping make this possible, and I look forward to an alcoholic beverage or two in an English pub.

The sponsors of Teen World Flight: from our principal partner Telstra to the local takeaway store that collected unwanted spare change, you are all phenomenal individuals, companies and organisations that took a step beyond interest in seeing Teen World Flight become a success. I wish I could share the story of every sponsor and the faces and friendships behind the logos on the airplane. Thank you for making my dream come true and for changing the lives of so many.

Uncle Charles and the *60 Minutes* family: you all became more than a TV crew, we had a great time together and the program was a culmination of the moments we had together throughout the Teen World Flight journey. I still find it hard to believe I took a selfie with Charles Woolley while trying to survive a tuktuk ride through the streets of Colombo. Thank you!

I would like to thank the many experienced minds who offered advice and experience, whether as pilots, businessmen or anything else. This advice led to successful planning and a safe flight. I admire each and every one of you and hope in the future to give someone else the benefit of my experience as generously as you have given yours to me. I truly hope that all of you have enjoyed the ride.

—Ryan Campbell, June 2014

CPSIA information can be obtained
at www.ICGtesting.com
Printed in the USA
JSHW031929190522
26003JS00001B/3

9 781734 382105